In Sync 4

Ingrid Freebairn
Jonathan Bygrave
Judy Copage

PEARSON
Longman

Contents

Contents

Student Book

Contents

Contents

Lifestyles

1

What are you doing here?

Grammar	Simple present and present continuous
	Tag questions
Vocabulary	Clothes, styles, accessories, and patterns
Function	Shop for clothes

Get started

1 Where do you buy your clothes? Do you like shopping for clothes? Why or why not?

Presentation

2 [1 02] Listen and read along. Where does Sophie make her T-shirts?

Lisa: Come on, Sergio. The market **closes** in half an hour. What are you looking for?

Sergio: **I'm looking** for a shirt. I have to go to a wedding on July 2nd. I **want** something plain but nice.

Lisa: Hey, that T-shirt's nice. I **like** baggy T-shirts, and I **love** the design on it.

Sergio: But I **need** a shirt, not a T-shirt. Anyway, the design **looks** a little weird.

Sophie: Hey, Lisa! How's it going?

Lisa: Oh, hi, Sophie. What **are you doing** here?

Sophie: **I'm working**. I **make** these clothes at home, and then I **sell** them here every other Saturday.

Lisa: You don't know Sergio or Carlos, do you?

Sophie: No, I don't. Hi, guys. Nice to meet you.

Sergio: Hi. I **like** your clothes. They're really original.

Sophie: Thanks. That**'s** a cool T-shirt, **isn't it**?

Sergio: This one? Oh, um . . . yes. It's great! I'll take it.

Carlos: But Sergio, you**'re looking** for a shirt, not a T-shirt!

Phrases

[1 03] Listen and repeat.

- What are you looking for? • something [plain]
- Anyway • How's it going? • every other [Saturday]

Comprehension

3 Answer the questions.

1 What does Sergio want to buy? *a shirt*
2 What does Lisa like about the T-shirt?
3 What does Sergio think of the T-shirt at first?
4 What day of the week does Sophie work?
5 What does Sergio decide to buy?

Sophie

Carlos

Lisa

Sergio

Vocabulary: Clothes, styles, accessories, and patterns

4a **Review.** How many words can you remember for clothes, styles, accessories, and patterns? Write lists in your notebook. Then check the Word bank on page 128.

b **Extension.** Listen and repeat. Look at the items in the photo. Match the items with the words in the box. Write the numbers next to the words. Which item is not in the photo?

_1_ bandana	___ baseball cap	___ bracelet
___ cargo pants	___ headband	___ leggings
___ polo shirt	___ sandals	___ sweater
___ sweatpants	___ sweatshirt	

C Describe what the people in the photo are wearing.

Solve it!

5 Read the presentation again. When will Sophie next work at the market?

Grammar

> **Simple present and present continuous**
>
> **Simple present**
>
> I **want** something plain but nice.
> I **make** these clothes at home.
> I **sell** them here every other Saturday.
> The market **closes** in half an hour.
>
> **Present continuous**
>
> I**'m looking** for a shirt.
> I**'m shopping** for a wedding gift.

☞ Go to page 132, Master your grammar.

Practice

6 Complete the newsletter with verbs in the simple present or present continuous.

• extend • go • ~~know~~ • make (x2) • sell • study

Seattle NEWSLETTER

Meet an enterprising young student from our town!

Sophie Timms [1] <u>*knows*</u> exactly what career she wants to follow. Sophie [2] _____ to Garfield High School. Right now, she [3] _____ Art, Design, and Technology. In her spare time she [4] _____ clothes and [5] _____ them at Pike Place Market on Saturdays. Now she [6] _____ T-shirts and sweatshirts, but next year she [7] _____ her range to include scarves and jewelry. Good luck, Sophie!

7 Look at the photo on pages 2–3 again. In your notebook, write sentences about the friends. What are they doing in the photo? What do they usually do? Use your imagination.

Sophie is working at the market. She usually makes clothes at home . . .

Grammar

> **Tag questions**
>
> **A:** That's a cool T-shirt, **isn't** it?
> **B:** Yes, it **is.**
> **A:** You**'re** in Lisa's class at school, **aren't** you?
> **B:** Yes, I **am.**
> **A:** You **don't know** Sergio or Carlos, **do** you?
> **B:** No, I **don't.**
> **A:** Sophie **has** a lot of T-shirts, **doesn't** she?
> **B:** Yes, she **does.**

☞ Go to page 132, Master your grammar.

Practice

8 Complete the statements with the correct tag questions.

1 Your name is Maria, _____ <u>*isn't it*</u> _____?
2 You live near me, _____?
3 You have a brother, _____?
4 Your favorite band is Oasis, _____?
5 You don't like Mariah Carey, _____?
6 You're learning to play the piano, _____?
7 You aren't enjoying this exercise, _____?
8 My questions aren't annoying, _____?

Pronunciation: Intonation in tag questions

9 🎧 Go to page 130.

Speak

10 PAIRS Ask your partner the questions from Exercise 8, changing the information where necessary. Make sure you choose the correct intonation.

A: *Your name is Maria, isn't it?*
B: *Yes, it is./No, it isn't.*

A: *You live near me, don't you?*
B: *Yes, I do./No, I don't. I live . . .*

Use your English: Shop for clothes

13 Read the sentences below.

Offer help
- Can I help you?/Do you need any help?

Say what you want
- Yes, please. I'm looking for a shirt/some jeans.
- Yes, do you have this shirt in a different color/ a larger size/a smaller size/size 14?
- No, thanks. I'm just looking.

Comment
- It's/They're too big/small/tight/long.
- I think I need a smaller/larger size.
- It looks good. How much is it?

Make a decision
- It's perfect/great. I'll take it, please.
- No, sorry. Thanks, anyway.

Presentation

11 Listen and read along. What kind of shirt is Sergio looking for?

Man: Can I help you?
Sergio: Yes, I'm looking for a shirt. Do you have this one in a larger size? This is a small.
Man: Just a minute. I'll see . . . Yes, here's a medium.
Sergio: Can I try it on?
Man: Sure. There's a fitting room over there.
Sergio: Thanks. . . . What do you think, Carlos?
Carlos: Well, it's not exactly my style, but that color looks good on you.
Sergio: It's fine for a wedding. How much is it?
Carlos: Let's see . . . It's $59.
Sergio: $59! Forget it!
Man: Would you like to buy the shirt?
Sergio: Um . . . No, sorry. Thanks, anyway.

Comprehension

12 What does Sergio do at the end of the conversation? Why?

Listen

14 PAIRS Listen again. Role-play similar conversations. You want to buy the following:

1 a sweater—smaller size?—$25
2 some cargo pants—different color?—$40
3 some sandals—larger size?—$10.50

Write

15 On a piece of paper, write a paragraph about your clothes. What do you usually wear? What are you wearing today?

I usually wear jeans and a T-shirt. Today I'm wearing . . .

> **Extra practice**
> - Student Book, page 112, Lesson 1A
> - Language Builder: WB, page 2; GB, page 101
> - Student CD-ROM, Unit 1

1B   He's broken 24 bones.

Grammar	Present perfect with *for* or *since*; Simple past
Vocabulary	Jobs
Function	Talk about dangerous jobs

Get started

1 What are some dangerous jobs? What makes them dangerous?

Vocabulary: Jobs

2 **Review.** Write a list of jobs in your notebook. Then check the Word bank on page 128.

Read

3 🔊 1.08 Listen and read along. Why was the year 2002 important for Jet? _____

Comprehension

4 Correct the statements.

1 Jet's job is ~~boring~~. *exciting*

2 Jet rides bulls in rodeo shows.

3 Jet has worked as a clown for 16 years.

4 Jet has never won an award.

5 Jet has never been injured.

6 Jet wants a safer job.

DANGEROUS JOBS — Rodeo clown

In our series about dangerous jobs, Tom Greenspan finds out about the work of a rodeo clown.

For danger and excitement, it's hard to beat Jet Rivers's job. Jet, who comes from Texas in the U.S., is a famous rodeo clown. In a rodeo show, a bull rider gets eight seconds to ride the bull. If he falls off or is injured, it is Jet's job to dance around in brightly colored clothes and distract the bull so that the rider can escape from the arena. The job is dangerous because the bull often turns and chases the clown. Jet first **became** interested in rodeo shows at the age of 16. "I went to a lot of shows and watched the clowns and I thought: That's what I want to do." He**'s worked** as a rodeo clown for nearly ten years. He **won** his first prize in 2002. Since then he**'s won** six other awards. He loves his job. "I know it's crazy, but I love the danger," says Jet. Since Jet started the job, he**'s broken** 24 bones. "But I'm getting lucky. I **haven't had** an accident for almost two years!"

Grammar

Present perfect with *for* or *since*; Simple past

Present perfect	Simple past
Jet **has worked** as a rodeo clown **for** ten years. **Since** Jet started, he's **broken** 24 bones.	Jet **became** interested in rodeo shows at the age of 16. He **won** a prize in 2002.

☛ Go to page 132, Master your grammar.

Practice

5 Look at the factfile. In your notebook, ask and answer questions about David's life. Use the simple past or present perfect and the cues.

1 **A:** *How long has he been a window cleaner?*
  B: *He has been a window cleaner since 2005.*

2 **A:** *When did he . . . ?*

DANGEROUS JOBS FACTFILE

High-rise window cleaner

Name: David Harris

1 be/window cleaner/ 2005 to now
2 finish/school/2000
3 travel/from Australia/2001
4 live/U.S./2002 to now
5 clean/5,000 windows/so far
6 clean/tallest building in New York/2008

💡 Solve it!

6 Complete the sentences with *since* or *for*. Then guess the three jobs.

1 I've flown more than 20 different kinds of planes ª_____*since*_____ I got my license in 1990. My favorite route is to Hong Kong, but I haven't been there ᵇ_____ six months.

2 I've loved cars ª_____ I was a boy, so my job is ideal. I've worked in this auto repair shop ᵇ_____ over six years now. I love it!

3 I've worked in this studio ª_____ three years. I've interviewed a lot of famous people ᵇ_____ I started work at CNN.

Listen

7 🎧 **1/09** Listen to Sean Tanner, a professional storm chaser, and complete the information.

Sean Tanner: storm chaser

1 Job: *storm chaser and photographer*
2 Comes from: _____
3 Age when saw first tornado: _____
4 Tornado season: _____
5 Previous job: _____
6 How many tornadoes seen: _____
7 Dangerous incidents:
   1 *nearly drowned in flood*
   2 _____
8 Currently on website:
   _____

Speak

8 **PAIRS** Discuss. Would you like to do any of the jobs in this lesson? Why or why not?

Write

9 Do you know anyone with a dangerous job? On a piece of paper, write a paragraph about what he or she has done at work. Use the present perfect with *for* or *since* and the simple past.

My uncle is a truck driver. He has had two accidents since he started . . .

> **Extra practice**
> • Student Book, page 112, Lesson 1B
> • Language Builder: WB, page 4; GB, page 101
> • Student CD-ROM, Unit 1

1c It's much more rewarding.

Grammar	Intensifiers *much, a lot, a little* with comparative adjectives and adverbs; *(not) as . . . as*
Vocabulary	Adjectives to describe work
Function	Talk about plans after graduation

A _____   B _____   C _____

Get started

1 Have people you know graduated from school? What are they doing now?

Read

2 Listen and read along. Match the photos to the teenagers' comments.

What are your choices after you graduate? Do you want to get a job or do something else?

The magazine *Getahead* conducted a survey. Here are some of the answers teens gave.

1 "I want to get a job and earn some money. But I don't want to work in a factory or a supermarket. I'd like to do something a little more interesting—maybe work as a sound technician in a recording studio. It's not as exciting as people think, but it's creative and it pays well. Unfortunately, there aren't many jobs in the music industry for high school graduates, and there are lots of better-qualified people around. I know I can get a job in a store a lot more easily than in a studio, but I don't want that."

Peter

2 "I don't want to get a job right away. I want some freedom. I'd like to take six months off and travel. Backpacking in another country seems much more interesting and exciting than getting a job at home, and you learn a lot. The trouble is, traveling is a lot more expensive than people realize. It's much cheaper to stay in the U.S. and get a job, and it costs a lot less to live at home."

Donna

3 "I'd like to go to college and get a degree. I need to work a little harder at school if I want to do that, but I'm sure it's worthwhile. I'm not sure that it's a very exciting choice, but in the end you get a much better job with a degree. Of course I want to earn money, but that can wait until I've graduated."

Robert

Comprehension

3 Complete the statements and name the speakers.

1 A college degree helps you to *get a much better job*.
2 Working in a supermarket is _____.
3 It costs a lot to _____.
4 There are many well-qualified people in
_____.
5 To get into college, I need to _____.

Vocabulary: Adjectives to describe work

4  Listen and repeat. Write *P* for the positive adjectives in the box. Write *N* for the negative adjectives.

N badly paid	__ boring	*P* creative
__ dangerous	__ dull	__ educational
__ exciting	__ glamorous	__ interesting
__ rewarding	__ safe	__ stressful
__ tiring	__ well-paid	__ worthwhile

Grammar

Intensifiers *much*, *a lot*, *a little* with comparative adjectives and adverbs; *(not) as . . . as*

Comparative adjectives

It's **much/a lot/a little cheaper** to live at home **than** to travel abroad.

This job is **(not) as exciting as** people think.

Comparative adverbs

I can get a job in a store **much/a lot/a little more easily than** in a studio.

It costs **much/a lot/a little more/less** to live at home.

They don't pay **as badly as** you think.

☛ Go to page 132, Master your grammar.

5 Look at the examples of comparatives in the magazine article. Underline the adjectives and circle the adverbs.

a little more interesting

Practice

6 Complete with a comparative form of the adjective or adverb, or *(not) as . . . as*.

1 Today is ___*much hotter than*___ yesterday. (hot/much)
2 This bed is _____ my old one. (comfortable/much)
3 Can you try to write _____? (carefully/a little)
4 I feel _____ today than yesterday. (bad/a lot)
5 Can you please drive _____? (slowly/a little)
6 Teaching isn't _____ web designing. (well-paid)
7 I see my grandparents _____ now than before. (frequently/a lot)

7 Compare the choices below. In your notebook, write sentences with the comparative form of adjectives in Exercise 4 and intensifiers.
Backpacking is much (a lot) more exciting than doing a temporary job.
Doing a temporary job isn't as exciting as backpacking.

Choices for high school graduates
1 Doing a temporary job/backpacking
2 Going to college/getting a full-time job
3 Doing volunteer work/working in a factory

Speak

8 PAIRS Which of the activities in Exercise 7 would you prefer to do after school? Why?

Write

9 On a piece of paper, write a paragraph about what you want to do when you leave school and why. Try to use intensifiers.

When I leave school, I want to . . .

> **Extra practice**
> • Student Book, page 113, Lesson 1C
> • Language Builder: WB, page 6; GB, page 102
> • Student CD-ROM, Unit 1

INTEGRATED CONSOLIDATION SKILLS

Across cultures

Before you read, go to page 11.

The changing face of American teen fashion

For most American teenagers, fashion matters. However, designer clothes are usually beyond their budget. Teens tend to spend their money in malls, street markets, and thrift stores, where they mix and match to create their own style and image.

Clothes in the U.S. cost much less than they used to. Since the year 2000, the price of clothing has dropped a lot. In one popular store, a pair of designer jeans costs as little as $28. The reason is that the factories, which are usually located in developing countries like India and China, are using the cheapest labor they can find—sometimes even child labor.

As a result of this, there has recently been more emphasis on *ethical fashion*. People are beginning to buy clothes made from recycled products and renewable sources. These clothes are often also part of fair trade organizations, which ensure that the people who manufacture the clothes are paid a fair salary. Even the top fashion magazines now have articles on ethical clothing.

Is ethical fashion realistic? Perhaps, but maybe the only really ethical solution is to buy fewer clothes!

Maddy

Fraser

José

Teenagers speak out

Maddy

"I spend most of my money in thrift stores. I love a good bargain! I like putting unusual clothes together to create a different look. In this photo I'm wearing clothes I found at a garage sale."

Fraser

"I live and breathe skateboarding. I don't worry about fashion. I usually wear baggy jeans or pants, hoodies, T-shirts, and a baseball cap or ski hat. The kind of sneakers I wear is important, but nothing is as important as skateboarding."

José

"I've read lots of stuff online about where clothes come from and how they are made, so I try to buy fair trade clothes. I just bought some sneakers from a store where they promise to plant one tree in Ethiopia for every pair of sneakers they sell. I like that."

New words and phrases
- designer • beyond someone's budget • tend to • mix and match • image • fashionable
- developing • child labor • emphasis • ethical • recycled • product • renewable • source
- fair trade • ensure • manufacture • wage • realistic • bargain • unusual • look (n)
- garage sale • live and breathe • worried • ski • stuff • plant (v)

Get started

1 What kind of clothes and styles are popular in your country right now?

Read

2 Read the article about the American teen fashion scene. Where do American teenagers usually buy their clothes?

Comprehension

3a Answer the questions.

1 How do most American teenagers feel about clothes?
Clothes are important to them.

2 Why do clothes cost less than they used to?

3 How do fair trade organizations help workers?

4 Which teenager is most interested in "ethical fashion"? Explain.

b Check (✓) the correct box.

Who:	Maddy	Fraser	José
1 likes to spend as little as possible on clothes?			
2 is interested in clothes manufacturing?			
3 likes to shop ethically?			
4 is more interested in sports than fashion?			
5 likes to look different from other people?			

Speak

4 PAIRS Discuss the questions.

1 Which of the three teenagers are you most similar to? In what way?
2 Apart from clothes, what other things are "fashion items" among your friends?
3 How interested are people in your country in ethical fashion?

Listen

5 🔊 1/12 Listen to Dan talking about his style and interests and complete the information.

1 Favorite item of clothing:
   hoodies
2 Why he likes them:
   _____
3 What else he wears:
   _____
4 Clothes for special occasions:
   _____
5 Favorite music: _____
6 Weekend activities: _____

Write

> **Learning strategy: Collect and organize your ideas**
>
> Before you start to write, take time to collect and organize your ideas. First, make a list of all your ideas in any order. Then organize them into groups under headings.

6a You are going to write an article called "The factors that influence my choice of clothes." First match the headings with the ideas (a–e).
• Advertising and the media [b]
• Opinions of friends [ ]
• Money [ ]
• Personal expression [ ]
• Comfort [ ]

> **I'm influenced by:**
> a) how much the clothes cost.
> b) what magazines say is fashionable.
> c) the clothes that my friends like.
> d) how comfortable/practical/adaptable the clothes are.
> e) whether the clothes reflect my lifestyle and opinions.

b Now put the ideas in order of importance for you.

c Write the article on a piece of paper. Use your notes from Exercises 6a and 6b to help you.

CLIL PROJECT, page 157

I didn't recognize you.

Grammar Simple past
Function Show concern and reassure

Get started

1 Have you ever seen an accident? What happened?

Presentation

2 Listen and read along. How did Sophie fall?

Sergio: Are you OK? **Did** you **hurt** yourself?

Sophie: No, I'm fine. Don't worry.

Sergio: It's Sophie, isn't it? We **met** last weekend at the market.

Sophie: Yes, I remember. You **bought** one of my T-shirts.

Sergio: That's right. I **didn't recognize** you in your helmet. Are you sure you're OK?

Sophie: Yes, no problem.

Sergio: What **happened**?

Sophie: I **swerved** to avoid a skateboarder and I **lost** my balance.

Sergio: I bet you're glad you **wore** kneepads.

Sophie: Yes, I am. I **fell** twice yesterday, but I'm beginning to get the hang of it.

Sergio: When **did** you **start** learning?

Sophie: Not long ago. A Chilean friend **came** to stay for a few days over the summer, and she **gave** me some lessons. Well, I'd better get going.

Sergio: How about getting a cup of coffee first?

Sophie: I **didn't have** breakfast this morning, so I'd love one.

Phrases

Listen and repeat.

- no problem
- I bet you're glad . . .
- get the hang of it
- I'd better get going.

Comprehension

3 Complete the sentences.

1 Sergio first met Sophie
   _____*at the market*_____.

2 Sergio didn't recognize her at first because she had
   _____

3 Sophie fell when she tried to avoid
   _____.

4 Sophie wanted to try rollerblading after a friend
   _____

5 Sergio and Sophie decide to
   _____.

Grammar

Simple past	
Regular verbs	**Irregular verbs**
I swerv**ed** to avoid a skateboarder.	We **met** last weekend.
I **didn't recognize** you. When **did** you **start**?	I **ate** breakfast already. **Did** you **hurt** yourself?

☛ Go to page 133, Master your grammar.

4 Underline nine irregular past tense forms in the presentation on page 12.

Practice

5 Complete the article with the simple past form of verbs from the box.

> • ~~be~~ • become • break • enter • give
> • grow up • name • practice • start • win

Danny Way
Professional skateboarder

Danny Way is one of the most famous skateboarders in the world. He ¹ _was_ born and ² _____ in Portland, Oregon. He ³ _____ skateboarding at the age of four. He ⁴ _____ skateboarding as much as possible, and soon he was very good at it. He ⁵ _____ his first competition at the age of 11, and surprisingly, the judges ⁶ _____ him first prize. Between 1986 and 2009, he ⁷ _____ many medals. The magazine *Thrasher* ⁸ _____ him the Skater of the Year— twice! In 2005, he ⁹ _____ the first person to jump over the Great Wall of China on a skateboard! But Danny has had some hard times, too. He gets injured a lot, and in 2008 he ¹⁰ _____ his back. But after 20 years, he's still skating.

Speak

6 PAIRS You are a reporter interviewing Danny Way. Look at Exercise 5 and write some questions. Then role-play an interview.

A: *Where were you born, Danny?*

B: *In Portland. That's where I grew up.*

Pronunciation: Intonation of *Wh-* questions

7 🎧 Go to page 130.

Use your English: Show concern and reassure

8 Read the sentences below.

Show concern	Reassure
• Are you OK/all right?	• Don't worry. I'm fine.
• Are you sure?	• Really, I'm OK.
• Did you hurt yourself?	• No problem.
• Can I do anything?	
• Can I give you a hand?	

Question	Explanation
• What happened?	• I lost my balance.

Listen

9 🎵 17 PAIRS Listen to the conversation. Then read the situations below and role-play conversations.

1 You see your friend, Student B, picking up his or her books from the sidewalk. Show concern and ask what happened.
2 Your younger brother's or sister's knee is bleeding. Ask what happened.

Write

10 On a piece of paper, write a paragraph about a time when you hurt yourself. What happened? Did anyone help you?

I hurt myself last weekend. I fell . . .

> **Extra practice**
> • Student Book, page 113, Lesson 2A
> • Language Builder: WB, page 10; GB, page 104
> • Student CD-ROM, Unit 2

2B   He was struggling . . .

Grammar	Past continuous and simple past with *while* and *when*
Vocabulary	Phrasal verbs with *up*
Function	Talk about two past actions happening at the same time

No easy path to success

Today Matt Damon is one of Hollywood's most famous movie stars. But in the early 1990s he was struggling to be a success, and, over the years, life has not always been easy.

In 1996, he had to lose 40 pounds for his role as a drug-addicted soldier in *Courage under Fire*. While he was dieting, he became ill and had to take medication for several years afterwards.

In 2000, he cracked a rib while he was playing golf in *The Legend of Bagger Vance*. Then, 12 years after losing weight for *Courage under Fire*, he had to gain 30 pounds to play a businessman in *The Informant*.

Matt grew up in Massachusetts in the U.S. and started acting while he was still a student. He was studying English at Harvard University when he got a part in the movie *Geronimo: An American Legend*. When he heard the good news, he immediately dropped out of Harvard, hoping that Hollywood would take notice of him. It didn't. It wasn't until he won an Oscar with his friend, Ben Affleck, for *Good Will Hunting* in 1997 that Hollywood began to show interest. After excellent performances in *The Talented Mr. Ripley, Saving Private Ryan,* and *Ocean's 11*, he was offered the lead role in 2002 as the assassin Jason Bourne in *The Bourne Identity*. From then on, his career moved in one direction only—upward.

Get started

1 Have you seen any of Matt Damon's movies? Which was your favorite? Why?

Read

2  Listen and read along. When did Matt Damon win his first Oscar?

Comprehension

3 Number the events (a–h) in the order in which they happened. Matt Damon:

_____ a) lost a lot of weight for a part in a movie.

__1__ b) went to Harvard University.

_____ c) was chosen for the lead role in *The Bourne Identity*.

_____ d) put on weight to play a businessman.

_____ e) won his first Oscar.

_____ f) hurt his rib on a golf course.

_____ g) acted in *Geronimo: An American Legend*.

💡 Solve it!

4 Matt Damon was 38 years old when he starred in *The Informant*. In what year was he born?

14

Vocabulary: Phrasal verbs with *up*

5 Listen and repeat. Then complete the sentences with phrasal verbs from the box.

> • get up • grow up • hurry up • look up • pick up
> • show up • stand up • take up • wake up

1 Please _____ *stand up* _____ when the teacher comes into the room.
2 She was born in Chicago, but she didn't _____ there.
3 I always _____ at seven, but I don't _____ then. I'm too lazy!
4 _____! We're going to be late.
5 He plays football, but he doesn't want to _____ another sport.
6 I'm going to _____ that word in the dictionary.
7 Did she _____ in time for class?
8 Can you please _____ that book?

Grammar

Past continuous and simple past with *while* and *when*

Past continuous

In the early 1990s, he **was struggling** to be a success.

Past continuous + simple past with *while* and *when*

While he **was dieting**, he **became** ill.
He **was studying** English **when** he **got** a part in a movie.
He **cracked** a rib **while** he **was playing** golf.

Simple past + simple past with *when*

When he **heard** the news, he **dropped** out of Harvard.

☛ Go to page 133, Master your grammar.

Practice

6 In your notebook, combine the sentences in columns A and B of the chart using *while* or *when* and the past continuous or simple past.

While Matt Damon and Ben Affleck were growing up, they planned to make lots of movies together.

	A	B
1 (while)	Matt Damon and Ben Affleck/grow up	They/plan to make lots of movies together
2 (when)	The director of *Ocean's 11*/call Matt	Matt watch/a DVD at home
3 (while)	He eat/his lunch	He/read the whole script
4 (while)	He/prepare for the role of Mr. Ripley	He/start to learn the piano
5 (when)	He/audition for *Ocean's 11*	Julia Roberts/walk through the door
6 (while)	He/film a *Bourne* movie	He/take up ten-pin bowling

7 Complete the questions with the past continuous or the simple past form of the verb *do*.

1 A: *What were you doing* when you heard the news?
   B: I was having lunch.
2 A: _____ when he saw the burglar?
   B: He called the police.
3 A: _____ when the lights went out?
   B: They were having dinner.
4 A: _____ when he injured his ankle?
   B: He was working in the yard.
5 A: _____ when it started to snow?
   B: We stopped playing and went home.
6 A: _____ when she saw the shark?
   B: She was swimming in the sea.

Speak

8 PAIRS With a partner, ask and answer the questions in Exercise 7. Invent new answers.

Write

9 Go to the Writing bank on page 144 and complete the exercises. Then, on a piece of paper, write a short biography of your favorite movie star.

> **Extra practice**
> • Student Book, page 113, Lesson 2B
> • Language Builder: WB, page 12; GB, page 104
> • Student CD-ROM, Unit 2

He had fallen overboard.

Grammar	Simple past and past perfect *after/before* + gerund (*-ing* form)
Vocabulary	Transportation and travel
Function	Talk about traveling

Get started

1 Do you think traveling is fun? Why or why not?

Read

2 🎧 Listen and read along. What incident happened or nearly happened in each story?

Comprehension

3 Match the stories (A–C) to the sentences (1–6).

1 Someone did something brave. *B*
2 There was a risk of fire. _____
3 People were traveling by sea. _____
4 A man saved another person's life. _____
5 Someone got wet. _____
6 Someone called the fire department. _____

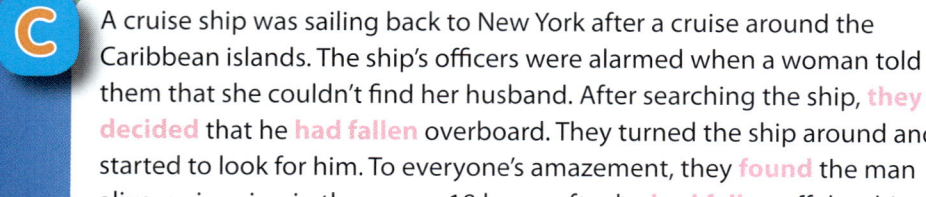

Travel Traumas!

A Railroad officials at a station outside Boston in the U.S. were surprised when a note landed on the platform from a passing train. The note said: "Mr. Grant, of 48 First St, Boston, left a pot on the stove. Please call the police." **Before telling** the police, the station manager called the fire department, who **went** immediately to the house. Mr. Grant **left** the pot on the stove, but luckily he **hadn't turned on** the gas.

B The pilot of a four-seater plane **had to leave** his cockpit in mid-flight to free a parachutist who **had** accidentally **gotten caught** in the wheels of the plane. The pilot was flying at 3,280 feet when he suddenly saw a man waving at him from the back of his plane. **After putting** the plane on automatic pilot, he got out of his seat, crawled to the back of the plane, and cut the lines of the parachute. The man landed safely, using his emergency parachute.

C A cruise ship was sailing back to New York after a cruise around the Caribbean islands. The ship's officers were alarmed when a woman told them that she couldn't find her husband. After searching the ship, **they decided** that he **had fallen** overboard. They turned the ship around and started to look for him. To everyone's amazement, they **found** the man alive, swimming in the ocean, 18 hours after he **had fallen** off the ship.

Grammar

Simple past and past perfect

The fire department **went** to the house.
Mr. Grant **had left** the pot on the stove.
They **found** the man 18 hours after he **had fallen** off the ship.

after/before + gerund (*-ing* form)

After putting the plane on automatic pilot, he got out of his seat.
Before telling the police, he called the fire department.

☞ Go to page 133, Master your grammar.

Practice

4 Complete the paragraph with the correct form of the verbs in parentheses.

Last week, I ¹ _____*went*_____ (go) back to the town where I ² _____ (live) as a child. I was wondering if it ³ _____ (change). Yes, it ⁴ _____ (have)! After ⁵ _____ (go) to see our old house, we ⁶ _____ (go) to look at my old elementary school. I was shocked! They ⁷ _____ (knock) it down! They ⁸ _____ (not build) a new school, but a huge supermarket.

5 In your notebook, combine the sentences in two ways with *after* and *before*.

1 He (have) lunch. Then he (go) for a walk.

> *After having lunch, he went for a walk.*
> *Before going for a walk, he had lunch.*

2 She (have) some lessons. Then she (take) her driving test.
3 I (meet) some friends in town. Then I (catch) a train to Boston.
4 He (ask) a friend for advice. Then he (buy) a bike.
5 They (look) at three websites. Then they (book) their flights.
6 I (sell) my car. Then I (buy) a motorcycle.

6 Solve it!

Read Paragraph C in Exercise 2 again. Cruise ships travel at 18 miles per hour. How far had the ship traveled before it turned around to pick the man up?

Vocabulary: Transportation and travel

7 Review. Write the headings *Land*, *Sea*, and *Air* in your notebook. List all the forms of transportation you can remember under the headings. Then check the Word bank on page 128.

Listen

8 🎧 Listen to Nico's story. Follow the cues and say how the story ended.

- rock concert/California
- alarm/hurry/subway/airport
- check-in desk/flight closed/phone call/not take off on time

Speak

9a Retell Nico's story using the questions below and the cues in Exercise 8.

1 Where was Nico going?
2 What had he forgotten to do?
3 What did he find when he arrived at JFK?
4 Did he get on the plane?

b PAIRS Describe the most interesting trip you have ever taken. Say where you went, how you traveled, and what happened.

Write

10 On a piece of paper, write a paragraph about a problem you had while traveling. Use the simple past and the past perfect.

I had a problem on my trip to Los Angeles. The train ride was terrible because I had forgotten my money ...

> **⊳ Extra practice**
> - **Student Book, page 114, Lesson 2C**
> - **Language Builder: WB, page 14; GB, page 105**
> - **Student CD-ROM, Unit 2**

Curriculum link: History

Before you read, go to page 19.

Heroes of the air

Amelia Mary Earhart 1897–1937 (U.S.)

Achievement: _____

In 1917, when she was 20. Amelia Earhart went to an air show with her father. While she was watching the planes circling in the sky, she realized she had found her vocation. She wanted to be a pilot. The next day, she took her first trip in a plane and her career had begun. In 1932, she became famous as the first woman to fly solo across the Atlantic Ocean. Five years later she began her most ambitious project—to be the first woman to fly around the world. Tragically, she and her plane disappeared just before completing the journey. Where did she disappear? Nobody knows, and it's still a mystery today.

Sally Ride 1951– (U.S.)

Achievement: _____

It was no surprise that Sally Ride chose a career in space travel. As a young woman she had always been interested in science and went on to study physics at Stanford University. Not long after graduating, she spotted an advertisement in a newspaper. The space agency NASA was looking for people to work in the American space program. More than 5,000 people applied, and Sally was one of the successful candidates. She joined NASA in 1978. On June 18, 1983, she became the first American woman in space as a crew member on the space shuttle *Challenger 7*.

Richard Branson 1950 – (U.K.)

Achievement: _____

Sir Richard Branson, who owns a large media and travel company, has always enjoyed a challenge. As well as setting up successful companies, he is well known for trying to break world records in travel. In 1987, Branson and his friend Per Lindstrand were the first people to cross the Atlantic Ocean in a hot-air balloon. The balloon, which Per had designed, took off from the U.S. on July 2 and landed on July 3 in Ireland 31 hours later. They had broken all records for long-distance ballooning and changed the sport forever.

New words and phrases

• air show • circle (v) • vocation • solo • ambitious • tragically • space • spot (v)
• space agency • space program • apply • candidate • crew • member • space shuttle
• media • challenge (n) • set up • break (a record) • hot-air balloon • forever

Get started

1 Which famous people do you know who are connected with travel and transportation?

Read

2 Read the article on page 18. Complete the "Achievement" for each person.

Comprehension

3 In your notebook, write sentences about why these years were important for each person.

1 Amelia Mary Earhart: 1917
   It was the year when she took her first trip in a plane.
2 Amelia Mary Earhart: 1932
3 Sally Ride: 1978
4 Sally Ride: 1983
5 Richard Branson: 1987

4 Answer the questions.

1 What made Amelia Mary Earhart decide to become a pilot?
   an air show
2 When did she begin her journey around the world? _____
3 How did Sally Ride find her job with NASA? _____
4 How many candidates applied for a job there? _____
5 What does Richard Branson do for a living? _____
6 In which country did he land the hot-air balloon? _____

Learning strategy: Dictionary skills (1)

If you need to use a dictionary, use a good American-English dictionary. When you look up the meaning of a new word, you will also see how to pronounce the word and what part of speech it is.

5a Look at the dictionary entry for *vocation* and answer the questions.

vocation /voʊˈkeɪʃən/ *n* [c] a job that you do because you have a very strong feeling that doing this job is the purpose of your life

1 How do you pronounce the word?
2 What part of speech is it? Is it count or non-count?
3 What does it mean?

b Look up: *solo*, *ambitious*, *candidate*, and *media* in a dictionary and write the information in your notebook. Write an example sentence for each word.

Listen

6 Listen to the radio program about transportation heroes. Complete the chart.

Transportation heroes	Country	Achievement
The Wright brothers Orville Wright (1871–*1948*)	U.S.	1 Designed and built the first real _____ in 19_____. 2 _____ a steering system.
Henry Ford (1863–_____)	_____	1 Produced _____. 2 By 1918, _____. 3 Invented _____.
NASA (created in _____)	_____	1 In 19_____, it put _____. 2 It developed the _____ shuttle. 3 It helped to build the _____.

Speak

7a GROUPS Discuss: Which of the famous people do you think is the most important in the history of transportation? Why?

b Think of heroes from the history of your country. Do a group survey and find out who is the most popular person.

Write

8 On a piece of paper, write a short article about one of the heroes from your survey in Exercise 7b. Use the questions below.
- What did this person do before he or she became famous?
- What important event helped to make him or her famous?

CLIL PROJECT, page 157

Grammar (40 points)

1 Complete the sentences with the correct form of the verbs in parentheses. **(10 points)**

0 How often ___*do you go*___ (go) to the movies?

1 My sister _____ (see) her boyfriend a lot.

2 I _____ (do) my homework now.

3 How long _____ (you/know) Sam?

4 I _____ (run) to school this morning.

5 A: Where's the ice cream?
   B: Sorry. I _____ (finish) it!

6 She (recently/take up) _____ the piano.

7 Jay wasn't there when I called. He _____ (already/leave).

8 Kevin arrived while we _____ (have) lunch.

9 After _____ (see) the movie, he bought the DVD.

10 I was watching TV when I _____ (hear) a bang.

2 Write sentences in your notebook with the present perfect and *for* or *since*. **(7 points)**

0 I/not see/Richard/three/years
   I haven't seen Richard for three years.

1 We/not be/to the movies/last December

2 I/live here/ten years

3 Jeremy/wear glasses/several years

4 My cousin Joe/have his driver's license/2005

5 She/send 10 text messages/she woke up

6 My dog/not eat anything/three days

7 He/know Emma/six months

3 Complete with the simple past, past continuous, or past perfect tense. **(8 points)**

It was the month of May, and three Russian soccer fans [0] *were driving* (drive) from St. Petersburg to Vladivostok, an 8,000 mile journey, to see their team play in the Cup Final. Their team [1] _____ (win). After the game [2] _____ (finish), they [3] _____ (start) the trip back. While they [4] _____ (cross) the mountains, their old car completely [5] _____ (break down) and they had to take the train home. Later, when the soccer club [6] _____ (hear) how far the fans [7] _____ (drive), they [8] _____ (give) them a new car!

4 Complete the statements with the correct tag questions. **(10 points)**

0 He has a bicycle, ___*doesn't he*___?

1 You know the answer, _____?

2 She doesn't like me, _____?

3 They weren't angry, _____?

4 Josh can swim, _____?

5 Helen eats meat, _____?

6 The boys aren't coming, _____?

7 I haven't met Julian yet, _____?

8 This movie is awful, _____?

9 Marianne has a new laptop, _____?

10 You didn't buy those jeans, _____?

5 Complete the comparative sentences. Use the cues. **(5 points)**

0 Venezuela is ___*much hotter than*___ Chile. (hot/much)

1 I don't feel better. In fact, I feel _____ yesterday. (bad/a little)

2 The final was _____ the semi-final. (exciting/not as)

3 Yesterday's test was _____ last year's. (easy/a lot)

4 Delivering newspapers is _____ working in a hospital. (rewarding/not as)

5 The beaches in Ecuador are _____ the beaches in the U.S. (good/a lot)

Vocabulary (40 points)

6 Copy the chart into your notebook. Put the words into the correct categories. **(10 points)**

Clothes and accessories	Footwear	Jobs	Transportation
fleece	*sandals*	*beautician*	*truck*

- ~~beautician~~ • boots • bracelet • coat • dress
- electrician • ferry • ~~fleece~~ • helicopter
- high heels • leggings • mechanic • moped
- politician • receptionist • ~~sandals~~ • shoes
- ski instructor • sneakers • sweater
- sweatshirt • tights • ~~truck~~ • van

7 Complete the adjectives to describe the jobs. (11 points)

0 You don't earn very much money. It's _badly paid_.

1 There's nothing to do all day. It's d_____l.

2 It's useful work. It's w_____e.

3 You use a lot of energy. It's t_____g.

4 You can get hurt. It's d_____s.

5 You feel good when you get results. It's r_____g.

6 You travel to exciting places. It's g_____s.

7 You learn a lot while you do it. It's e_____l.

8 You just sit at the cash register all day. It's b_____g.

9 You get a chance to make things. It's c_____e.

10 There's always too much to do. It's s_____l.

11 You get a good salary. It's w_____-p_____.

8 In your notebook, rewrite the sentences with the correct phrasal verbs. (8 points)

0 I always ~~grow up~~ at seven o'clock.

I always _get up_ at seven o'clock.

1 I need to *pick up* that word in a dictionary.

2 Please *take up* when the teacher comes in.

3 I always *look up* when the cat jumps on my bed.

4 What time should I *hurry up*?

5 *Turn up*! We're going to be late!

6 Where did you *get up* as a child?

7 My dad is going to *stand up* golf.

8 Could you *wake up* that paper from the floor?

9 Circle the correct verbs. (11 points)

What a journey! We ⁰(*set off*)*took off* at six in the morning and Mom took us to the station. We ¹ *got on/ get on* the train and ² *arrived/reached* at Mill Creek 15 minutes later. There we ³ *took off/got off* and ⁴ *changed/ caught* trains. We went to buy some coffee and we nearly ⁵ *caught/missed* our train! We ⁶ *reached/arrived* King Street Station at 7:30. From there we ⁷ *missed/ caught* a train to the airport. The plane ⁸ *took off/set off* at 11 A.M. and we ⁹ *landed/reached* at JFK airport six hours later. After we ¹⁰ *got off/set off* the plane, we ¹¹ *got on/got in* a taxi and went straight to our hotel.

Use your English (20 points)

10 Circle the correct phrases. (12 points)

A: Do you ⁰_____?

  a) want to help b) need to help c) (need any help)

B: Yes, do you have this sweater ¹_____ different color?

  a) in a b) in c) with

A: Yes, we have it in light blue.

B: Can I ²_____, please?

  a) try on b) try c) try it on

A: Sure. Over there . . . What do you think?

B: It's a little small. ³_____ in a larger size?

  a) I want b) Do you have it c) Is it

A: Yes, here's a size 8.

B: Thank you. What ⁴_____, Anna?

  a) do you think b) you think c) do you like

C: I'm sorry, but that color ⁵_____ you.

  a) isn't right b) doesn't fit c) doesn't look good on

B: OK. ⁶_____.

  a) Anyway b) Thanks anyway c) No

11 Complete the conversation with words from the box. (8 points)

- don't • fine
- give • ~~happened~~
- hurt • I'm • no
- right • sure

A: What ⁰ _happened_ ? Are you all ¹_____?

B: Yes, ² _____ OK. I was rollerblading and I fell.

A: Did you ³ _____ yourself?

B: No, ⁴ _____ worry.
I'm ⁵ _____. It's just my arm.

A: Really? Are you ⁶ _____?

B: Yes, ⁷ _____ problem.

A: Can I ⁸ _____ you a hand with that bag?

B: OK. Thanks.

SELF-CHECK	
Grammar	_____ /40
Vocabulary	_____ /40
Use your English	_____ /20
Total score	_____ /100

There won't be any running water.

Grammar	Future tenses: *will, be going to,* present continuous form *be about to* + infinitive
Vocabulary	Food and kitchen equipment
Function	Talk about future plans

3 Responsibility

Get started

1 What is your favorite food? What kitchen equipment do you use to make it?

Vocabulary: Food and kitchen equipment

2a Review. In your notebook, make lists of all the food words you know. Use the categories below. Then check the Word bank on page 128.

- dairy • drinks • fish • fruit • meat • other
- restaurant food • snacks/fast food • vegetables

b Extension. Listen and repeat. Label the pictures. Which words are not in the pictures?

Dishes
- bowl • cup • plate • saucer

Silverware
- fork • knife • spoon

Cooking utensils
- can opener • cheese grater • cutting board
- frying pan • ~~kettle~~ • peeler • saucepan
- scale • sieve

1 *kettle*	2 _____	3 _____
4 _____	5 _____	6 _____
7 _____	8 _____	9 _____

Pronunciation: Intonation in lists

3 🎧 Go to page 130.

NEW SHOWS FOR THE FALL

Teen Island Challenge

What **are** you **going to do** this summer? Do you want to do something different?

If your answer is yes, then things **are about to get** exciting. Channel 9 **is screening** a new reality TV show this year called *Teen Island Challenge.*

We're looking for 20 teenagers between the ages of 16 and 18 to take part. We**'ll fly** you to a Carribean island at the end of July and leave you there with a camera crew. But don't worry, we**'ll come** back and get you a month later.

So what happens? Well, it's an uninhabited island. It **will be** a tough challenge because there **won't be** any electricity or running water. You**'ll sleep** in tents, and you**'ll have** some camping lamps. We**'ll give** you some basic food for the first week, such as flour, sugar, oil, canned meat, and canned vegetables. You**'ll have to** find or catch all your fresh food. Your kitchen **will consist of** an open fire and four saucepans.

Read

4 Listen and read the advertisement above. In which months will the TV show be taped?

💡 Solve it!

5 How many months are there between the audition and the end of the challenge?

Comprehension

6 Answer the questions.

1 What is *Teen Island Challenge*?  *a TV show*
2 Who can take part in it?
3 What is the island like?
4 What kind of food is there?
5 How can you book an audition?

Speak

7 PAIRS Discuss. Would you apply for this reality TV show? Why or why not?

We**'re holding** auditions on January 31 in New York. There's been a lot of interest in it already. It**'s going to be** a hit show. Book your audition now!

Call Gaby at Roll-up Productions at 1(800) 555-0000.

Grammar

Future tenses: *will, be going to,* present continuous form

What **are** you **going to do**?
It**'s going to be** a hit show.
Don't worry. We**'ll come** back and get you.
It **will be** a tough challenge.
There **won't be** any running water.
We**'re** hold**ing** auditions on January 31.

be about to + infinitive

Things **are about to get** exciting.
Note: Use the verb *to be* + *about* to + infinitive for something that will happen very soon.

☛ Go to page 134, Master your grammar.

Practice

8 Read the e-mail from someone who auditioned for the TV show. Circle the correct form of the verbs.

Hi Georgina,
[1] You**'ll never guess**/'re never guessing what's happened. Last week I auditioned for a new TV show called *Teen Island Challenge,* and they accepted me! [2] I'm being/**'m going to be** one of 20 teenagers spending a month on an uninhabited island. [3] We're flying/**'re about to fly** to the island on July 30. Before I go, my friend [4] Ralph**'s going to teach**/teaches me how to make a fire! He's really good at that kind of thing.

[5] It is/**'ll be** an amazing experience. [6] I'll take/**'m taking** a video camera and keep a diary.

Wish me luck! Keira

9 Complete the sentences. Use *will, be going to,* or the present continuous form and the verb in parentheses.

1 **A:** Oh, no! I left my wallet at home.
  B: I*'ll go* _____ (go) back and get it for you.
2 **A:** Paul and I _____ (play) soccer tomorrow. We play every Thursday.
  B: That's cool. Can I come?
3 **A:** Do you want to go for a walk?
  B: No, thanks. Look at the sky. It _____ (rain).
4 **A:** Can I go out?
  B: No. Grandma _____ (arrive) soon.
5 **A:** This is a secret. Don't tell my mom.
  B: Don't worry. I _____ (say) anything.

Speak

10 PAIRS You are going to take part in *Teen Island Challenge.* You can take three things from Exercise 2b. What are you going to take? Why?

Write

11 On a piece of paper, write a paragraph about your summer plans. What are you going to do? What do you think will happen?

I'm going to visit my cousins this summer …

 Extra practice
• Student Book, page 114, Lesson 3A
• Language Builder: WB, page 18; GB, page 108
• Student CD-ROM, Unit 3

3B You have to push yourself.

Grammar	*must, need, should, ought to, have to, had better*
Vocabulary	Part-time jobs
Function	Talk about rules

Get started

1 Have you ever had a part-time job? What did you do? Did you enjoy it? Why or why not?

Read

2 🎧 Listen and read along. Which jobs are mentioned in the chat forum?

---

http://www.holidayjobs.net   Q- Google

Looking for summer jobs!

>Hi, guys. I need to earn some money and I want to get a part-time vacation job. Does anyone out there have any suggestions? I don't want to deliver newspapers (too many early mornings!) or babysit—that's too much responsibility. **PaulK89**

>Have you thought of mowing lawns or helping to weed people's yards? You **have to** be in good shape and energetic, but it's easy and you **don't have to** have any special gardening skills. **Clare**

>There's lots of part-time work out there, but you **have to** be open to new ideas. You **must not** think, "Oh, I can't do painting and decorating, I've never done that." You **have to** push yourself. **Joseph**

>Sure, but you **shouldn't** say you can do something when you can't. That's dishonest. And it can get you into trouble. **Laura Jane**

>I agree. You **shouldn't** lie about your skills, but you don't need to be too honest or you'll never get a job. **Joseph**

>Maybe you **should** do something with computers, like my sister. She's teaching older people how to use their computers. You **have to** be polite and friendly—and patient, of course—but it's not hard and you can choose your hours. **Clare**

>Sounds good. What can I charge per hour? **PaulK89**

>I'm not sure, but you**'d better not** charge too much. **Clare**

Comprehension

3 Read the comments below. Write the name(s) of the people in the chat forum who agree with them.

1 Trying new things is good. ____*Joseph*____

2 Getting up early is no fun. _____

3 Don't lie about what you can do. _____

4 You don't need special skills to weed yards. _____

5 Teaching requires patience. _____

6 Taking care of children is a lot of responsibility. _____

Vocabulary: Part-time jobs

4a 🔊 Listen and repeat. Divide the jobs into those that involve
a) dealing with people or
b) physical work. Write *a* or *b*.

- *a* babysitting
- ___ delivering newspapers
- ___ dog walking
- ___ helping in a retirement home
- ___ mowing lawns
- ___ painting and decorating
- ___ teaching computer skills
- ___ washing cars
- ___ weeding yards
- ___ working in a store

b Say which jobs you think are easy, difficult, boring, or fun.

I think babysitting is easy.

> **Note**
> **Gerund (*-ing* form) as subject**
> Babysitt**ing** is easy.

Grammar

> ### *must, need, should, ought to, have to, had better*
>
> You **must** be open to new ideas.
> You **must not** lie about your skills.
> You **should/ought to** do something with computers.
> You **shouldn't** say you can do something when you can't.
> You **have to/need to** be in good shape.
> You **don't have to/don't need to** have any gardening skills.
> You **have to** push yourself.
> You**'d better not** charge too much.

☛ Go to page 134, Master your grammar.

Practice

5a PAIRS Ask and answer questions about the jobs in the chart. Use *(not) have to*.

1 A: *I'd like to teach computer skills. Do I need to get up early?*
  B: *No, you don't. And you don't have to work . . .*

	get up early	work late	have special skills	be polite
1 teach computer skills	✗	✗	✓	✓
2 do babysitting	✗	✓	✗	✓
3 do decorating	✓	✗	✓	✓
4 work in a store	✗	✗	✗	✓

b Describe the jobs.

1 *A person who teaches computer skills doesn't have to get up early or work in the evening. He or she has to have . . .*

6 Complete the hostel rules with *have to*, *don't have to*, *must not*, *should*, or *shouldn't*.

Red Forest Hostel Rules

Please read all the hostel rules carefully.
- Breakfast is at 8 A.M., lunch at 12:30 P.M., and dinner at 7 P.M. If you want a good choice of food, you [1] ___*have to*___ be on time for all meals.
- You [2] _____ eat lunch, but it's included in the price.
- Cleaners come in every day, but you [3] _____ make your own bed.
- You [4] _____ keep any food in your room. This is important.
- You [5] _____ probably lock any valuables in the safe.
- There's a CD player, but you [6] _____ play loud music after 11 P.M.
- You [7] _____ bring too much money—there isn't much opportunity to go shopping!
- There's singing around the campfire every Friday evening. You [8] _____ join in, but it's usually fun.

Speak

7 PAIRS With a partner, ask and answer questions about the rules in Exercise 6.

Write

8 On a piece of paper, write a paragraph about the rules at a job you had or in a place you stayed. Use the hostel rules in Exercise 6 as a model.

> **Extra practice**
> - **Student Book, page 114, Lesson 3B**
> - **Language Builder: WB, page 20; GB, page 109**
> - **Student CD-ROM, Unit 3**

You can't make me stay at home.

Grammar *make, let, allowed to*
Function Invite, accept, and refuse
with excuses

Get started

1 Do you have to follow lots of rules? Who makes
the rules?

Presentation

2 Listen and read along. What two things
are happening on Saturday?

Lisa: Hi, Sergio.

Sergio: Hi, Lisa. Do you want to go to the Rock FM
concert in the park on Saturday?

Lisa: Yes, that sounds great. I'll check with my
mom. Mom, can I go to a concert with Sergio
this Saturday?

Mom: Sorry, but I need you to take care of Danny.
Your dad and I have tickets for the theater.

Lisa: Oh, Mom! That's so unfair! Please **let me go.**
You can't **make me stay** at home on a
Saturday evening!

Mom: Sorry, Lisa, but we've had these tickets for
weeks.

Lisa: Oh, all right. Sergio, I'd like to, but I can't.
I have to take care of my little brother.

Woman: Excuse me. You're **not allowed to use** your
cell phone in this car.

Lisa: Oh, sorry. I didn't see the sign. I have to go
now, Sergio. Bye!

Comprehension

3 In your notebook, answer the questions.

1 What does Lisa want to do next Saturday?
2 What are Lisa's parents doing that evening?
3 Why is this a problem?
4 What is the woman annoyed about?

Grammar

make, let, allowed to

You can't **make me stay** at home!
Please **let me go** to the concert.
You're **(not) allowed** to use your cell phone.

☛ Go to page 134, Master your grammar.

Practice

4a In your notebook, explain what the signs mean, using *allowed to* or *not allowed to*.

1 *You're not allowed to use your cell phone.*

1 use/cell phone   **2** go   **3** park

4 eat   **5** turn left   **6** ride/bike

b In your notebook, write the same sentences, using *they let* or *don't let*.

1 *They don't let you use your cell phone.*

 ## Solve it!

5 Look at the photo of the train. What else is not allowed?

6 In your notebook, report the airport instructions with *make* and the pronouns in parentheses. Change the possessive adjectives where necessary.

1 "Could you take off your shoes?" (She/him)
   She made him take off his shoes.

2 "Please wait in the departure lounge." (They/us)

3 "Everyone must show their ID." (They/me)

4 "Please fasten your seatbelts." (He/them)

5 "Everyone must turn off their phones." (She/us)

Listen

7 1/30 Lisa is taking care of her younger brother, Danny. Listen and answer the questions.

1 What does Danny have for dinner? *burger and fries*

2 What vegetable(s) does he eat? _____

3 What time does *Batman* start? _____

4 How many stories does Lisa read to Danny? _____

5 What does she let him do? _____

Speak

8 **GROUPS** Discuss with the class your rules at home and the jobs your parents make you do.

Use your English: Invite, accept, and refuse with excuses

9 Read the sentences below.

Invite
- Do you want to go to the Rock FM concert?
- Can you come over and watch a DVD?
- Would you like to go to the movies tomorrow?

Accept
- Yes, that sounds great.   • Thanks. I'd love to.

Refuse
- I'd like to, but I can't. I'm really sorry.
- I'd love to, but I can't.

Make excuses
- I have to take care of my brother.
- My grandparents are coming to dinner.

Listen

10 1/31 **PAIRS** Listen to the conversation. Then role-play the conversations twice using the cues, first accepting, then refusing.

Invitation	Excuse
1 go shopping with me this afternoon	go to the dentist
2 go for pizza with us on Sunday	aunt and uncle coming over for the day
3 study together	take the dog for a walk

Write

11 On a piece of paper, write the rules in your home. Use the expressions from Exercise 9 and the following words to help you get started.

a) TV   b) video games
c) makeup and jewelry   d) staying out late

I'm allowed to watch TV, but I'm not allowed to watch it when I have homework . . .

 **Extra practice**
- **Student Book, page 115, Lesson 3C**
- **Language Builder: WB, page 22; GB, page 109**
- **Student CD-ROM, Unit 3**

A refugee's story

INTEGRATED
CONSOLIDATION
SKILLS

Values for living

Before you read, go to page 29.

REFUGEE CASE STUDY

Koor Deng

Koor Deng was born in a country in Africa. Koor was the eldest of six children.

When Koor was 15 years old, civil war returned to his country. It became a dangerous place to live. Soldiers and armed men were everywhere, and friends and neighbors in Koor's town no longer trusted each other.

Koor's mother was a strong woman, and she looked after her family with pride. Koor's father was a teacher, and the whole family respected him. The family didn't want to leave their house, but after a year the situation became very dangerous, and they decided that they had to go. One morning they packed some possessions and left their town on foot. Koor's uncle came with them. They walked for weeks. Eventually they crossed the border and came to a refugee camp. Conditions in the camp were very difficult. There was no electricity and very little water or food.

After four months in the camp, Koor's parents and uncle discussed the situation with Koor.

"We are refugees now," Koor's father said. "Life here is very hard. We must stay to look after your brothers and sister, but you are 16. You are old enough to leave."

"But where can I go?" asked Koor.

"I think you should go to the U.S.," Koor's father said. "We can apply for a refugee visa. Then we will borrow the money for your plane ticket. When you are in the U.S., you can finish your education and get a job. Then perhaps you can help us."

"That will take a long time, and how will we pay back the money?" Koor's uncle said, "I think Koor ought to go back to our country. He can go to the capital and find a job. Then he can earn money and help us all."

"The capital is 1,000 miles from here," Koor's mother said. "It's a big city, and he'll be on his own there. It is better for him to stay here and help us."

"I don't want to leave you," Koor said, "but I want to help. I will do what is best for the family."

FACTFILE
- There are about 16 million refugees in the world.
- Most refugees lose everything: their homes, their possessions, their friends, and often their family.

New words and phrases

- refugee • eldest • civil war • peaceful
- fear • armed • trust *(v)* • pride • respect *(v)*
- situation • eventually • border • refugee camp
- visa • pay back

Get started

1 What students do you know from other countries?

Read

2 Read the story on page 28. Where does Koor's father want Koor to go?

Comprehension

3 Answer the questions.

1 Where is Koor from? *Africa*
2 What happened when Koor was 15?
3 In what ways was Koor's town dangerous?
4 Where did Koor's parents take the family?
5 What was the refugee camp like?
6 What did Koor's father want Koor to do?
7 What did Koor's mother and uncle want?

Speak your mind!

Learning strategy: Take time to prepare

Before you start speaking, prepare what you want to say. Try to use new language to make your point.

4 GROUPS Role-play: Choose one of the roles below and prepare what you want to say.

Student A: You are Koor's father. You want him to apply for a refugee visa and go to the U.S. You think he will be safe there.

Student B: You are Koor's mother. You want him to stay and help the family in the refugee camp. He is young, and you don't want him to be alone.

Student C: You are Koor's uncle. You think Koor should go to the capital of your country. You have some friends there who can help him.

5 Act out the role play. Decide what Koor should do.

Listen

6 Listen and answer the questions.

1 What did Koor decide to do in the end?
move to the U.S.

2 How does Lauren feel about Koor?

3 How does Ashton feel about Koor? Why?

4 Where is Ashton's family from?

5 What does the teacher say about Koor's life?

6 What do Lauren and Ashton promise to do?

Write

7 Imagine you are Koor. You have been in the U.S. for a month. Write a letter to your parents.

Paragraph 1: Ask how the family is and say that you miss them.

Paragraph 2: Tell them about your life in the U.S.
– U.S.: strange, but nice
– people: very friendly
– have two friends already: Ashton and Lauren
– have a Saturday job in pizza restaurant

Paragraph 3: Talk about your plans for the future.
– will send money soon
– sister can come to the U.S. soon

CLIL PROJECT, page 157

The most fun I've had in a long time

Grammar	Present perfect with *already, before, never, ever, yet*
	Superlatives with the present perfect
Function	React to good and bad news

Phrases

34 Listen and repeat.

- that great • try • up for it • really easy
- Bad luck. • It's my turn. • Way to go!

Get started

1 What kinds of fairs are there in your town? Do you like to go?

Presentation

2 **33** Listen and read along. Who gets a present?

Sophie: Look! I won a necklace!

Lisa: Cool! I've never won anything at a fair.

Sophie: Never mind. The prizes aren't that great.

Lisa: What did you do to win it?

Sophie: I knocked three cards down with three balls. You know, this is the most fun I've had in a long time.

Carlos: Why don't you try, too, Lisa? It's only 50 cents a try.

Lisa: I can't. I've already spent all my money.

Sergio: Hey, we haven't tried this game yet. Are you up for it, Carlos?

Carlos: I don't know. I've never played it before.

Man: You get three darts, and you have to hit the cards.

Carlos: OK. I'll try.

Sergio: It's really easy. Watch this . . . Oops! Missed!

Carlos: Bad luck. It's my turn now. . . . Yes!!

Sophie: That's awesome, Carlos! Way to go!

Man: Here you are, sir.

Carlos: I won a giant teddy bear!

Sophie: That's the biggest bear I've ever seen!

Carlos: Here, Lisa. It's a present for you.

Lisa: Oh! That's . . . um . . . great, Carlos. Thanks.

Comprehension

3 Write the names in the chart. Write *Sophie, Lisa, Carlos,* or *Sergio.*

Activity	Name
Who:	
1 won a necklace?	*Sophie*
2 doesn't win prizes at fairs?	
3 threw balls and knocked down cards?	
4 is very confident about the game?	
5 is better at the game?	
6 wins a teddy bear?	

ARE YOU LUCKY TODAY?

$2 = 3 DAR
LAND THE DART IN THE CARD
DARTS IN THE WHITE OR THE BLACK
DARTS MUST BE IN SEPARAT
2 IN WINS M
3 IN WINS
NO CROSSING THE RED LI
ONE PRIZE LIMIT PER

Grammar

Present perfect with *already, before, never, ever, yet*

I've **never won** anything at a fair.
She **has already spent** all of her money.
Have you **ever tried** this game?
We **haven't tried** this game **yet**.
I've **never done** it **before**.

Superlatives with the present perfect

This is **the most** fun I've **had** in a long time!
That's **the biggest** bear I've **ever seen**!

☛ Go to page 135, Master your grammar.

Practice

4 Complete the video game review with the present perfect or simple past.

```
000
◄ ► c ⊠ + ● http://www.gamesreview.net          Q▾ Google
```

Guitar Star 3   Our rating: ☆☆☆☆☆

¹ Have you _____*played*_____ (you/play/yet) **Guitar Star 3** _____*yet*_____? I ² _____ (buy) it last week, and it's probably the best game I ³ _____ (ever/play). It was easy to install and I ⁴ _____ (not have) any problems with the instructions so far. Even if you ⁵ _____ (never/play) the guitar in your life, you can still enjoy this game. When I started, I ⁶ _____ (choose) the easiest songs and ⁷ _____ (sing) with the lyrics on the screen. There are six levels of difficulty, but I ⁸ _____ (not get/yet) to Level Six _____. I ⁹ _____ (finish) Level Three last night. It's a fantastic game!

5 Write sentences in your notebook using the present perfect with *ever* and a superlative.

1 That/nice thing/someone/say to me!
   That's the nicest thing someone has ever said to me!
2 That/bad CD/I/hear.
3 This/good/vacation/we/have.
4 This/delicious meal/I/eat.
5 That/difficult game/I/play.
6 Those/expensive jeans/I/ever buy.

Use your English: React to good and bad news

6 Read the phrases below.

React to good news
• Wow! That's great/wonderful!
• That's really cool/amazing!
• Way to go! • Good job!
• Awesome!

React to bad news
• Oh, no! That's awful/too bad!
• That's horrible! • Cheer up!
• I'm really sorry to hear that.

Pronunciation: Falling intonation in exclamations

7 🎧 Go to page 130.

Listen

8 🎧 **PAIRS** Listen to the conversation. Then role-play more conversations. Use the cues.

1 I/already/lose my new phone.
   A: *I've already lost my new phone.*
   B: *Oh, no! That's awful.*
2 These are/good/grades/I/ever/have!
3 I'm really tired. I/not/sleep/for two days.
4 I/already/get/tickets for the concert.

Write

9 On a piece of paper, write a paragraph about one of your sentences from Exercise 5.

My dad said I was smart. That's the nicest thing ...

Extra practice
• **Student Book, page 115, Lesson 4A**
• **Language Builder: WB, page 26; GB, page 112**
• **Student CD-ROM, Unit 4**

4B He's been playing for 10 years.

Grammar	Present perfect and present perfect continuous with *for* and *since*
	Present perfect for numbers and amounts
Vocabulary	Music words
Function	Talk about past events that are still important today

Get started

1 Can you name any racing car drivers? How do you think they spend their free time between races?

Read

2  Listen and read along. Name Lewis Hamilton's favorite a) musicians, b) type of music, c) guitar solo.

Solve it!

3 How old was Lewis Hamilton when he joined the McLaren Youth Program?

Comprehension

4 Correct the sentences.

1 Lewis Hamilton is a famous ~~guitarist~~. *racing car driver*

2 His favorite way of relaxing is to read.

3 He likes singers only from the 60s and 70s.

4 He has had a large number of guitar lessons.

5 He would like to be a rock star.

Lewis Hamilton – *free-time formula*

Lewis Hamilton **has been** a professional racing driver **since** the Formula One team McLaren signed him to their Youth Program. He **has won** about four Formula One races each season and **has traveled** around the world. When he is in a hotel or on the move, his favorite way to pass the time is to pick up his electric guitar.

The British driver **has been playing** the guitar **for** 10 years. "You have a lot of time to kill when you're traveling," Lewis said. "Like everyone else, I watch DVDs, read books, and surf the net, but I soon get bored with all that, so I always take my guitar with me. It's the only way I can really relax."

He practices songs by Tracy Chapman, Oasis, Bob Dylan, Lenny Kravitz, and Jimi Hendrix, but his favorite is Bob Marley's *No Woman No Cry*. "I like rock, funk, hip-hop, R & B, soul, and jazz, but I was basically brought up on reggae. **I've been listening** to Bob Marley ever **since** I was a child."

So does he have ambitions to be a rock star after a career in Formula One? "No," he said with a laugh. "I'll never be that good. I had a few guitar lessons when I started, but I **haven't had** any lessons **for** years now. Anyway, if I had the choice, I'd be a rapper, not a rock star."

FACTFILE	Lewis Hamilton: early life and career
1985	Born in Stevenage, U.K.
1990	Got an electric car as a present
1995	Won his first go-carting championship
1998	McLaren signed him/Took up the guitar
2002	Passed his driving test
2003	Won the F3 U.K. championship
2007 Jan	Drove in his first F1 race
June	Won his first F1 race
Oct	Moved to Switzerland
2008	Won the F1 world championship
2010	Won second/third place in the F1 world championship

Grammar

Present perfect with *for* and *since*

I **haven't had** any lessons **for** years now.
He**'s been** a racing car driver **since** McLaren
  signed him.

Present perfect continuous with *for* and *since*

He**'s been playing** the guitar **for** 10 years.
I**'ve been listening** to Bob Marley ever **since**
  I was a child.

Present perfect for numbers and amounts

He **has won** four Formula One races each
  season.

☛ Go to page 135, Master your grammar.

Practice

5 Read the factfile on page 32. In your notebook,
ask and answer questions with *How long?* Use the
present perfect or present perfect continuous and
the cues below. Answer with *for*, and then with *since*.

1 like cars?
  A: *How long has he liked cars?*
  B: *He's liked cars for almost 20 years./*
    He's liked cars since the age of five.
2 play/the guitar?
3 have/his driver's license?
4 drive/in Formula One races?
5 be/part of McLaren's team?
6 win/races?
7 live/in Switzerland?

6 Complete the sentences with the correct form
of the verb and *for* or *since* where necessary.

1 We ____*have been living*____ (live) in the center of
  town _____*since*_____ the end of last year.
2 How many cups of coffee _____
  (she/drink)?
3 She _____ (have) glasses
  _____ she was 10 years old.
4 My mother _____ (look) for her
  keys _____ over an hour.
5 How many hours _____ (he/sit)
  at that computer?
6 I _____ (play) tennis three times this week.

Vocabulary: Music words

7a **Review.** In your notebook, write all the
musical instruments you can remember next to the
headings. Then check the Word bank on page 128.

String: *guitar*   **Wind:** *trumpet*   **Other:** *piano*

b 🎧 1 39 **Extension.** Listen and repeat. Look at the
words in the box. Circle the people.

> **Musical terminology**
> • album • backup singer • band • beat
> • charts • lead singer • lyrics • producer
> • rapper • single • song • songwriter

c Now give an example of each of the following:

1 a popular hit single ____*Down*____
2 a lead singer and a band you like _____
3 a current album _____
4 a good track on the album _____
5 a song with a strong drum beat _____
6 a song with good lyrics _____

Listen

8 🎧 1 40 Listen to an interview.
Then answer the questions.

1 How did Kanye West start his
  career in music? *as a producer*
2 Which famous artists has he worked
  with? _____
3 When did he release his first album? _____
4 What other talent does he have? _____
5 How long has the Kanye West Foundation been in
  Chicago? What does it do? _____

Speak

9 PAIRS Use the questions and answers from
Exercise 8 to role-play conversations about
Kanye West.

Write

10 On a piece of paper, write about your favorite
musician. Include facts like those in Exercise 8.

> ⊙ **Extra practice**
> • Student Book, page 115, Lesson 4B
> • Language Builder: WB, page 28; GB, page 113
> • Student CD-ROM, Unit 4

The website everyone is talking about

Grammar	Restrictive and nonrestrictive relative clauses
Vocabulary	Phrasal verbs with *on*
Function	Talk about music technology

Entertainment innovations

Your round-up of the hottest events and coolest gadgets in the world of entertainment, by Caroline Brett

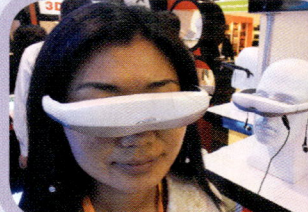

1 Silent discos

A silent disco is an event **where** clubbers get a pair of wireless headphones when they enter the club. The DJ broadcasts music to the clubbers' headphones and everyone dances. The first disco took place at a festival **where** neighbors had previously complained about the noise. Silent discos are now becoming very popular. People **who** want to talk can take their headphones off. Amazing!

2 Hi-tech specs

These super cool glasses let you watch movies or music videos any time and anywhere you want! When you put them on, it's like having a huge TV screen in front of your eyes. Headphones, **which** are built into the glasses, allow you to listen in stereo at the same time. Boredom will be a thing of the past with these new hi-tech specs!

3 Online music lessons from the stars

The latest website everyone is talking about offers video tutorials for trainee musicians. The teacher in each video is the person **who** actually wrote the song! Stars like KT Tunstall and Paul McCartney, **whose** Beatles songs are famous, are just two of the artists already on the website. Any musician **whose** songs are popular can submit a video. So next time you want to learn a new song, log on to the website and pick up your guitar!

Get started

1 How do you think music technology will change over the next 20 years?

Read

2 Listen and read along. Then match each entertainment innovation in the article to a category.

a) a website _____   b) an event _____

c) a gadget _____

Comprehension

3 Write the number of the innovation that each comment refers to.

1 "I learned to play a new song." _____3_____

2 "This place is usually really noisy, but not this evening." _____

3 "I used them to watch the latest James Bond movie." _____

4 "We were all dancing to the same song, but the room was quiet!" _____

5 "They've made my boring bus trip much more fun." _____

6 "Some of the teachers are really famous." _____

Speak

4 PAIRS Discuss the questions.

1 Which innovation do you think is the most interesting?

2 Which one would you most like to experience? Why?

3 Do you have an idea for a different entertainment innovation? Describe it.

Grammar

Relative clauses

Restrictive relative clauses

People **who/that** want to talk can take their headphones off.

It's a new website **that** offers video tutorials.

Any musician **whose** songs are popular can submit a video.

It was a club **where** neighbors had complained about the noise.

A website (**that**) everyone is talking about . . .

Clubbers can choose the DJ (**who/that**) they want to listen to.

Nonrestrictive relative clauses

Damon Albarn, **who** is the lead singer of Blur, is also on the website.

Headphones, **which** are built into the glasses, allow you to listen.

Paul McCartney, **whose** Beatles songs are famous, is on the website.

☛ Go to page 135, Master your grammar.

Practice

5 In your notebook, write sentences using the correct tense and relative pronouns (*whose*, *where*, *who*, *which*, or *that*). Use commas where necessary.

1 The movie/everyone (talk) about right now/(be) *School Rules*.

   The movie that everyone is talking about right now is School Rules.

2 The teenage actor/(play) the lead role/(be) Jay Fox.

3 Some movie-lovers/see the movie last night/give it five stars.

4 Jay/mother (be) from Italy/(arrive) in Los Angeles last night.

5 Jay said, "I'd like to thank my mother/(encourage) me to become an actor."

6 The movie/(start) Jay's career two years ago/(be) *Rock Star*.

7 That movie (become) a big success in Canada/Jay (be) born.

6 In your notebook, rewrite the text below. Combine the sentences with relative pronouns to make restrictive or nonrestrictive relative clauses.

1 *A TV station in the U.S. is offering instant fame to teenagers who want to be celebrities.*

A new reality show

¹ᵃ A TV station in the U.S. is offering instant fame to teenagers. ¹ᵇ The teenagers want to be celebrities. ²ᵃ The station created its own TV recording booths. ²ᵇ The booths are like phone booths but bigger. ³ᵃ They then put the booths in shopping malls and other places. ³ᵇ Young people go to these places. ⁴ᵃ The booths are very popular. ⁴ᵇ They have a TV camera inside. ⁵ᵃ Young people can perform a song or dance. ⁵ᵇ The young people are often very talented. ⁶ᵃ The results appear on a show. ⁶ᵇ The show is on TV the same evening.

Vocabulary: Phrasal verbs with *on*

7 Listen and repeat. In your notebook, replace the underlined phrases below with phrasal verbs from the box.

- count on • hold on • keep on • log on
- put on • try on • ~~turn on~~ • work on

1 Do you <u>switch on</u> the TV when you get home?

   Do you turn on the TV when you get home?

2 Do you always <u>wear</u> clothes <u>to see how they look</u> before you buy them?

3 Can you always <u>rely on</u> your best friend to help you?

4 When you <u>enter your user name and password</u> to a website, do you often make a mistake?

5 Do you <u>continue</u> talking when the teacher arrives?

Write

8 On a piece of paper, write a paragraph about a type of new technology that you use. Try to use relative clauses.

I have a cell phone that plays music . . .

> **Extra practice**
> • **Student Book, page 116, Lesson 4C**
> • **Language Builder: WB, page 30; GB, page 113**
> • **Student CD-ROM, Unit 4**

Across cultures

Get started

1 What kind of books do you like reading? What have you read recently?

Read

2 Read the texts. In what year is the book set?

Comprehension

3a Read the review again. In your notebook, write the questions for these answers.

1 H.G.Wells *Who wrote The Time Machine?*
2 1894
3 A science fiction book
4 In a time machine
5 In the year 802,701

3b Answer the questions.

The review

1 What does the Time Traveler notice about the size, strength, and intelligence of the Eloi?
   They are small, weak, and not intelligent.
2 What happens to the time machine?
3 How are the Morlocks different from the Eloi?
4 How does the Time Traveler get his machine back?

The excerpt

5 What does he notice about the natural world?
6 How healthy were people?
7 What social change did he find surprising?
8 In what way can difficulties in life be good?

A BOOK I'VE ENJOYED

The Time Machine
by H.G.Wells

The Time Machine is a science fiction book by H.G.Wells, who was a famous British author. He wrote the book in 1894. It is about a journey through time in a time machine. The book forecasts space travel and nuclear wars as well as predicting genetically modified foods.

The main character is an inventor who lives in London. He's called simply "the Time Traveler." He builds a time machine and sets off on a journey that takes him into the future. He arrives in the year 802,701. He expects to find a better world with more intelligent people and great inventions. Instead, he discovers a world where people have become happy, child-like creatures. These people, the Eloi, are not only physically smaller but also less intelligent than people in the present day. What's more, they have become weak. While he gets to know the Eloi, the Time Traveler forgets about his time machine. He suddenly realizes that it has mysteriously disappeared. During his search for it, he meets a second group of creatures, the Morlocks, who live underground. They are the workers and they are strong, but they are also evil and violent. After fighting the Morlocks, the Time Traveler finds his time machine, which the Morlocks have stolen and hidden. He returns to the present time to tell his friends the story of his time travel.

I just finished this book, and I enjoyed every minute of it. It's one of the most exciting books I've read in a long time.—*Terri Edwards (16)*

Listen

> **Learning strategy: Listen for mood**
>
> The intonation and tone of voice of a speaker can help you to understand his or her mood and what he or she is saying.

4 🔊 1/43 Listen to the conversation about *The Time Machine*. Answer the questions.

1 What does Harry need to do?
   write a book review

2 Why does Harry's dad love the book?
   _____

3 Is the book popular today? How do you know?
   _____

4 What does Wells think humans are like?
   _____

An excerpt from *The Time Machine*
The Time Traveler has just met the Eloi.

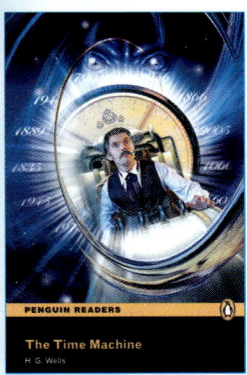

"At the top of a hill, I sat down and looked at our world. Here I could see that these changes had been made. The air was free of unpleasant insects, the earth was free of weeds. Everywhere there were fruits and pleasant flowers. Beautiful birds flew here and there. And I saw no diseases during my stay.

There had been social changes as well. I saw people living in fine buildings, beautifully dressed, but I hadn't yet found them doing any work. The shop, the advertisement, buying and selling—all of these things which are so important to us had all disappeared.

I thought of the small size of the people and their low intelligence. People had been strong, energetic and intelligent, and had used this energy to change their living conditions. Difficulties make people strong and clever and help them to work together. But where were these dangers now?"

> **New words and phrases**
> - forecast *(v)* • nuclear war • predict
> - genetically modified • creature • weak
> - mysteriously • evil • violent • fight *(v)*
> - insects • weeds • disease • low intelligence
> - energetic • living conditions • difficulty/ies

Speak

5 **PAIRS** Discuss the questions.

1 Have you read any science fiction books or seen any science fiction movies? Did you enjoy them?
2 Imagine you travel in a time machine to the year 3020. What changes do you think you would see?

Write

> **Writing tip: Conjunctions** *as well as, what's more, not only . . . but also*
>
> We can combine two ideas in one sentence by using pairs of conjunctions, e.g., **not only . . . but also**. We can add points with **as well as** and **what's more**.
>
> *The book forecasts space travel and nuclear wars* **as well as** *predicting genetically modified foods.*
>
> *They are* **not only** *physically smaller* **but also** *less intelligent.* **What's more**, *they have become weak.*

6 In your notebook, combine the sentences in three ways.

1 She is intelligent. She is very beautiful.
   As well as being intelligent, she is very beautiful.
   She is not only intelligent but also very beautiful.
   She's intelligent. What's more, she's beautiful.
2 He speaks Spanish. And he speaks French.
3 He has a new job. And he has a new laptop.
4 I've read *The Time Machine*. I've seen the movie.

7 Go to the Writing bank on page 145 and complete the exercises. Then write a short review of a book.

The War of the Worlds is another work of science fiction by H. G. Wells. It was written in 1898 . . .

_____
_____
_____
_____
_____
_____
_____
_____
_____

CLIL PROJECT, page 157

Grammar (40 points)

1 Circle the correct verb form. (5 points)

0 A: I left my keys inside.

B: Don't worry. I ____ and get them for you.

a)'m going to go   b)('ll go)

1 A: Have you booked your summer vacation yet?

B: Yes, we have. We ____ two weeks in Mexico.

a) 're spending   b) 'll spend

2 A: Have my books arrived yet?

B: No. We ____ you when they arrive.

a) are about to call   b) 'll call

3 A: My brother is going to college next year.

B: Really? What ____?

a) does he study   b) is he going to study

4 A: What time is it? The game starts at three.

B: It's five minutes to three. It ____.

a) 's about to start   b) 'll start

5 A: They're losing 2-0. The manager looks angry.

B: I'm sure he ____ at the team after the game.

a) 'll shout   b) 's about to shout

2 Complete the sentences with verbs from the box. (8 points)

> • don't have • don't need to • have • must (x2)
> • must not • should (x2) • shouldn't

Winter Sports Camp Rules

* Everyone ⁰ ___*must*___ wear a helmet. This is essential when you ski or snowboard.
* All beginners ¹ _____ go to ski school. Good skiers and boarders ² _____ go if they don't want to.
* You can go into the village after skiing, but you ³ _____ be back later than 7 P.M.
* You ⁴ _____ to make your bed every morning, but you ⁵ _____ to clean the room. The housekeepers will do this.
* Everyone ⁶ _____ wear a high protection sunscreen.
* If you're a beginner, you ⁷ _____ stay on the easy green and blue slopes. You ⁸ _____ try any red slopes unless you are very confident.

3 Complete the sentences with the correct form of *make*, *let*, or *allowed*. (5 points)

0 Did your parents ____*let*____ you stay out late?

1 Our teacher _____ us take a test yesterday.

2 My brother won't _____ me use his football.

3 When his car broke down, he _____ us push it.

4 Don't _____ him use your laptop. He'll break it.

5 Were you _____ to eat a lot of candy as a child?

4 Complete the conversation with the present perfect or the present perfect continuous and *for* or *since*. (10 points)

Int: How long ⁰ _*have you been*_ (be) in the heavy metal band Headz Up?

Leo: I ¹ _____ (be) the drummer ² _____ two years.

Int: When did you start to play the drums?

Leo: A long time ago. In fact, I ³ _____ (play) the drums ⁴ _____ I was a teenager.

Int: Do you have a new album?

Leo: Yes, we ⁵ _____ (work) on a new album ⁶ _____ February. It's almost finished.

Int: ⁷ _____ you always ⁸ _____ (love) heavy metal?

Leo: No, I haven't. I ⁹ _____ always ¹⁰ _____ (prefer) classical music, but I earn more in this band!

5 In your notebook, combine the sentences to include restrictive or nonrestrictive relative clauses. (12 points)

0 I've seen the man before. (He was talking to you.)

I've seen the man who was talking to you before.

1 The girl is Paul's sister. (She was at the party.)

2 Leonardo da Vinci was born in 1452. (His most famous painting is the *Mona Lisa*.)

3 That's the restaurant. (We had our first date.)

4 That's the café. (Your brother recommended it.)

Vocabulary (40 points)

6 Complete the sentences with an item of kitchen equipment. (7 points)

0 You grate cheese with a ___cheese grater___ .
1 You peel potatoes with a p_____ .
2 You fry onions in a f_____ p_____ .
3 You open cans with a c_____ o_____ .
4 You boil water in a k_____ .
5 You eat soup from a b_____ .
6 You slice onions with a k_____ .
7 You measure the weight of something on a
s_____ .

7 Circle the word that doesn't belong and choose a category from the box for the other three words. (18 points)

> • dairy • desserts • drinks • ~~fish~~ • fruit
> • meat • musical instruments • restaurant food
> • snacks • vegetables

0 shrimp (yogurt) salmon ___fish___
1 cucumber chips cake cookie _____
2 lasagna garlic bread clarinet
spaghetti Bolognese _____
3 chicken beef steak ravioli _____
4 lamb violin cello keyboard _____
5 milk butter onion cheese _____
6 cola fruit juice mineral water melon
_____
7 fruit salad shrimp cheesecake apple pie
_____
8 tea mushroom beans potato _____
9 peach trumpet grape strawberry
_____

8 Correct the phrases for part-time jobs.
(8 points)

0 babyhelping ___babysitting___
1 delivering yards _____
2 washing newspapers _____
3 weeding computers _____
4 working in a computer _____
5 teaching lawns _____
6 painting and walking _____
7 mowing stores _____
8 dog painting _____

9 Complete with phrasal verbs. (7 points)

> • ~~count on~~ • hold on • keep on • log on
> • put on • try on • turn on • work on

0 She's really reliable. You can ___count on___ her.
1 Did you _____ this shirt
before you bought it?
2 Hurry up! _____ your
jacket. We're leaving.
3 As soon as they get home they
_____ the TV!
4 I need to _____ my tennis
skills more.
5 You need a password to _____
to that website.
6 _____ tight! I don't want
you to fall off.
7 Don't stop! _____ trying.

Use your English (20 points)

10 Complete the sentences. Then put the conversation in order.

☐ a) **Ben:** 0 ___That's___ too bad. Are you going out?
☐ b) **Ben:** That museum is great! 1 _____
you come out in the evening?
☐ c) **Jo:** Fine 2 _____. And you?
☐ d) **Jo:** His favorite — hot dogs. Hey,
3 _____ you want to go out
4 _____ Sunday instead?
☐ e) **Ben:** What are you going to cook?
☐ f) **Jo:** Yes, we're going 5 _____ the
Train Museum.
☐ g) **Ben:** Yes, Sunday 6 _____ great.
☑ h) **Ben:** 7 _____, Jo. How are you?
☐ i) **Ben:** Not 8 _____, thanks. Do you
9 _____ to go bowling
tomorrow afternoon?
☐ j) **Jo:** I'd 10 _____ to, but I can't.
It's my dad's birthday.
☐ k) **Jo:** No, I can't. I'm going to cook dinner for
Dad in the evening.

SELF-CHECK	
Grammar	___ /40
Vocabulary	___ /40
Use your English	___ /20
Total score	___ /100

Unless they do something, . . .

Natural world

5

Grammar	Conditionals with *if, unless, provided that, as long as*
Vocabulary	Landforms and the environment
Function	Talk about two sides of an issue

Get started

1 Have you ever been to a large music concert or festival? What was it like? How many people were there?

Read

2 🔊 Listen and read along. How many e-mails are in favor of the rock festival?

Comprehension

3 Complete the information.

1 Location of festival: _____*fields close to Mayton*_____
2 Number of people expected: _____
3 Local residents' plans: _____
4 Arguments against the festival: _____
5 Arguments for the festival: _____

Plans for rock festival worry locals

by our local correspondent **ALAN BLACK**

THE PLAN to hold a large music festival on fields close to the village of Mayton has worried local residents.

The festival will bring more than 100,000 people to the area over three days in August. Latest reports show that the local community is planning to take legal action to prevent the festival. Unless the local council does something to reassure residents, the festival might not happen at all. But what do the villagers really think? Here are just some of the hundreds of e-mails we've received this week.

"I'm appalled! If the council agrees to hold this festival here in our beautiful village, the river might end up full of garbage."
Mr. S. Yang

"I think people are making too much fuss over nothing. Provided that people clean up and put all their garbage in cans, there won't be a problem. It's a great chance for music fans to see their favorite singers and bands!"
Adele Smith

"I'm not crazy about the idea at all. I know all about music festivals—the music usually goes on all night. Unless I move out of the village, I won't get any sleep because of the noise."
Mrs. Maria Fernandez

"As long as the concert is well organized, the village won't suffer, and it might even benefit from the money that music fans will spend in our stores. If we stop this festival, the village will lose a great opportunity to make some money."
Mr. Brian Schmidt

Vocabulary: Landforms and the environment

4 Review. Complete the words. In your notebook, list other words that you know for landforms and the environment. Then check the Word bank on page 128.

1 c _o_ _a_ st   3 w__terf__ll   5 v__lle__   7 oc____n

2 r__v__r   4 d__s____t   6 mo__nt__n   8 h____b__r

Grammar

Conditionals with *if, unless, provided that, as long as*

If the council **agrees** to hold the festival here, the river **might end up** full of garbage.

Unless I **move** out of the village, I **won't get** any sleep!

Provided that people **clean up**, there **won't be** a problem.

As long as the concert **is** well organized, the village **won't suffer**.

☛ Go to page 136, Master your grammar.

Practice

5 Complete the conversation with the correct form of the verbs.

Sergio: Mrs. Brown, ¹ _____*will*_____ it *be* OK if we ² _____ (have) a party in class at the end of the semester?

Mrs. B: Well, I think it ³ _____ (be) all right, provided that you ⁴ _____ (clean up) after you've finished.

Sergio: Of course we will. We're going to have music, too, unless that ⁵ _____ (be) a problem.

Mrs. B: No, it ⁶ _____ (not/be) a problem, as long as you ⁷ _____ (not/disturb) the other classes.

Sergio: We won't play it too loud, don't worry.

Mrs. B: OK. I'll have to check with the principal. If he ⁸ _____ (say) no, you ⁹ _____ (have to) forget it.

6 In your notebook, write sentences using the words or phrases in parentheses.

1 not rain > we go to the beach tomorrow (if)

   If it doesn't rain, we'll go to the beach tomorrow.

2 you/promise to be/careful > I/let you ride my bike (as long as)

3 he/leave now > he/be late for class (unless)

4 you/concentrate > you/not have any problems on the test (if)

5 the students/take notes > they/forget the lesson (unless)

6 you/not invite/Mark > I/not come to your party (if)

7 you/give it back soon > I/lend you my camera (provided that)

Speak

7 PAIRS Role-play a discussion about a rock festival. Make notes before you speak. Use the ideas below to help you.

<u>For</u> (Student A)
· will be good entertainment
· will bring money to stores

<u>Against</u> (Student B)
· too much noise
· a lot of garbage

Write

8 On a piece of paper, write an e-mail to the local newspaper giving your opinion of the planned festival. Use conditionals.

Dear Points of View,
I think the festival will be fun as long as
people don't . . .

> **Extra practice**
> · **Student Book, page 117, Lesson 5A**
> · **Language Builder: WB, page 34; GB, page 115**
> · **Student CD-ROM, Unit 5**

By the time the rain comes . . .

Grammar	Future time clauses with *when, until, as soon as, by the time, before*
Vocabulary	Extreme weather and natural disasters
Function	Talk about disasters

Controlling
the weather

Storm, one of the superhero characters in the X-Men movies, has the ability to control the weather. She can create a hurricane, cause a thunderstorm, and start a downpour.

Rod Taylor

Rod Taylor, 17, works on an Australian sheep farm, and he needs a friend like Storm. The current drought in Australia is making his job impossible.

"**By the time** the rain **comes**," it will probably be too late," Rod says. "Some of the sheep have already died, and now we have to sell the rest. **When** that **happens**, I'll be out of a job."

Get started

1 What kinds of extreme weather or natural disasters do you have in your country?

Read

2 Listen and read along. Why is it expensive to stop rain for one evening?

Comprehension

3 Answer questions 1–4 with *Rod*, *Liu*, or *both*.

Who:

1 grows food on his or her farm? _____*Liu*_____
2 gets too little rain? _____
3 wants to leave his or her farm, but can't? _____
4 is hoping that the weather will change? _____

Answer questions 5–8 with *cloud-seeding*, *rocket-firing*, or *both*.

Which method:

5 could help Rod? _____
6 makes rain fall? _____
7 is expensive? _____
8 doesn't need a plane? _____

Vocabulary: Extreme weather and natural disasters

4a Listen and repeat.

- avalanche • blizzard • downpour • drought
- earthquake • famine • flood • gale • hail(storm)
- heat wave • hurricane • landslide • lightning
- snow(storm) • storm • thunder and lightning
- thunder(storm) • tornado • tsunami
- volcanic eruption

4b Now write the words from Exercise 4a in the chart below.

Extreme weather	Natural disasters
blizzard,	*avalanche,*

Grammar

Future time clauses with *when, until, as soon as, by the time, before*

When that happens, I'll be out of a job.
I won't be able to move **until I have some money**.
I'm going to move to the city **as soon as I can**.
By the time the rain comes, it will be too late.
Liu will have to save some money **before she leaves**.

☛ Go to page 136, Master your grammar.

Liu Wei

In another part of the world, in southwest China, 16-year-old **Liu Wei** has the opposite problem. Liu works on her parents' farm, but last month a flood destroyed their crops. "I'm going to move to the city *as soon as I can*," Liu says. "But I won't be able to move *until* I *have* some money. The flood has destroyed everything, so there won't be any money this year."

Can scientists help people like Rod and Liu? Sometimes they can create rain by "cloud-seeding." Planes drop chemicals onto clouds to make them rain. But it's expensive, and in a drought, the right kind of clouds are rarely in the sky. Scientists can use the same principle to try to stop floods. They fire chemical-filled rockets into the sky. This makes the clouds drop their rain early, away from areas that might flood. It works, but you need 1,000 rockets to stop the rain for one evening in one place. So for now, Rod and Liu can only hope for a natural change in the weather.

Practice

5 Complete the conversation with the correct form of the verbs in parentheses.

Mom: What time is your train to Portland?

Gerry: Eleven o'clock. I [1] _____'ll leave_____ (leave) for the station as soon as this show [2] _____ (end).

Mom: That's no good. It [3] _____ (be) after 10:30 by the time you [4] _____ (leave). That's too late.

Gerry: OK. I'll leave now.

Mom: Is Jake going to meet you when you [5] _____ (arrive)?

Gerry: I'm not sure. I [6] _____ (not know) until he [7] _____ (call) me.

Mom: What about food? By the time your train [8] _____ (arrive) in Portland, you [9] _____ (be) starving.

Gerry: Don't worry. I [10] _____ (buy) a sandwich before I [11] _____ (catch) the train. And I [12] _____ (call) you as soon as I [13] _____ (get) there.

6 Complete the sentences with the correct time conjunctions: *until, as soon as,* or *by the time.*

1 I'll stay here _____until_____ the rain stops. Then I'll go.

2 _____ scientists find an answer, it'll be too late.

3 _____ the sun comes out, I'll start the barbecue.

4 Hurry up, or the movie will be over _____ we get there.

5 You can't go out _____ you've done your homework.

6 We'll buy a boat _____ we have enough money.

Speak

7 GROUPS Complete the sentences to make them true for you; then discuss.

1 I'll feel really happy when . . .

2 I'm going to stay in school until . . .

3 As soon as I have enough time, I'm going to . . .

4 Before I get old, I'm going to . . .

5 By the time I'm 25, I . . .

Listen

8 (2 05) Listen to a news report about a tornado. Answer the questions.

1 Where was Patricia when the tornado started?
At school.

2 What did the tornado look and sound like?
_____

3 What damage did the tornado do?
_____

4 Where was Howard when the tornado started?
_____

5 What happened to Howard during the tornado?
_____

Write

9 Have you ever been in extreme weather? On a piece of paper, write a paragraph about your experience. Use the news report in Exercise 8 as a model.

> **Extra practice**
> • **Student Book, page 117, Lesson 5B**
> • **Language Builder: WB, page 36; GB, page 115**
> • **Student CD-ROM, Unit 5**

5c In case it gets cold

Grammar	*in case* + simple present
Vocabulary	Camping equipment
Function	Make and respond to requests

Get started

1 Which outdoor activities do you enjoy: camping, swimming, hiking, mountain climbing, biking?

Presentation

2 🎧 2/06 Listen and read along. What does Carlos want to borrow and why?

The four friends are planning to go camping.

Sophie: I need a warm sleeping bag **in case** it **gets** cold in the tent at night. I think that one might be good.

Man: Yes, can I help you?

Sophie: Could I see that sleeping bag?

Man: Sure. I'll open it up for you.

Sergio: What about you, Lisa? What are you looking for?

Lisa: A waterproof jacket **in case** it **rains** all the time.

Carlos: Sergio, do you think you could lend me $10? I want to buy this book, but I only have a dollar on me.

Sergio: Sure. Here you are.

Carlos: Thanks. That's great. I'll give it back to you tomorrow. Excuse me. I'd like this book, please.

Man: Certainly. Here's your change. Two dollars.

Carlos: Thanks. Great! Now we won't get bored if the weather turns bad.

Sergio: What book is it?

Carlos: "101 Things to Do in a Thunderstorm."

Sergio: How sad is that!

Phrases

🎧 2/07 Listen and repeat.

- [I'll] open it up
- What are you looking for?
- I only have a dollar on me.
- How sad is that!

Comprehension

3 Complete the sentences.

1 Sophie wants a warm sleeping bag because it might ___*get cold*___.

2 She asks a sales assistant to _____.

3 It might rain, so Lisa wants to _____.

4 Carlos doesn't have enough money, so he asks Sergio to _____.

5 Carlos buys a book because _____.

 Solve it!

4 Read the presentation again. How much did the book cost?

Grammar

in case + simple present

I need a warm sleeping bag **in case** it
  gets cold.
I want a jacket **in case** it **rains**.

☞ Go to page 136, Master your grammar.

Practice

5 Carlos is going on a bike ride. Match the object with the reason he's taking it. Then write the sentences in your notebook with *in case*.

1 e) *He's taking a bottle of water in case he needs*
  a drink.

1 ~~a bottle of water~~
2 a camera
3 a waterproof jacket
4 a package of chocolate cookies
5 a swimsuit and a towel
6 a map

a) maybe he'll want to go for a swim
b) perhaps he'll get hungry
c) he might get lost
d) he may want to take some photos
e) ~~he will probably need a drink~~
f) it might rain

Vocabulary: Camping equipment

6a PAIRS Listen and repeat. Then look at the words in the box below. Decide on the five most important items to take on a camping trip.

• backpack • bandages • camping stove
• can opener • compass • flashlight
• hiking boots • insect repellent • matches
• penknife • sleeping bag • sunscreen • tent
• waterproof jacket

b Say why the friends need each item. Use *in case* or the infinitive of purpose with *to*.

They need a camping stove in case they want to
cook some food.
They need a camping stove to cook some food.

Use your English: Make and respond to requests

7 Read the sentences below.

Make a polite request
• Do you think I could borrow $6?
• Would you mind lending me $6?
• Could you go to the store for me?

Agree to a request
• Sure. Here you are.
• Of course not. No problem.
• Yes, of course.

Thank and make a promise
• Thanks. I'll give it back tomorrow.
• Thank you. That's really nice of you.

Refuse with a reason
• I'm sorry, I can't. I don't have $6.

Accept the reason
• It doesn't matter. • OK. Don't worry about it.

Pronunciation: Rising intonation in polite requests

8 🎧 Go to page 130.

Listen

9 🎧 PAIRS Listen to the conversation. Then have a similar conversation using the cues.

A: Ask to borrow B's cell phone. Say why.
B: Agree.
A: Promise to give it back in a minute.
B: Ask if A can return some DVDs for you. Say why.
A: Refuse politely with a reason.
B: Accept the reason.

Write

10 On a piece of paper, write a paragraph about an outdoor vacation you want to take. What do you need to take in case it rains/snows/is hot/is cold?

I need to take an umbrella in case it rains . . .

> **Extra practice**
> • **Student Book, page 118, Lesson 5C**
> • **Language Builder: WB, page 38; GB, page 116**
> • **Student CD-ROM, Unit 5**

Before you read, go to page 47.

Curriculum link: Geography

Frozen rivers

GLACIER FACTFILE

- A glacier is a big river of ice, water, and rocks.
- There are nearly 100,000 glaciers in Alaska.
- Glaciers move very slowly, about 200 feet per year.
- Glaciers are getting smaller because of global warming, but they still cover about 10% of the earth's land and hold about 77% of the earth's fresh water (7,000,654,295 cubic miles).

How is a glacier formed?

On the tops of mountains it can snow at any time of the year. As more snow falls, the snow on the ground begins to get deeper and more compact until it forms a glacier. Glaciers move very slowly downhill. If they reach the ocean, huge chunks will occasionally break off. These pieces then become icebergs, which float in the sea and can be dangerous to ships. The oceanliner *Titanic* sank because it hit an iceberg.

Where are glaciers found?

Glaciers are found in regions with continuous snowfall and constant freezing temperatures. Most glaciers are in high mountain regions such as the Himalayas or the Alps. Glaciers are even found in California and Tanzania in central Africa.

Does anything live on a glacier?

The top of a glacier is only rocks, ice, soil, and snow, so do any animals live there? Surprisingly, they do. Seals and polar bears live on glaciers near the sea. Insects and ice worms also live there.

What is the connection between glaciers and global warming?

If temperatures continue to rise, glaciers will begin to melt, releasing huge amounts of water over time. As a result, sea levels will begin to rise. If sea levels rise more than about 3 feet, major cities such as London, New York, and Tokyo could flood.

Computer-generated image of New York flooding

New words and phrases

- frozen • glacier • global warming • cover (v) • form (v) • compact (adj) • downhill
- chunk • float (v) • region • continuous • snowfall • constant • soil • seal
- polar bear • worm • rise • worldwide • melt • release (v) • sea level • major

Get started

1 Look at the pictures of glaciers. Have you ever seen one? What are they like?

Read

2 Read the article on page 46. What kinds of regions have glaciers?

Comprehension

3 In your notebook, write the questions for these answers.

1 100,000 *How many glaciers are there in Alaska?*
2 200 feet
3 10%
4 7,000,654,295

4 Answer the questions.

1 How does snow eventually become a glacier?
   It gets deeper and more compact until . . .
2 What can happen when a glacier meets the sea?
3 Why can this be dangerous for ships?
4 Why is it surprising that animals live on glaciers?
5 What will happen if the glaciers melt?

> **Learning strategy: Dictionary skills (2)**
>
> When you look up a word in a dictionary, look at the example sentences to see the different meanings of the word in context.

5a Read the dictionary entry and answer the questions.

> **float** / floʊt / v. **1** to stay or move on the surface of a liquid without sinking: *The boat floated slowly along the river.* **2** to move slowly in the air: *I looked at the clouds floating in the sky. The sound of her singing floated down from her bedroom window.*

1 Which of the two definitions of *float* is the correct one for the word in the first paragraph in the article? _____
2 Look at the example sentences. Which other things can float? _____

b Now look up *compact* (adj), *cover* (v), and *release* (v) in a dictionary. Write your own example sentences for each word in your notebook.

Listen

6 Before you listen, check the meaning of these words: *steel, hole, radio operator*. Then listen to a lecture about the *Titanic* disaster. Answer the questions in your notebook.

1 When did the disaster happen? *April 12, 1912*
2 Where was the iceberg probably from?
3 What was the weather like on that night?
4 What was the first explanation for the sinking?
5 What was the later explanation?
6 Why couldn't the ship stop in time?

Speak

7 PAIRS Imagine you are a radio operator who survived the sinking of the *Titanic*. Role-play a conversation with a newspaper reporter.

The reporter wants to know:

1 where you were when the ship hit the iceberg
2 if you received any messages about icebergs
3 what you did with the messages
4 why you didn't give the messages to the captain
5 what you did when the ship hit the iceberg

Write

8 On a piece of paper, write a paragraph about icebergs, using the information below.

Definition	large piece of ice/break off from glacier/float in the sea
Weight	100,000 to 200,000 tons
Speed	average/10 miles a day
Size	average amount above water = 15% under water = 85%

CLIL PROJECT, page 157

If I were invisible for a day, . . .

Imagination

6

Grammar	Conditional: *if* clause + past
Vocabulary	Transitive phrasal verbs
Function	Talk about imaginary situations

Get started

1 What would you do if you were invisible for a day?

Read

2 Listen and read along. Who do you think has the most interesting idea? Why?

_____

Comprehension

3 Read the survey again. Who wants to:

1 go to another country? _____*Paul*_____
2 learn about government secrets? _____
3 know if someone has a new girlfriend? _____
4 see the president's house? _____
5 text a movie star? _____

💡 Solve it!

4 Look at the photos and text carefully. What month did Sienna and her boyfriend split up?

IF YOU WERE INVISIBLE FOR A DAY, WHAT WOULD YOU DO?

THE TIME: Saturday morning
THE PLACE: Seattle

Heather, 17

"I'm a big fan of Will Smith, so I'd go to the set of his latest movie and watch him. If I felt really brave, I might try to get his cell number and send him a text message."

Paul, 16

"If I were invisible for a day, I'd fly to Peru. I've always wanted to see Machu Picchu. I'd sit in first class and fly for free. But if I had only one day, I'd be lost in the mountains!"

Bonnie, 15

"I'd walk into the CIA offices. The CIA is the Central Intelligence Agency. I'd check out all their top-secret documents. I'd love to know what's really going on in the world."

Dean, 17

"I'd visit the president in the White House and, if he was at home, I'd sit next to him while he was working. I'd play basketball on the White House courts. If I had time, I might check out the other rooms in the White House."

Sienna, 16

"My boyfriend and I split up two months ago. I've gotten over it . . . but I'd like to know what he's doing now. Has he asked another girl out? If he didn't know I was there, I could follow him around and find out what he's up to."

Grammar

Conditional: *if* clause + past

If he **didn't know** I was there, I **could follow** him around.

If I **felt** brave, I **might get** his cell number.

What **would** you **do if** you **were** invisible?

If I **were** invisible, **I'd fly** to Peru.

Note

*If I **was** invisible* is also possible but more informal.

☛ Go to page 137, Master your grammar.

Practice

5 In your notebook, complete the sentences with the correct form of each verb, using *would*, *might*, or *could*.

1 If you (meet) Justin Bieber at a party, what (you/say) to him?

   If you met Justin Bieber at a party, what would you say to him?

2 If we (move) to another town, I (may) miss all my friends.

3 I (can) call her if I (have) her phone number.

4 If I (be) a better singer, I (can) enter the TV *American Idol* contest.

5 Do you think Carla (say) no if I (ask) her out?

6 If you (not pass) your English test tomorrow, (you/tell) your parents?

7 You (may not) feel so tired if you (not stay) up so late every night.

6 PAIRS Invent questions for the answers starting with *What would you do if. . . .* Use your imagination.

1 I'd shut the closet quickly.

   What would you do if you found a rat in the back of your closet?

2 I might take a photo of him.

3 I'd ask for my money back.

4 I might try to fix it myself.

5 I'd jump in and rescue it.

Vocabulary: Transitive phrasal verbs

7 🎧 2/14 Listen and repeat. Complete each sentence with a phrasal verb from the box below and the object. When possible, write two alternative sentences in your notebook.

• ask out • ~~check out~~ • find out • give back
• pick up/put down • put on/take off
• turn on/off • turn up/down

Note

• With most transitive phrasal verbs, the object can come before or after the particle.
  *She picked up **the book**./She picked **the book** up.*

• However, object pronouns (e.g., *it, him, her*) must come before the particle.
  *She picked **it** up.*

1 I need a new shirt. Let's _____. (that new store)
  Let's check out that new store./Let's check that new store out.

2 Ricky likes Carla. He _____ last week. (her)

3 There's nothing good on TV. Can you _____? (it)

4 It's freezing outside. Make sure you _____! (your coat)

5 Here's your DVD. Sorry I forgot to _____. (it)

6 Be careful! Please _____ (the vase)! It's very valuable.

Speak

8 PAIRS Ask and answer the questions.

1 If you were a famous person for a day, who would you be and why?

2 If you were an animal for a day, what animal would you be and why?

3 If you could ask a famous celebrity out to dinner, who would you choose?

4 If you were Superman for a day, what would you do?

Write

9 On a piece of paper, write a paragraph about what you would do if you were a famous person.

If I were Barack Obama, I would fly all over . . .

> **Extra practice**
> • **Student Book, page 118, Lesson 6A**
> • **Language Builder: WB, page 42; GB, page 118**
> • **Student CD-ROM, Unit 6**

If only I had my camera!

Grammar	*wish/if only* + simple past
Function	Ask for and give advice

Get started

1 What things in your life do you wish were different?

Presentation

2  Listen and read along. Where will Lisa leave Sophie's ticket?

Lisa: Yum! This is delicious. I **wish** I **didn't like** ice cream so much!

Sergio: I'm bored. I **wish** I **had** my laptop with me.

Carlos: Let's go in. We can't wait for Sophie anymore. She's already 20 minutes late.

Lisa: I have her ticket. What do you think we should do?

Sergio: Have you tried calling her?

Lisa: Yes, but all I got was her voicemail.

Carlos: If I were you, I'd see if you can get a refund for her ticket.

Sergio: I think we should wait another five minutes.

Lisa: OK. But I **wish** there **was** somewhere to sit.

Sergio: That's your cell. It's probably Sophie.

Lisa: Hi, Sophie! Missed the bus? All right. I'll leave your ticket at the entrance. See you in 15 minutes. Bye!

Later:

Lisa: Aww! Look at that monkey with its mother. It's so cute! **If only** I **had** my camera with me!

Sergio: Why don't you use your cell phone?

Lisa: OK. Come on, monkey, smile! Hey! Hands off! It tried to grab my phone!

Phrases

Listen and repeat.
- See you in . . . • Hands off! • Come on.

Comprehension

3 Check (✓) the correct name(s).

	Lisa	Sergio	Carlos	Sophie
1 loves ice cream	✓			
2 is tired of waiting				
3 is late				
4 will pick up a ticket				
5 takes a picture				

 **Solve it!**

4 Approximately how late will Sophie be?

Grammar

***wish/if only* + simple past**

I **wish** I **didn't like** ice cream so much!
If only I **had** my camera with me.

☞ Go to page 137, Master your grammar.

Practice

5 Complete the sentences with the correct form of the verbs in parentheses.

1 I wish I _____*had*_____ (have) a sister, not a brother.
2 If only I _____ (can) remember his name!
3 I wish we _____ (not have) math today.
4 If only they _____ (not make) such a mess.
5 I wish I _____ (like) coffee, but I don't.
6 If only she _____ (not be) vegetarian!

6 Sergio's cousin has moved to the country and enrolled in a new school there. Look at his list of complaints. Write sentences with *I wish* or *If only*.

Why I don't like my new life here!

1 ~~My school is too far from our house.~~

2 We live in the country.

3 We can't afford to live in town.

4 My bike is so old.

5 I have to walk everywhere.

6 The teachers give us too much work.
---

1 *I wish my school wasn't so far from our house.*
   If only my school wasn't so far from our house.

2 _____

3 _____

4 _____

5 _____

6 _____

Use your English: Ask for and give advice

7 Read the sentences below.

Ask for advice
• What should we do?
• What do you think I/we should do?
• What would you do (if you were me)?

Give advice
• Why don't you . . . ?
• Have you tried calling her?
• I think we/you should wait another . . .
• If I were you, I'd see if you can get a refund.

Accept advice
• That's a good idea. Maybe you're right.

Reject advice
• I'm not sure (that's a good idea).
• I don't think that sounds like a good idea.

Listen

8a **GROUPS** Listen to the conversation. Then have a similar conversation following the instructions below.

Student A: Your laptop is broken. Ask for advice.

Student B: Tell A to take it back to the store where he or she bought it.

Student C: Tell A to ask a friend to look at it.

Student D: Tell A to buy a new laptop.
---

b Agree on the best advice for Student A.

Write

9 Go to the Writing bank on page 146 and complete the exercises. Then, on a piece of paper, write an informal letter to a friend giving him or her advice.

⊳ **Extra practice**
• **Student Book, page 119, Lesson 6B**
• **Language Builder: WB, page 44; GB, page 118**
• **Student CD-ROM, Unit 6**

6c If you keep playing video games, . . .

Grammar	Verb + infinitive or gerund
Vocabulary	Noun suffixes *-ion, -ment, -ity*, and *-y*
Function	Talk about video games

http://www.asktheexperts.nt

Ask the Experts!

This week: video games

Professor Rodgers from the University of Chicago gives us his opinion.

Video games are very popular, but they are also controversial. If you play more than five hours a day, you risk becoming isolated from your friends, and your health can suffer, too. But if you only play a few hours a week, games can bring improvement in many areas.

1 Your eyesight

When you **start to play** video games, your eyes sometimes have difficulty following all the movements on the screen, but if you **keep playing** them, your eyes move faster. This can be useful if you play ball sports.

2 Your body coordination

To play the games, you need accuracy and precise hand, finger, and thumb movements. This strengthens your hands and improves your hand/eye coordination. This can help you if you play a musical instrument.

3 Your schoolwork

Games that require a lot of reading on the screen can **help to improve** your ability to read fast. This can be good for all subjects at school, especially English.

Post your comments on this article

I had my first guitar lesson last week. My teacher was surprised that I **managed to play** the chords so easily. The reason for my success? Two years playing video games!

Julia, Chicago

I'm from Ecuador, and most of my games are in English. I have fun with them, but at the same time I'm **practicing reading** and generally improving my English.

Sonia, Quito

I play tennis and now I can see the ball better than I used to. I think that's happened since I **started playing** video games.

Jack, New York

Get started

1 Do you like playing video games? Why or why not?

Read

2 Listen and read along. How does Sonia improve her English?

Comprehension

3 Read the website again and complete the chart.

Benefits of video games	How?	Reader's examples
1 *Improve eyesight*	*Eyes follow movements on the screen*	*Jack–playing tennis*
2 *Improve body coordination*		
3		

Speak

4 **PAIRS** Describe your favorite video game. Why do you like playing it?

Grammar

Verb + infinitive or gerund

Verb + infinitive

This can **help to improve** your ability to read.

These verbs are followed by the infinitive: *agree, decide, expect, forget, help, hope, manage, offer, promise, want, would like*

Verb + gerund

You should **keep playing** video games.

These verbs are followed by a gerund: *admit, avoid, can't stand, deny, enjoy, finish, give up, keep, practice, stop*

Verb + infinitive or gerund

I have **started to play** video games.
I have **started playing** video games.
The verbs *hate, like, love, prefer,* and *start* can be followed by either.

☛ Go to page 137, Master your grammar.

Practice

5 Circle the correct form of the verbs.

1 My brother hopes (*to get*)/*getting* a new video game for his birthday.

2 I promised *staying/to stay* at home and study tonight, but I'm going to miss *to go out/going out* with my friends.

3 My grandfather has just learned *using/to use* a cell phone, and now he never stops *to text/texting* me.

4 I expect *passing/to pass* all my finals, but I don't expect *to get/getting* very good grades.

5 When my computer crashed, I had just finished *to write/writing* a long essay, but I had forgotten *to save/saving* it!

6 If you want *finding/to find* some information quickly, try *surfing/to surf* the net.

6 Complete with the correct form of the verbs.

Many parents ¹ ___*don't like seeing/don't like to see*___ (don't like/see) their teenage children in front of a TV screen and ² _____ (would like/stop) them playing video games. Parents complain that their teenage children ³ _____ (avoid/go out) and ⁴ _____ (not want/exercise). Although teens sometimes ⁵ _____ (admit/spend) too much time playing video games, they still ⁶ _____ (refuse/give up) their favorite activity.

Vocabulary: Noun suffixes *-ion, -ment, -ity,* and *-y*

7 Write the nouns for the following verbs and adjectives in your notebook. Then listen and check.

Verbs: 1 move—*movement* 2 improve 3 coordinate 4 decide 5 disappoint 6 correct 7 explain 8 excite 9 imagine 10 organize 11 entertain 12 discover

Adjectives: 13 difficult 14 accurate 15 able 16 brave 17 real 18 possible 19 similar

Pronunciation: Word stress in three- and four-syllable words

8 Go to page 130.

Listen

9 Listen. Write *Dan, Rachel, Arturo,* or *Lara.*

1 I like doing something I can't do in real life. ___*Dan*___
2 Video games are unhealthy. _____
3 I like discussing games with friends. _____
4 Soccer is more fun. _____
5 The feeling of speed is great. _____

Write

10 On a piece of paper, write a paragraph about the pros and cons of video games. Use information from the listening in Exercise 9 to help you.

> **Extra practice**
> • Student Book page 119, Lesson 6C
> • Language Builder: WB, page 46; GB, page 119
> • Student CD-ROM, Unit 6

53

Values for living

Before you read, go to page 55.

Before you read, go to page 55.

INTEGRATED
CONSOLIDATION
SKILLS

Vote for Nicole Roberts!

Every June, Merton High School has a prom, or party for grades 11 and 12. The student president, who is elected by the students, organizes this party. Nicole and Toby are getting ready to go.

"This party is going to be amazing," Toby said.

"I hope so," said Nicole.

But when they got to the prom, Nicole and Toby were disappointed. The music wasn't very good and the school hall wasn't decorated.

"This is terrible," Toby said, "There's no atmosphere at all."

"I know what you mean," Nicole replied. "If I were student president, I wouldn't hold the prom in the school hall. I'd have it in a more exciting place, I'd decorate it, and I'd hire a good DJ."

"Why don't you run for student president in September?" Toby said. "I think you'd be great, and you'd organize a wicked prom!"

Three months later, Nicole decided to take Toby's advice. She put up some posters around the school asking students to vote for her. She promised to organize the best prom ever, in a great place.

Nicole won the election. In February, she started to organize the prom. She had a budget of $500. She called a lot of places, but they all charged around $1,000 for the evening. Finally, Nicole found a local youth club that only charged $200. She booked the club and a DJ and ordered some decorations and some drinks.

But a month before the prom, disaster struck. There was a fire at the youth club and Nicole had to find a new place quickly. She talked to Mr. Bradshaw, the art teacher at school.

"If I were you, I'd use the school hall again," he said.

"But I promised the students a better place," Nicole said.

Then she had an idea. She talked to Toby about it.

"There are about 60 students in grades 11 and 12. If I sold tickets for $20 each, I'd have enough money to book a good place," Nicole said.

"That's not fair," Toby said. "Some people can't afford $20. I think you should keep looking for a cheaper place."

"But I haven't got time to look," Nicole said. "Our finals are in three weeks."

Nicole's mom agreed.

"If I were you, I'd cancel the prom. Your finals are the most important thing now."

Nicole didn't know what to do.

New words and phrases
- elect • disappointed • decorate (v)
- decorated (adj) • atmosphere • prom • hire
- run for • election • vote for • budget • charge
- strike (v) • afford • finals

Get started

1 Is it ever OK to break a promise? Explain.

Read

2 Read the story on page 54. Why does Nicole have to find a new place for the prom?

Comprehension

3 Answer the questions.

1 When is the prom? *In June*
2 Why was the prom disappointing?
3 How did Nicole win the election?
4 How much money did Nicole have for the prom?
5 What place did she find?
6 What was the disaster?
7 What are her options now?

Speak your mind!

Learning strategy: Disagree politely

When you listen to people, if you disagree, disagree with them politely. Use phrases such as *Yes, that's true, but . . .* or *I see what you mean, but . . .*

4a GROUPS Role-play: Choose one of the roles below and prepare what you want to say.

Student A: You are Mr. Bradshaw, the art teacher. You think Nicole should use the school hall again. It's free, and she can spend more money on music, decorations, and food.

Student B: You are Toby. You are sure that there are other cheap places. You think Nicole should contact cafés, restaurants, and other youth clubs.

Student C: You are Nicole's mom. You want her to cancel the prom because of finals. You think that the other students will understand and that they won't blame Nicole.

b Act out the role play. Decide what Nicole should do.

5 GROUPS Can you think of a different solution to Nicole's dilemma?

Listen

6 Nicole is talking to Toby at the prom. Listen and answer the questions.

1 Where is the prom? _____ *at the school hall*
2 How is the place better than last year?
3 What did the 11th-grade art students do?
4 What food is available?
5 Why did Nicole have enough money for food?
6 What has Nicole learned?
7 Would Nicole run for student president again? Why or why not?

Write

7 On a piece of paper, write an informal letter from Nicole to her friend, Ethan, in New York. Tell him about the party. Don't forget the address and date.

Paragraph 1
—thank Ethan for last letter.
—apologize for delay in replying—busy

Paragraph 2
—tell him about the prom.

Paragraph 3
—say when you hope to see him next.

Ethan Clooney
1350 East 54th Street
New York, NY 10022

CLIL PROJECT, page 157

Grammar (40 points)

1 Circle the correct conjunction to complete the advice for a camping trip. (6 points)

0 *If*/*Unless* you go to the top of the mountain, you'll see some great views.

1 Take a thick sweater with you. *If/Provided that* the weather turns cold, you won't freeze.

2 Use the garbage cans. *If/As long as* you don't clean up, the local people will get very angry.

3 Watch out for mosquitoes. *As long as/Unless* you wear insect repellent, they won't bite you.

4 *If/Provided that* your backpack is too heavy, you'll get tired quickly.

5 Don't walk in the forest alone. *Provided that/ Unless* you stay with the group, you'll be safe.

6 Don't go out at night *if/unless* you take a flashlight.

2 Complete the conversation with the correct form of the verbs in parentheses. (7 points)

Ben: Hi, Mom, I'm on my way home. I ^{0} ___*'ll call*___ (call) you just before the train ^{1} _____ (leave).

Mom: OK. When I ^{2} _____ (know) what time you're arriving, I ^{3} _____ (meet) you at the station.

Ben: ^{4} _____ (there/be) any food when I ^{5} _____ (get) home?

Mom: Yes. We ^{6} _____ (not eat) until you ^{7} _____ (arrive).

3 Match sentences 1–4 to sentences a–e. Then combine them using *in case* in your notebook. (8 points)

(0–e) *We're bringing umbrellas in case it rains.*

0 We're bringing umbrellas.
1 Why don't you take a packed lunch?
2 I always use a dictionary.
3 His neighbor has an extra front door key.
4 Take your gloves and scarf.

a) The weather might turn cold.
b) He might lose his own.
c) You might get hungry on the train.
d) I might need to look up a word.
e) It might rain.

4 Write *if* clause + past sentences in your notebook. (8 points)

0 What/you do/if/win/the lottery?
   What would you do if you won the lottery?

1 If you/not have/a TV/you miss it?

2 If he/lie to me, I/(may) not trust him again.

3 If I/win/the prize, I/(can) treat you all to pizza.

4 you/scream if you/see a spider in your room?

5 Write sentences in your notebook using *wish/if only* + the simple past. (6 points)

0 I'm too tall (wish)
   I wish I wasn't so tall!

1 I don't like parties. (wish)
2 My ears stick out! (if only)
3 I can't dance! (if only)
4 I have red hair and I hate it! (wish)
5 I'm not very confident. (if only)
6 I don't know how to talk to girls. (wish)

6 Complete the diary entry with the gerund or infinitive. (5 points)

I've already started ^{0} ___*thinking*___ (think) about the summer. If I manage ^{1} _____ (pass) my finals, I'll be really happy. Then I'll try ^{2} _____ (find) a summer job, because I don't enjoy ^{3} _____ (sit) around with nothing to do. I don't mind ^{4} _____ (do) a boring job as long as I earn some money. I'll keep ^{5} _____ (work) until I get enough money to go on vacation.

Vocabulary (40 points)

7 Replace the underlined phrases with phrasal verbs from the box and replace the orange words with pronouns. Write the sentences in your notebook. (10 points)

• ask out • check out • find out • turn down
• give back • take off

0 I asked the waiter to lower the music.
   I asked the waiter to turn it down.

1 Harry invited Sally to go on a date.
2 Please return my DVD if you've watched it.
3 Let's go see the new music store.
4 Get some information about the new movies.
5 I had to remove my shoes.

8 Complete the sentences with words from the box. (12 points)

> • avalanche • desert • downpour • earthquake
> • famine • floods • forest • gale • heat wave
> • ~~mountain~~ • rocks • stream • thunderstorm

0 Everest is the highest ___mountain___ in the world.
1 _____ fires are a problem in California.
2 We need an air-conditioner because of the _____.
3 A huge _____ covered the small village in snow.
4 A strong _____ blew the roof off our house.
5 The ship sank because it hit some _____.
6 We drank water from the _____ in the valley.
7 The house began to shake. It was an _____.
8 A lot of food will help with the _____.
9 They got very wet in the sudden _____.
10 The _____ was very loud last night.
11 Camels often live in the _____.
12 After heavy rain, there is a danger of _____.

9 Match the phrases (1–8) to the camping equipment (a–i) in the box. (8 points)

> a) a sleeping bag   b) a compass
> c) some bandages   d) a backpack
> e) some insect repellent   f) some matches
> g) a flashlight   h) a camping stove   i) ~~a can opener~~

___i___ 0 open cans   _____ 5 see in the dark
_____ 1 cook   _____ 6 cut your finger
_____ 2 Mosquitoes!   _____ 7 things to carry
_____ 3 time for bed   _____ 8 make a fire
_____ 4 don't get lost

10 Complete the sentences with the noun form of the words in the box. (10 points)

> • accurate • ~~brave~~ • decide • difficult
> • entertain • imagine

0 Alexander the Great was famous for his ___bravery___.
1 Have you made a _____ about your vacation yet?
2 I'm having a lot of _____ with this exercise.
3 To write exciting stories, you need a good _____.
4 You should see that show. It's great _____.
5 What is the _____ of the news reports?

Use your English (20 points)

11 Match each sentence (0–7) to the correct response (a–h). (14 points)

> ___g___ 0 Do you think you could lend me your dictionary?
> _____ 1 What do you think I should do?
> _____ 2 Can I see what's inside the package?
> _____ 3 I wonder where Jack is.
> _____ 4 Oh, look! Someone left their ice cream.
> _____ 5 I think we should forget about the movie and go for pizza.
> _____ 6 Would you mind closing the window?
> _____ 7 Oh, no. I only got three correct answers.

> a) Of course not. No problem.
> b) Hands off! That's mine!
> c) Sure. I'll open it up for you.
> d) But I've already bought the tickets.
> e) Don't worry. It's better than nothing!
> f) If I were you, I'd apologize to her.
> g) I'm sorry, I can't. I'm using it.
> h) Knowing him, I'd say he's gotten lost.

12 Complete the conversation with phrases from the box. (6 points)

> • ~~Could you~~ • Don't worry about it • Here
> • I'll give it back • on me • rather not,
> • would you mind

A: 0 ___Could you___ lend me your Taylor Swift CD?
B: Sure. 1 _____ you are.
A: Thanks. That's great. 2 _____ on Monday.
B: No problem.
A: And 3 _____ lending me $5 to buy a magazine?
B: I'd 4 _____ if you don't mind. I only have $5 5 _____.
A: OK. 6 _____.

SELF-CHECK	
Grammar	_____ /40
Vocabulary	_____ /40
Use your English	_____ /20
Total score	_____ /100

He asked me if I had a website.

Grammar	Reported statements and questions
Function	Take/leave phone messages

Get started

1 Do you have voicemail? What does your outgoing message say?

Presentation

2 🔊 2/24 **Listen and read along. What does Sophie want Sergio to do?**

Sergio's voicemail: Hi, you've reached Sergio. I can't take your call right now, but leave a message and I'll get back to you.

Sophie: Hi, Sergio, it's Sophie. I need to talk to you about websites. Can you call me when you get this message? Thanks!

Half an hour later:

Sergio: Hi, Sophie. I just got your message.

Sophie: Hi, Sergio. Thanks for calling back. Lisa **told me that you were learning** how to design websites. Is that true?

Sergio: Yes. Why do you ask?

Sophie: Well, a guy named Mr. Scott came to the market stall and **said that he'd like** to sell my T-shirts. He **said that he owned** a clothing store.

Sergio: Cool! If he takes 40 T-shirts, you'll get 300 dollars!

Sophie: Actually, he wanted 60 T-shirts! Anyway, he **asked me if I had** a website where he could look at more of my stock. I **told him I was building** one and that it **would be** ready next week.

Sergio: And let me guess—the website's still not ready and you want some help?

Sophie: Yes, please.

Sergio: OK. You can give me a free T-shirt!

Sophie: Great! Thanks, Sergio. I have the perfect T-shirt for you right here!

Phrases

🔊 2/25 **Listen and repeat.**

- Thanks for calling back • Well, . . .
- Actually, . . . • let me guess . . .

Comprehension

3 Answer the questions.

1 What is Sergio learning to do? *design websites*
2 Where does Mr. Scott want to sell Sophie's T-shirts?
3 How many does he want to buy?
4 What small lie did Sophie tell Mr. Scott?
5 What payment does Sergio want for helping Sophie?

💡 Solve it!

4 How much does one of Sophie's T-shirts cost?

Grammar

Reported statements and questions

Reported statements

"I **own** a clothing store." ➜
He said (that) he **owned** a clothing store.
"I'm build**ing** one." ➜
I told him (that) I **was** build**ing** one.
"I **bought** a T-shirt here." ➜
He said (that) he **had bought** a T-shirt there.

Reported questions

"**Do** you **have** a website?" ➜
He asked me **if/whether** I **had** a website.
"How many T-shirts **do** you **want**?" ➜
I asked him how many T-shirts he **wanted**.

Notes

These words often change in reported speech:
• today ➜ that day
• tomorrow/next week ➜ the following day/week
• yesterday/last week ➜ the previous day/week
• this/these ➜ that/those
• here ➜ there

☛ Go to page 138, Master your grammar.

Practice

5 You are Sophie. In your notebook, report your conversation with Mr. Scott.

Mr. Scott asked me if I worked there . . .

Mr. Scott: Excuse me. Do you work here?
Sophie: Yes, I do. I work here with my aunt.
Mr. Scott: Are the T-shirts yours?
Sophie: Yes, they are. Why?
Mr. Scott: I'm looking for T-shirts for my store. Will you give me a discount?
Sophie: I can do that if you order more than 40 T-shirts.
Mr. Scott: Good. How much of a discount can you give me for 60 T-shirts?

Speak

6 PAIRS Ask two students the questions. Report the answers to your partner.

1 What kind of websites do you like?
2 Have you ever bought anything online?

Pronunciation: Sentence stress in reported speech

7 🎧 Go to page 131.

Use your English: Phone messages

8 Read the phrases below.

Outgoing voicemail messages
Say whose phone it is
• Hi, you've reached . . .
• Hello. This is . . .

Explain that you can't answer the call
• I can't take your call right now, . . .

Ask the caller to leave a message
• . . . but leave a message and I'll get back to you.
• . . . so please leave a message after the tone.

Incoming voicemail messages
Say who it is
• Hi, Sergio, it's Sophie.

Say why you are calling
• I need to/wanted to talk to you about . . .
• I was just calling to chat.

Ask the person to call you back
• Can you call me back? Thanks.
• Call me when you get this message.

Listen

9 🎧 2/28 PAIRS Listen again to the conversation. Then make similar messages using the cues below.

Student A: Make your own outgoing message.

Student B: Leave messages for your partner:
   a) You need some help with your homework.
   b) Invite your friend to go bowling on Saturday.

Write

10 On a piece of paper, write a message that you recently left for someone. What did the person's message say? What did you say?

Ronaldo's voicemail message said that he was busy . . .

> **Extra practice**
> • Student Book, page 120, Lesson 7A
> • Language Builder: WB, page 50; GB, page 122
> • Student CD-ROM, Unit 7

You promised not to accept a ride.

Grammar	Reporting verbs
Function	Restate what someone has said

Get started

1. *Assertive* people are confident, and people pay attention to them. Would you like to be more assertive? Why or why not?

Read

2 Read. Then take the quiz and see how you score.

Comprehension

3 Match the quiz questions (1–4) to the topics (a–h).

_4_ a) your taste in movies

_____ b) safety in a car

_____ c) a domestic accident

_____ d) respecting your parents' wishes

_____ e) a disappointing meal

_____ f) not wanting to say you're scared

_____ g) complaining about food

_____ h) a friend being unfair

QUIZ

How assertive are you?

How good are you at communicating what you really feel and think?

Imagine yourself in these situations. What did you do?

1 You were at a friend's house yesterday, and his parents were out. Your friend was making some coffee when he broke the glass pot from the coffee machine. He suggested sharing the cost of a new one with you. Did you:

A agree to pay half?
B offer to pay five dollars toward it?
C refuse to pay anything because it wasn't your fault?

2 A few days ago you asked some friends to come over for the evening. You ordered some takeout pizzas from Pizzas2Go, but when the pizzas arrived, they were almost cold. Did you:

A admit to your friends that the pizzas weren't hot enough but eat them anyway?
B apologize to your friends and give them sandwiches instead?
C complain to the company and ask for more pizzas?

3 After an evening out with a friend, you missed the last bus home. You offered to get a taxi, but your friend asked her 18-year-old cousin to come and pick you up in his car. You recently promised your parents not to accept a ride from anyone under the age of 21. The cousin arrived in the car. Did you:

A accept the ride and hope for the best?
B accept the ride but ask the friend's cousin to drive very carefully?
C refuse the ride politely and call for a taxi?

4 You and your friends were watching TV the other day. Your friends wanted to watch a horror movie, but horror movies give you bad dreams. Did you:

A agree to watch the movie and say nothing?
B say you were not feeling very well and leave?
C ask them to change the channel and explain why?

YOUR SCORE

Mostly As: You hate to hurt people's feelings. You need to stand up for yourself sometimes.

Mostly Bs: You are diplomatic. You try not to hurt or offend anybody, but you don't do things you don't want to do.

Mostly Cs: You are assertive. You would make a good leader, but be careful you don't sound rude or aggressive.

Grammar

Reporting verbs

He **asked them (not) to** call.
She **told him (not) to** accept a ride.
He **invited her to** come and stay.

You **promised (not) to** accept a ride.
He **offered to** pay half.
He **refused to** pay anything.

He **admitted** break**ing** the glass pot.
He **denied** break**ing** the glass pot.
He **suggested** call**ing** his cousin.
He **didn't apologize for** be**ing** late.

She **explained that** it was too dangerous.
He **complained that** the pizzas were cold.
He **admitted/denied that** he had broken it.

☛ Go to page 138, Master your grammar.

Practice

4 Complete the sentences using the cues in parentheses.

1 He offered _____to take_____ (take) her to the station.
2 She apologized for _____ (be) rude.
3 The boys admitted _____ (steal) the peaches.
4 The students complained that the school lunches _____ (not be) very healthy.
5 We told _____ (she/not/wait) for the bus.
6 I asked _____ (he/give) me Charlie's phone number.
7 Our math teacher agreed _____ (give) us less homework the following week.
8 I refused _____ (wait) any longer for Sophie.

5 Report what the people said using verbs from the box.

- accept • agree
- apologize • ~~ask~~ • offer
- refuse • suggest • tell

> Jeremy, could you open the door for me?

1 _She asked him/Jeremy to open the door for her._

> Sarah, don't feed the dog any cookies.

2 _He . . ._

> Thanks for the offer of a ride. I'll take it.

3 _He . . ._

> Emma, would you like a cup of coffee?

4 _She . . ._

> I'm sorry I broke your sunglasses.

5 _He . . ._

> Why don't we take a break?

6 _He . . ._

> I'm not going to answer the phone.

7 _She . . ._

> OK. I'll do the dishes.

8 _He . . ._

Listen

6  Listen. Lisa's parents are grounding her for two weeks. Circle the correct answers.

1 Yesterday Lisa went to a   a) party.   b) movie.
   c) concert.
2 To get home, her father wanted her to
   a) call him.   b) get a taxi.   c) walk home.
3 At the end of the evening, Lisa went to a
   a) restaurant.   b) park.   c) friend's house.
4 The taxi company told her she had to wait
   a) an hour.   b) 30 minutes.   c) a few minutes.
5 In the end, she   a) waited for the taxi.
   b) walked home with a friend.   c) got a ride in a car.
6 The next time she has a problem, Lisa's father wants her to   a) wait longer for a taxi.
   b) check the times of the buses.   c) call him.

Speak

7 PAIRS Discuss. Do you think Lisa was right or wrong not to wait for the taxi? Why or why not?

Write

8 On a piece of paper, write a paragraph about a problem you had with your parents or someone else. Use reporting verbs.

My mother was angry at me last night. She complained that my room was too messy. I . . .

> ⊙ **Extra practice**
> • Student Book, page 120, Lesson 7B
> • Language Builder: WB, page 52; GB, page 122
> • Student CD-ROM, Unit 7

61

Grammar	Subordinating conjunctions that show contrast
Vocabulary	Relationship words and phrases
Function	Agree or disagree with someone

HOT TOPIC

Parent–teen relationships

Is the parent–teen relationship really a nightmare? This week, we interviewed some of our readers about their relationships with their parents.

It's definitely not a nightmare relationship, but I do feel that my mom and dad worry about me too much. Every time I leave the house, they ask: "Are you dressed warmly enough? Do you have your phone with you?" I know it's because they care about me, but sometimes it gets on my nerves. **Helen, 15**

In spite of our reputation, teenagers aren't always moody and difficult. I get along well with my parents. **Despite** having a few arguments about my room and the hours I spend on the computer, we have a good relationship, and they usually give good advice. **On the other hand**, they're not perfect, and they can get things wrong sometimes. **Gareth, 15**

My parents and I are close. **However**, I sometimes wish they treated me more like a grown-up. The other day we were discussing which classes I should take next year, and **although** they listened to what I had to say, they wanted to choose for me. It's like they don't trust me to make the right decision. **Jade, 16**

Get started

1 Which of the topics below do you talk about with your parents? With your friends?

> • school • your friends • money
> • your interests and hobbies

Read

2 🎧 2/30 Listen and read along. Which teenager's story is closest to your own experience?

Comprehension

3 Correct the mistakes.

1 Helen ~~has~~ *doesn't have* a bad relationship with her parents.

2 Helen's parents don't worry about her.

3 Gareth never argues with his parents.

4 Gareth's parents are always right.

5 Jade thinks her parents treat her like an adult.

6 Jade wanted her parents to choose her school classes.

Vocabulary: Relationship words and phrases

4a Review. Complete the phrases with words from the box. Then check the Word bank on page 129.

> • fall • get along • get/from
> • get/to • ~~have~~ • out (x2) • up (x2)

1 ___*have*___ an argument with someone
2 break _____ with someone
3 _____ engaged/married _____ someone
4 ask someone _____
5 _____ _____ well with someone
6 _____ in love with someone
7 go _____ with someone
8 _____ divorced _____ someone
9 make _____ with someone

b 🎧 **Extension. Find the forms of these phrases in the article. Complete them with the correct words. Then listen and check.**

1 _____treat_____ someone like [a grown-up]
2 care _____ someone
3 worry _____ someone
4 get on someone's _____
5 _____ someone [to make the right decision]
6 _____ close

Grammar

Subordinating conjunctions that show contrast: *although, in spite of/despite, however, on the other hand*

Although they listened to me, they wanted to choose for me.
In spite of being worried about me, she didn't get angry.
Despite a few arguments about my room, we have a good relationship.
However, I sometimes wish they treated me more like a grown-up.
On the other hand, they're not perfect.

☛ Go to page 138, Master your grammar.

Practice

5 In your notebook, rewrite the sentences using the conjunctions.

1 I worked hard, but I failed the class. (in spite of)
In spite of working hard, I failed the class.
2 My dad is strict, but my mom lets me do what I like. (however)
3 I have a good relationship with my mom, but I get annoyed with her sometimes. (despite)
4 I always tell my parents where I'm going, but they still worry about me. (although)
5 I love rock music, but some classical music is good, too. (on the other hand)
6 I'm shy, but I have a lot of friends. (although)
7 We're best friends, but we still have arguments. (in spite of)

6 Read the article below. In your notebook, combine the sentences using conjunctions.
1a + 1b although
Although many teenagers argue with their parents, most of us prefer a quiet life.
2a + 2b however   4a + 4b on the other hand
3a + 3b despite   5a + 5b in spite of

My parents and me

❝ 1a Many teenagers argue with their parents. 1b Most of us prefer a quiet life. 2a We sometimes have arguments in our family. 2b Most of the time they aren't serious. 3a I am over 16. 3b I'm not allowed out after 10 o'clock. 4a I like to be independent. 4b It's good to know that my parents care about me. 5a I want to be treated like an adult. 5b I still sometimes cry on my mom's shoulder when I'm upset about something. ❞

Speak

7 GROUPS Discuss: Do you agree or disagree with these statements?

1 Parents often treat teenagers like young children.
2 Teenagers are often moody for no reason at all.
3 The only people teenagers can be close to are their friends.

Write

8 On a piece of paper, write a paragraph about the differences between you and someone in your family or a friend. Use conjunctions.
My brother is two years older than I am. Although we are close, we don't do things together very often. Our tastes are so different . . . .

 Extra practice
• Student Book, page 120, Lesson 7C
• Language Builder: WB, page 54; GB, page 123
• Student CD-ROM, Unit 7

CONSOLIDATION INTEGRATED SKILLS

Across cultures

Get started

1 Look at the three messages below. How are they similar? How are they different?

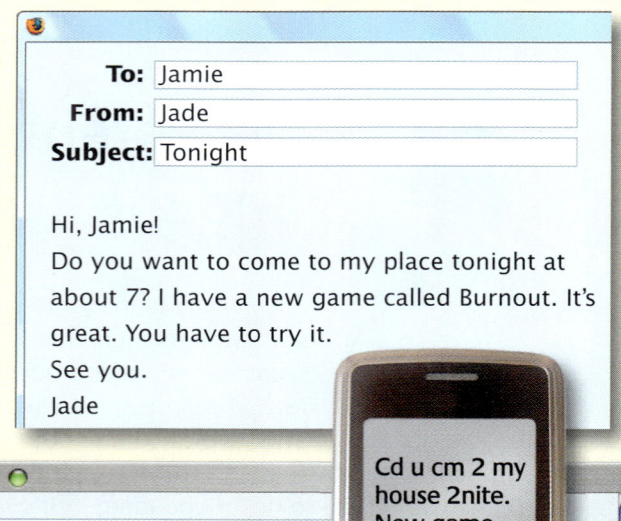

To: Jamie
From: Jade
Subject: Tonight

Hi, Jamie!
Do you want to come to my place tonight at about 7? I have a new game called Burnout. It's great. You have to try it.
See you.
Jade

Jade X: 2:40 P.M.
Hey are u there? I wanted to know what u r doing tonight.

Jamie_09:
Nothing. Why?

Jade X:
Wanna come over to play my new game, Burnout? It's really fun.

Cd u cm 2 my house 2nite. New game. CU L8r. Jade.

Learning strategy: Using slang

English speakers often use slang (informal language) when writing text messages and chatting online. Try to learn English slang, but don't use it in formal writing.

Speak

2 PAIRS Discuss: How would you communicate in these situations, and why?

1 You want to break up with the boy or girl you have been going out with for six months.
   I would meet him and talk to him because . . .
2 It's your grandmother's birthday.
3 You took great photos, and you want to share them with your friends.

New words and phrases
- survey • keep in touch with • digital
- photographic • record (n) • landline • cancel
- peaceful • lifeline • keep an eye on • screen
- webcam • contact (n) • regularly • phone bill

Read

3 Read the web article. Why was Carol's present for her daughter a waste of money?

http://www.ittalk.net

IT Talk: A Guide to the 21ˢᵗ century

Teens prefer writing to talking by Claudia Pitcher

The average teenager sends about 20 to 30 texts a day, according to the latest survey. Communicating with one another is one of the most popular hobbies among teenagers today.

In the U.S.:
- 90% of teenagers own a cell phone.
- 85% go online every day.
- 75% use online social networking websites like Facebook to share photos and keep in touch with friends.
- IM (Instant Messaging) online is more popular than e-mail. 97% of 15–17-year-old teens have used IM.
- 66% use their cell phones and digital cameras to keep a photographic record of their lives.
- 28% have blogs—online diaries of their everyday lives.

Comprehension

4 In your notebook, list the following:

1 three uses of the cell phone
2 two things you can do with a social networking website
3 the activities Kevin does in his room
4 three reasons why David thinks modern forms of communication are a good thing

Two case studies

Three years ago **Carol Weston** got her older daughter Lizzie, then 15, her own landline telephone. Soon afterwards, she canceled it. "Lizzie preferred her cell phone or the computer and I realized we were wasting money on the second landline. It's now nice and peaceful because the phone doesn't ring very often. However, I never know anymore which of her friends is calling!"

For 15-year-old **Kevin Martinez**, his laptop is his lifeline. Kevin spends two or three hours a day online. He listens to music and keeps an eye on the sports news. He also checks Facebook four or five times to keep in touch with friends. He says a screen-free life would be difficult to imagine. "I think it would be hard for any boy of my age."

Comments

I text at least 20 times a day. And my mom texts all the time. She even texts me to tell me when dinner's ready!—**Holly, 15, Chicago, IL**

As a parent of a teenager, I'm all in favor of the Internet, e-mail, webcams, and cell phones—for several reasons. First, I have much more contact with my children than I ever did with my own parents. Second, my kids keep in touch with their grandparents regularly via e-mail. And last, the phone bill for the landline is much lower nowadays!—**David, 41, Dallas, TX**

💡 Solve it!

5 Look again at the statistics about the U.S. If there are 30 students in an American class, how many have cell phones?

Listen

6 🎧 2/32 Listen to a radio discussion. Write *D* (Denise) and/or *R* (Roger) next to each statement.

_D/R_ 1 Teenagers prefer writing to talking as a way of communicating.
_____ 2 Teenagers are losing the skill of talking.
_____ 3 Writing text messages and blogs can help teenagers develop their writing skills.
_____ 4 Teenagers like writing online because their audience is real.
_____ 5 Teenagers are careless about spelling when they write text messages.
_____ 6 Teachers can't correct homework fast enough to keep students' interest.
_____ 7 To get a job, teenagers need to learn to write and spell correctly.

Write

> **Writing tip:** *First, second,* **and** *last*
>
> Use these words to list points.
>
> *There are several reasons.* **First**, *I have much more contact with my children.*
>
> **Second**, *my kids keep in touch with their grandparents via e-mail.*
>
> **Last**, *the phone bill for the landline is much lower nowadays!*

7 In your notebook, write sentences using *first*, *second*, and *last*. Use the cues.

1 Cell phones have a number of uses. First, . . .
2 Teens can communicate with their friends online in several ways.
3 There are three main reasons why young people like social networking websites.

8 On a piece of paper, write an e-mail, a text message, and an IM conversation to a friend. Invite the friend to do something. Use Exercise 1 to help you.

CLIL PROJECT, page 157

Such an embarrassing story

Challenges

8

Grammar	*so* + adjective/adverb *(that)* . . .
	such a/an + adjective + noun *(that)* . . .
	so many/much + noun *(that)* . . .
	Verb + *so much (that)* . . .
Vocabulary	Adjectives of emotion
Function	Talk about new experiences

Snorkeling

– NEVER AGAIN!

Tracey Adams from the U.S. tells us her story about her first experience of snorkeling!

This is **such an embarrassing story that** I cringe when I think about it. The first and only time I tried to snorkel was in Florida. I was on vacation with some friends. It was **so hot that** we spent every day on the beach. One day I bought a snorkel, mask, and fins. I had heard **so many amazing things** about snorkeling **that** I wanted to try it. I put on my fins and walked to the water. That was mistake number one. Never walk in your fins. It's **such a clumsy way of moving that** you look very silly.

Then I put the mask and snorkel on my head and dove under the waves. That was mistake number two. I didn't realize you had to keep the top of the snorkel above the water! I got **so much water** in my mouth **that** I had to pull my head out again. My friends were beginning to enjoy the show!

I tried once more: "Remember to breathe. There's a . . . OH, NO! IT'S A MONSTER!" I screamed and stood up **so quickly that** I fell over backward. My friends **laughed so much** they nearly cried. The "monster" was just a small sea turtle. I was **so embarrassed that** I went right back to the beach and gave the snorkel away to my brother. Never again!

Get started

1 Have you ever done any of these water sports? Which would you like to do?

> • swimming • snorkeling • scuba diving
> • windsurfing • waterskiing • paragliding

Read

2 [2 33] Listen and read along. What equipment did Tracey have to buy?

Comprehension

3 Answer the questions.

1 What did Tracey want to do? *snorkel*
2 What were her two mistakes?
3 What scared her?
4 How did her friends react?
5 How did Tracey feel about her experience?

Vocabulary: Adjectives of emotion

4a [2 34] Listen and repeat. Write the adjectives from the box in two groups in your notebook.

Negative: *afraid*   **Positive:** *amused*

> • afraid • amused • angry • annoyed
> • anxious • ashamed • bored • calm
> • cheerful • confused • depressed
> • embarrassed • excited • frightened
> • frustrated • happy • lonely • nervous
> • proud • sad • scared • shocked
> • terrified • thrilled • worried

b Choose three negative and three positive adjectives. Write sentences in your notebook.

c Make a list of the adjectives ending in *-ed*. Which of these can also end in *-ing*?

amused–amusing

d Choose two adjectives and write sentences using *-ed* and *-ing* endings.

Grammar

8A

so + adjective/adverb (that) . . .

It was **so hot (that)** we swam every day.
I stood up **so quickly (that)** I fell over backward.

such a/an + adjective + noun (that) . . .

This is **such an embarrassing story (that)**
   I cringe when I think about it.
The fish were **such pretty colors (that)**
   I wanted to photograph them.

so many/much + noun (that) . . .

I had heard **so many amazing things (that)**
   I wanted to try it.
I got **so much water** in my mouth **(that)** I had
   to pull my head out.

Verb + so much (that) . . .

They **laughed so much (that)** they nearly cried.

☛ Go to page 139, Master your grammar.

Practice

5 In your notebook, write sentences in two ways. Use *so* and *such . . . (that) . . .* and the words in parentheses.

1 (scary movie) I closed my eyes.

   The movie was so scary that I closed my eyes.
   It was such a scary movie that I closed my eyes.

2 (embarrassing performance) She never sang karaoke again.
3 (sad story) She started to cry.
4 (nice people) We asked them to join us.
5 (exciting idea) I couldn't sleep.
6 (depressing book) He stopped reading it.
7 (confusing stories) The police became suspicious.
8 (frustrating experience) Tracey vowed never to snorkel again.

6 Melinda has just entered a music talent contest. Read her notes. In your notebook, combine the sentences with *so* or *such*.

1 *I was so worried that I nearly didn't go to the audition.*

My audition nerves!

1 I was very worried. I nearly didn't go to the audition. (so)
2 I had a really bad headache. I felt sick. (such)
3 There were hundreds of contestants. I was sure I didn't have a chance. (so many)
4 One of the guys behaved very badly. The judges asked him to leave. (so)
5 I was extremely nervous. I forgot the words. (so)
6 When I started to sing my voice shook a lot. I had to start again! (so much)
7 The judges were really nice. I wanted to give them a hug! (such)
8 It was an amazing feeling when I passed the audition. I nearly cried! (such)

Speak

7 PAIRS Ask and answer the questions.
Have you ever tried to do something for the first time? What did you try? What happened?

Write

8 On a piece of paper, write an e-mail to a friend describing one of the events you talked about in Exercise 7. Try to use *so* and *such*.

> ### Extra practice
> • Student Book, page 120, Lesson 8A
> • Language Builder: WB, page 58; GB, page 126
> • Student CD-ROM, Unit 8

I'm getting used to it.

Grammar	*used to/be used to/get used to*
Function	Ask for and give explanations

Get started

1 What are some differences between the U.S. and the U.K.?

Presentation

2 🎧 (2/35) **Listen and read along. What differences does Nathan mention between the U.S. and the U.K.?**

Sergio and Sophie are walking around Seattle with Nathan, a British friend who moved to the U.S. a month ago.

Sergio: Nathan, watch out for that car!

Nathan: Thanks. That was close! I'**m used to looking** right, not left. You guys drive on the wrong side of the road!

Sophie: Ha, ha! No, we don't! . . . Are a lot of things different for you here?

Nathan: Yeah, one or two things. In London, I took the tube, or subway, everywhere. But here, you don't have one. I'**m getting used to walking** everywhere! And another thing—it's really hard to find "a full English" here.

Sergio: "A full English"? What does that mean?

Nathan: It's a cooked breakfast of bacon, eggs, sausage, and baked beans.

Sergio: It sounds good. I **didn't use to like** baked beans, but I do now.

Sophie: Baked beans? No, thanks. I like grits better.

Nathan: Grits? I'm not sure what that is.

Sophie: It's a kind of hot breakfast food.

Nathan: You know, people think Americans and British people speak the same language, but we don't!

Comprehension

3 Answer the questions.

1 How long has Nathan been in Seattle?
   He's been in Seattle for a month.

2 Why does Nathan walk everywhere in Seattle?
   _____

3 What is "a full English"?
   _____

4 Who likes baked beans?
   _____

💡 Solve it!

4 Look at the photo and the presentation. What sides of the road do they drive on in the U.S. and in the U.K.?

Pronunciation: Word stress for emphasis

5 🎧 Go to page 131.

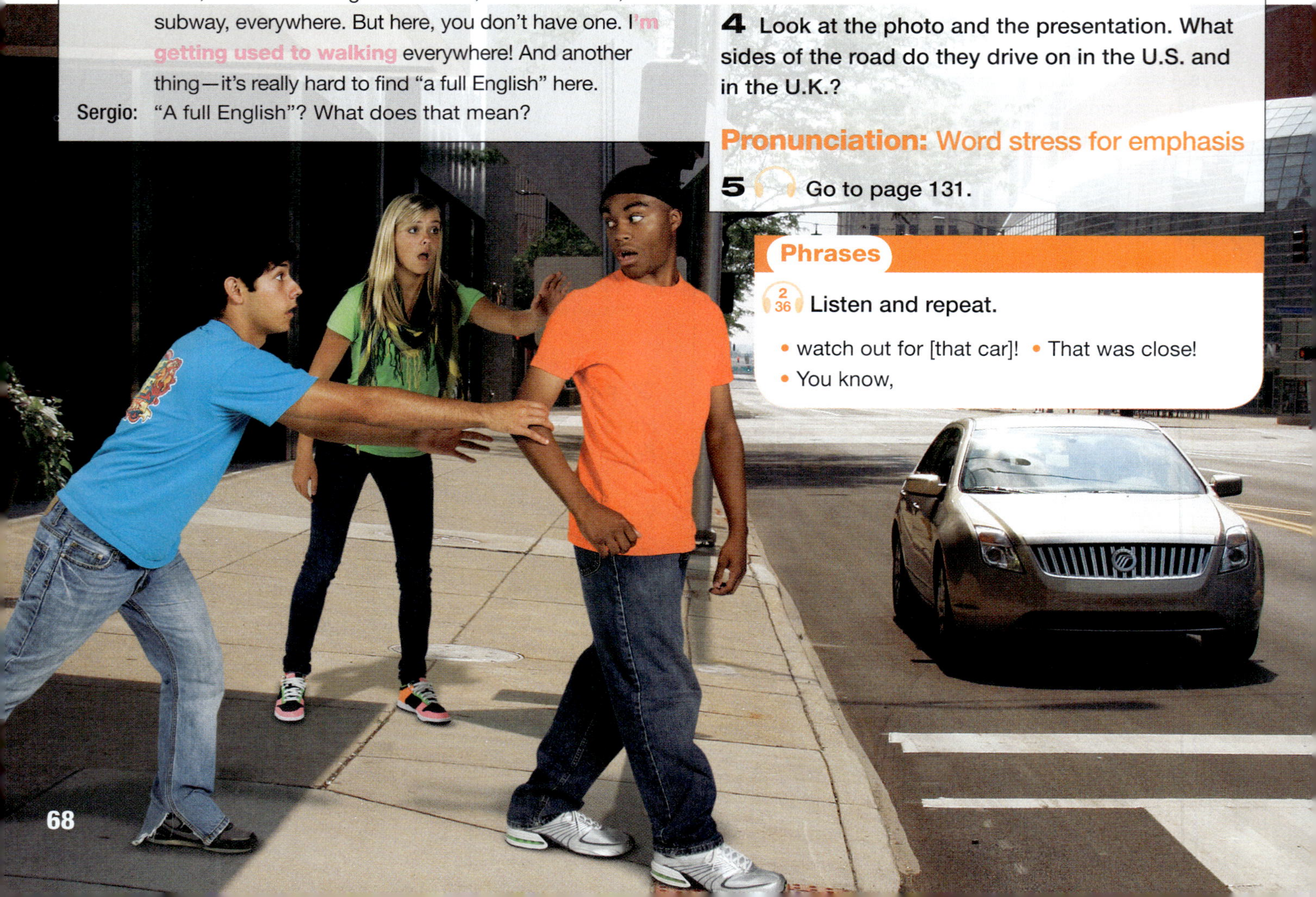

Phrases

🎧 (2/36) Listen and repeat.

- watch out for [that car]!
- That was close!
- You know,

Grammar

used to

Nathan **used to take** the subway in London.
Sergio **didn't use to like** baked beans.
Did he **use to eat** a cooked breakfast?

be used to

I'm **(not) used to** look**ing** right.

get used to

I'm **getting used to** walk**ing** everywhere.
Are you **getting used to** liv**ing** in the U.S.?

☛ Go to page 139, Master your grammar.

Practice

6a Some things in the U.S. are new for Nathan. In your notebook, write sentences using *used to*.

1 *He used to hate football, but now he likes it.*

Then	Now
1 hated football	like it
2 didn't like history	favorite subject
3 watched TV a lot	play video games
4 didn't walk very much	walk everywhere
5 was on the school rugby team	not play rugby at all

b Now write sentences with *(not) be used to*.

1 ✗ walk to school/✓ take the subway
   Nathan isn't used to walking to school. He's used to taking the subway.
2 ✗ eat grits for breakfast/✓ have bacon and eggs
3 ✗ dress casually/✓ wear school uniform
4 ✗ get up at 7 A.M./✓ stay in bed until 7:30.
5 ✗ drink a lot of coffee/✓ drink a lot of tea
6 ✗ be far away from grandparents/✓ see grandparents every week

c Look at Exercise 6b. List four things that Nathan is getting used to.

1 *He's getting used to walking to school.*
2 _____
3 _____
4 _____

Use your English: Ask for and give explanations

7 Read the sentences below.

Mention a special dish/food
• How about "a full English"?

Ask for an explanation
• "A full English"? What does that mean?
• What is/are grits?
• I have no idea/I'm not sure what that is.

Give an explanation
• It's a kind of cooked breakfast.
• It's/It tastes like potatoes.

Respond
• Really? I've never heard of it before.
• It sounds good/delicious/a little strange.

Listen

8a PAIRS Listen to the conversation. Then have similar conversations, using the cues.

A: *How about a Cornish pasty?*
B: *I'm not sure what that is.*

1 Cornish pasty: a pie with meat and potatoes in it
2 Black pudding: a kind of spicy sausage
3 Scones: they taste like sweet bread

b PAIRS Role-play. Describe a local food to an English-speaking visitor to your country.

A: *One of my favorite dishes is . . .*

Write

9 On a piece of paper, write a paragraph about yourself. What did you use to do? What are you getting used to doing?

I used to live in a small town. I'm getting used to . . .

 Extra practice
• Student Book, page 121, Lesson 8B
• Language Builder: WB, page 60; GB, page 126
• Student CD-ROM, Unit 8

Will I be able to touch a spider?

Grammar	*be able to*
Vocabulary	Phrasal verbs with *in*
Function	Talk about fears

Get started

1 Does anything scare you? What scares you and why?

PSYCHOLOGY TODAY: SEPTEMBER

What are you afraid of?

Around one in twenty people have a **PHOBIA**—an extreme fear of something. The most common phobias are spiders, social situations, and flying, but there are over 500 others, including a fear of frozen peas! We went to the Phobia Treatment Clinic in Los Angeles to find out how phobias affect people's lives and how the clinic can help.

Jacob

Jacob is 17, and he has a spider phobia. When he was younger, he **wasn't able to** look at a photo of a spider without crying. Three months ago Jacob and his parents moved into an old house. When Jacob saw that there were spiders everywhere, he couldn't stay in the house. He's temporarily living with his uncle and aunt. Jacob says: "It's going well at the clinic. **Will** I **be able to** touch a spider one day? I don't know, but hopefully I**'ll be able to** move in with my parents soon. That'll be enough for me!"

Nancy

Nancy is 16. She recently signed up for ten sessions at the clinic. Why? Because she has a huge fear of the dark. She's never **been able to** fall asleep with the light off, and she avoids going out in the evening. She also finds it difficult to sit in a dark theater.

Nancy says: "Here they teach you to overcome your fears, not give in to them. The doctors here think I**'ll be able to** go out in the evening with my friends soon. That'll be an incredible achievement for me!"

Read

2  Listen and read along. What are Jacob and Nancy afraid of?

Comprehension

3 Complete the sentences.

1 Jacob and Nancy both have ___*phobias*___.
2 When Jacob was a child, he couldn't _____.
3 He is now staying with _____.
4 He hopes he can soon _____.
5 Nancy can't _____.
6 It's not easy for Nancy to _____.
7 Nancy hopes that she can soon _____.

Solve It

4 In what month did Jacob move in with his uncle and aunt?

Vocabulary: Phrasal verbs with *in*

5a Listen and read. Complete the sentences with the correct form of phrasal verbs from the box.

> • break in • fit in • give in • hand in • ~~move in~~
> • sink in • stay in

1 My grandma is ___*moving in*___ with my parents.
2 Are you going out or _____ on Friday?
3 I can't believe I won! It will take time for it to _____!
4 Do you always _____ your homework on time?
5 Has a burglar ever _____ to your house?
6 Why did I say yes? I shouldn't have _____ so easily.
7 What clothes should you wear to _____ at school?

b PAIRS Ask and answer questions 2, 4, 5, and 7 in Exercise 5a.

Grammar

> **be able to**
>
> **Will** I **be able to** touch a spider?
> I hope I**'ll be able to** stay calm.
> He **wasn't able to** look at a spider.
> She**'s** never **been able to** fall asleep in the dark.

☛ Go to page 139, Master your grammar.

Practice

6 Complete the conversation with the correct forms of *be able to*.

Felix: 1 _____*Will*_____ your sister ___*be able to*___ come to my party?
Julia: No, she's sick. She 2 _____ get out of bed all day.
Felix: 3 _____ she _____ come next weekend?
Julia: Why do you want my sister to come?
Felix: Well, she 4 _____ come last time and . . .
Julia: Come on. You've never 5 _____ lie to me.
Felix: OK. It's my brother, Phil. He's in love with her.
Julia: Your brother? But he's only 13 and my sister's 17! She 6 _____ stop laughing when I tell her.

Listen

7 Listen to a report from a phobia clinic and complete the information.

PHOBIA Treatment Clinic

Reporter: Jon 1	_____*Robinson*_____
Clinic: 2 _____ floor of a building in New York	
Phobia: a fear of 3 _____	
Doctor's name: Miranda 4 _____	
Job: 5 _____ of the clinic	
Number of sessions: Between 6 _____ and _____	
Step 1: Jon stands 7 _____	
Step 2: Jon moves 8 _____ to the elevator until 9 _____	
Step 3: Jon puts 10 _____. Then he puts 11 _____ until he is 12 _____.	
Result: Jon can now 13 _____	

Speak

8 PAIRS Talk about things you're afraid of. Use the cues in the box.

A: *I'm terrified of snakes.*
  I wouldn't be able to pick one up.
B: *I don't mind them . . .*

> • big crowds of people • birds • flying • heights
> • open spaces • public speaking • rats • snakes

Write

9 On a piece of paper, write a paragraph about something you have never been able to do and something that you hope you will be able to do in the future.

I have never been able to rollerskate because I'm afraid of falling. I hope . . .

> **Extra practice**
> • Student Book, page 121, Lesson 8C
> • Language Builder: WB, page 62; GB, page 127
> • Student CD-ROM, Unit 8

8D Charity work

INTEGRATED CONSOLIDATION SKILLS

Curriculum link: Citizenship

You can make a difference

Have you ever thought of doing volunteer work or raising money for charity? Here are three famous charities that need donations and volunteers to do their work.

Doctors Without Borders (MSF USA) is an international organization that provides emergency medical help to people in need. It works in more than 70 countries. For example, it has a staff of more than 3,000 in Sudan, and in just one year MSF gave vaccinations to 700,000 Sudanese people.

The World Wildlife Fund (WWF), which has branches in over 90 countries, is the world's leading organization for protecting the environment and endangered animals. For example, in Uganda in central Africa, WWF helps to protect the mountain gorilla. There are only 700 mountain gorillas left in the world.

Habitat for Humanity fights poverty by building homes for poor families. The families help build the houses and then buy them for very cheap prices. The charity operates in 90 countries. In the United States alone, it has built homes for more than 30,000 families.

> **New words and phrases**
> • afford to • branch • construction • donations
> • emergency • impressed • leading • medical
> • protect • vaccinations • volunteers

Renée Brown, 17, St. Louis, MO

I volunteered for Habitat for Humanity last summer. I helped build a house for a poor family. I learned a lot about building, and I met a lot of great people on the construction site. But the best part was seeing how happy the family was when their new house was ready!

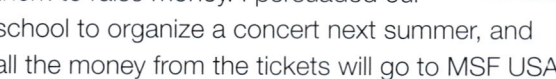

Neil Brooks, 15, Denver, CO

I didn't use to think about charities at all but, about a year ago, I was surfing the web for information about careers in medicine, when I found the Doctors Without Borders website and read about the work they do. I was so impressed that I decided to help them to raise money. I persuaded our school to organize a concert next summer, and all the money from the tickets will go to MSF USA.

Get started

1 Have you ever raised money for a charity or given money to a charity? Which charity was it?

Read

2 Read the article above. Which charities do Renée and Neil support?

Habitat for Humanity®

5a Find the word *raise* in the text about Neil and look it up in a dictionary.

1 What part of speech is it? _____
2 How many meanings are there? _____
3 Which meaning is the same as the meaning in the article? _____

b Now do the same for these words: *branch* and *fight*. In your notebook, write an example sentence for the different meanings of each word.

Listen

6 (2 43) Polly saw an ad for volunteer work. Listen and complete the sentences.

1 Spring Gardens is a conservation _____ that protects _____.
2 The work involves taking care of birds, _____, and _____.
3 No experience is necessary for the job. Green Planet will provide _____.
4 Polly is able to work for _____ every weekend.
5 Polly wants the job because she _____ and she is sometimes _____.

Speak

7 PAIRS OR GROUPS Look at the charities in the article and decide which charity you would like to help. Give your reasons and say what you could do.

Write

8 Go to the Writing bank on page 147 and complete the exercises. Then, on a piece of paper, write an application letter for a volunteer job. Use your ideas from Exercise 7.

CLIL PROJECT, page 157

Comprehension

3 Complete the chart.

	MSF	WWF	Habitat for Humanity
Number of countries	70		
Purpose	to provide medical help to people in need		
Example country	Sudan		
Action in that country	gave vaccinations to 700,000 people		

4 Answer the questions.

1 What did Renée do last summer?
2 What was the best part for Renée?
3 How did Neil find out about MSF USA?
4 What career is Neil thinking about?
5 What is his latest fundraising idea?

Grammar (40 points)

1 Write the sentences in reported speech. (12 points)

0 **Ana:** I'm going to study English in Boston.
Ana said that she was going to study English in Boston.

00 **Vera:** Is your English bad?
Vera asked her if her English was bad.

1 **Ana:** I need to improve my speaking.
_____

2 **Vera:** When are you going?
_____

3 **Ana:** I'm leaving next week.
_____

4 **Vera:** Are you looking forward to it?
_____

5 **Ana:** I've never been abroad before.
_____

6 **Vera:** I'm sure you'll have a great time.
_____

2 Rewrite the direct speech as reported statements. Use *He* and a reporting verb from the box. (6 points)

> • apologize • complain • deny • offer
> • promise • refuse • ~~tell~~

0 "Don't lose your key, Tom."
He told Tom not to lose his key.

1 "Do you want me to help with the shopping?"
_____

2 "I'm sorry I lost your CD."
_____

3 "I'm not going to pay $10 for a pizza."
_____

4 "The bus is late again!"
_____

5 "I won't make that mistake again."
_____

6 "I didn't break that plate."
_____

3 In your notebook, write sentences with conjunctions that show contrast. (5 points)

0 He loves music. He can't sing. (although)
Although he loves music, he can't sing.

1 I hate burgers. Pizza is good. (on the other hand)

2 She hates horror movies. She watched all of *Dark Nights*! (in spite of)

3 She had hurt her foot badly. She managed to walk into town. (however)

4 Horoscopes are silly. I read mine every day. (although)

5 I went to bed early. I'm still tired. (despite)

4 In your notebook, combine the sentences with *so* or *such*. (6 points)

0 I ate too much. I left awful afterwards. (so)
I ate so much that I felt awful afterwards.

1 The water was cold. My lips turned blue! (so)

2 They played badly. They didn't even score. (so)

3 It was a nice day. We had lunch outside. (such)

4 There are too many people. I can't move. (so)

5 It's a good book. I'm reading it again. (such)

6 The weather was bad. We stayed in. (such)

5 Complete the sentences with *used to, be used to,* or *get used to*. (6 points)

0 I'*m* not _____*used to riding*_____ (ride) a horse.

1 I _____ (walk) to school, but I don't now.

2 I can't _____ (drink) coffee.

3 I'm hungry. I'_____ (eat) more for lunch.

4 In 1850, people _____ (have) TVs.

5 I'_____ not _____ (live) in this town.

6 It was hard at first, but now I'_____ (wake up) at 6 A.M.

6 Complete the sentences with the correct forms of *be able to*. (5 points)

0 I'm glad you _____*were able to*_____ get away.

1 Since her accident, my aunt _____ walk well.

2 You must _____ swim if you want to come sailing.

3 I _____ see anything from the back of the room.

4 He _____ vote when he's 18.

5 I'll call you as soon as I _____ get to a phone.

Vocabulary (40 points)

7 Complete the paragraph with the correct forms of the phrases from the box. (20 points)

> • break up • fall in love • get along
> • get married • go out • ~~have a good relationship~~
> • not care • not treat • not trust • not worry

I ⁰ *'ve* always ___*had a good relationship*___ with my grandmother. She ¹ _____ me like a child and she ² _____ about me. I ³ _____ with her really well. Last year I ⁴ _____ with a girl and I ⁵ _____ with her for a month. I was very upset when she wanted to ⁶ _____, but Grandma told me she wasn't good enough for me, so I ⁷ _____ about it any more. I ⁸ _____ girls any more, and it'll be a long time before I want to ⁹ _____ and have kids!

8 Circle the correct answers. (15 points)

0 I'm *frightening* / (*frightened*) of spiders.
1 I was getting *worrying* / *worried* about you.
2 The book was really *boring* / *bored*.
3 Cold, wet weather s *depressing* / *depressed*.
4 They were *thrilling* / *thrilled* with the news.
5 That loud noise is really *annoying* / *annoyed*.
6 I felt *exciting* / *excited* on the plane.
7 I'm too *embarrassing* / *embarrassed* to sing in front of all those people!
8 I'm *confusing* / *confused*. Where are we now?
9 It's so *frustrating* / *frustrated* when my laptop crashes.
10 That rollercoaster looks *terrifying* / *terrified*.
11 I thought the movie was *amusing* / *amused*.
12 I feel *confident* / *proud*. I did it without help.
13 I know I did wrong. I feel *ashamed* / *shocked*.
14 I always feel *sad* / *nervous* before flying.
15 It's *lonely* / *alone* here when everyone has left.

9 Match each phrasal verb (0–5) to its meaning (a–f). (5 points)

> 0 give in __*f*__   1 break in ____   2 sink in ____
> 3 stay in ____   4 hand in ____   5 move in ____

a) not go out   b) give something (to the teacher)
c) start living in a new place   d) burgle a house
e) realize   f) agree in the end to do something

Use your English (20 points)

10 Complete the sentences with words or phrases from the box. (11 points)

> • Actually • Anyway • ~~calling~~ • close • delicious
> • kind of • Let me guess • mean • no idea
> • really • though • Watch

0 Is that you, Vicky? Thanks for *calling* back.
1 What's for lunch? _____ . . . Pizza!
2 A: "Grazie" is Italian for "thank you."
   B: Oh, _____?
3 There's a car coming. _____ out!
4 Let's order scones. They sound _____.
5 What does grits _____?
6 A: Are you free today?
   B: _____, I'm free all week.
7 I have _____ how to get there.
8 I don't want to go out. _____, I have no money.
9 Watch out! Wow! That was _____!
10 A Cornish pasty is a _____ meat pie.
11 The movie was boring. I liked the ending, _____.

11 Complete the phone messages. (9 points)

Adam

> Hi. You've ⁰ *reached* Adam. I can't ¹ t_____ y_____ c_____ right now. Please ² l_____ a message ³ a_____ the tone and I'll get ⁴ b_____ to you.

Luis

> Hi, Adam. ⁵ I_____ Luis here. I ⁶ w_____ to talk to you about next Saturday. Can you ⁷ c_____ me when you ⁸ g_____ this message? ⁹ T_____.

SELF-CHECK	
Grammar	____ /40
Vocabulary	____ /40
Use your English	____ /20
Total score	____ /100

Have you had it checked?

Grammar Causative *have*
Vocabulary Parts of a bike
Function Describe and deal with problems

Get started

1 Do you have a bike? What problems has it had?

Vocabulary: Parts of a bike

2 🎧 3/02 Listen and repeat. Match the words in the box to the items in the photo.

___ back light ___ brakes ___ chain ___ frame
___ front light *1* gears ___ handlebars
___ pedal ___ seat ___ tire ___ wheel

Presentation

3 🎧 3/03 Listen and read along. What three things are wrong with Carlos's bike?

Carlos: Hey, guys. Come and see my new bike. Well, it's not exactly new. It's second-hand.

Sergio: **Have** you **had** it **checked**?

Carlos: No, but it's in pretty good shape. Look!

Sergio: Good shape? It's a complete wreck!

Lisa: And you have a flat tire!

Sergio: You'd better **have** it **serviced** before you use it.

Later, at the bike shop:

Man: Hello, can I help you?

Carlos: Yes, I have a few problems with my bike. There's a flat tire. And the brakes don't work very well. Could you take a look at them?

Man: Sure. That won't be a problem.

Carlos: And would you mind checking the front wheel, too? It wobbles.

Man: I'll see what I can do. You may need to **have** it **replaced**. Anything else?

Carlos: No, I think that's all. How much will that be?

Man: Well, we're doing a special deal this month. You can **have** everything **done** for $50.

Carlos: $50? That's twice the amount I paid for the bike!

Phrases

🎧 3/04 Listen and repeat.

• it's not exactly [new] • in pretty good shape
• It's a complete wreck!

Comprehension

4 Complete part of Carlos's e-mail to a friend.

I just ¹ _____bought_____ a ² _____ bike. There are a few problems. There's a ³ _____ tire and the ⁴ _____ don't work. Also, the front ⁵ _____ wobbles, but the man at the bike store says he'll ⁶ _____ it if necessary.

💡 Solve it!

5 How much did Carlos's bike cost?

Grammar

> **Causative *have***
>
> **Have** you **had** it **checked**?
> You may need to **have** it **replaced**.
> You'd better **have** it **serviced**.

☞ Go to page 140, Master your grammar.

Practice

6 Look at Carlos's list. In your notebook, write what he is going to have done, using causative *have*.

1 He's going to have the brakes fixed.

1 Fix the brakes.	2 Fix the flat tire.
3 Replace the wheel.	4 Check the gears.
5 Lower the saddle.	6 Clean the frame.

7 In your notebook, complete with causative *have*.

1 My sister _is having her ears pierced_ (pierce/her ears) next week.
2 We had a burglary last night. My parents are going to _____. (change/the locks)
3 Ed _____ (take out/a tooth) yesterday.
4 We need _____ (repair/the TV).
5 Why don't you _____ (shorten/those pants)?
6 _____ (Bob/service/his car)?

Pronunciation: Sentence rhythm and stress

8 🎧 Go to page 131.

Use your English: Describe and deal with problems

9 Read the sentences below.

> **Say you need help**
> • I have a problem/a few problems with my bike.
> • There's something wrong with my bike.
>
> **Ask what the problem is**
> • What's wrong with it/them?
> • What seems to be the problem?
>
> **Explain the problem**
> • The front wheel wobbles.
> • The brakes don't work very well.
> • The front light is broken/loose.
>
> **Ask people to do things**
> • Can/Could you take a look at it/them for me?
> • Would you mind checking the brakes?
> • Do you think you could change it for me?
>
> **Respond**
> • Sure. That won't be a problem.
> • I'll see what I can do.
> • Sorry, but there's nothing I can do.

Listen

10 🎧 3/07 **PAIRS** Listen. Then have similar conversations. Use the cues below.

Problem	Store	Request	Response
1 Computer crashes	computer store	take a look at it?	install more memory
2 Dropped camera	camera store	repair it?	No—buy a new one

Write

11 On a piece of paper, write a paragraph about something you had repaired. What was wrong? What did you have done to fix the problem?

My TV didn't work well, so I had it repaired . . .

> **Extra practice**
> • Student Book, page 122, Lesson 9A
> • Language Builder: WB, page 66; GB, page 129
> • Student CD-ROM, Unit 9

9B To get the gold off

Grammar	Clauses of purpose: *to, in order (not) to, so that*
Vocabulary	Adjective suffixes with *-ful, -y, -ous, -ive, -al*
Function	Talk about movie plots

Get started

1 Look at the photo. What do you think the man is doing, and why?

Read

2 🔊 3/08 Listen and read along. Where was the gas tank?

Comprehension

3 Answer the questions.

1 In the movie, why was the gang escaping?
They had stolen gold.

2 How did the movie end?

3 What problem did people have to solve for the contest?

Italian job: problem solved!

The Chemistry Society has announced the winner of a contest to solve the problem at the end of the 1969 classic movie *The Italian Job*.

The problem

It is a beautiful sunny day in Italy, and Charlie Croker and his gang of professional robbers are celebrating. They have just stolen over three tons of gold and are on their way to Switzerland in a bus. Then the bus almost drives off a cliff. It ends up with the back of the bus hanging over the edge of the cliff. The gang are in the front end and their gold is in the back.

Charlie Croker, the gang leader, tries to reach the gold, but as he does so, the bus starts to rock. The situation is very dangerous. Croker turns around and says: "Hang on a minute, lads, I've got a great idea," but the movie ends before we find out what the idea was.

The solution

The society decided to give a prize for the most effective solution for getting the gold off the bus before it tips over the edge of the cliff. This was the winner's idea.

1 One man lowers another man out of a window **so that** he can let the air out of the front tires. This stops the bus from rocking.

2 **To** reduce the weight at the back of the bus, which is hanging over the cliff, another man empties the gas tank. **To** do this he crawls along the floor **in order not to** unbalance the bus.

3 One man gets off the bus and collects some heavy rocks. He puts them in the front of the bus **in order to** counterbalance the weight of the gold. When the bus is safely balanced, another man unloads the gold and the gang can get off the bus.

---

4 Match the steps of the winner's idea (1–3) to the pictures (A–C).

A _____

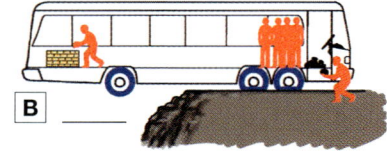

B _____

C _____

Grammar

Clauses of purpose: *to, in order (not) to, so that*

To reduce the weight, he empties the gas tank.
He puts the rocks in the front of the bus **in order to** counterbalance the gold.
He crawls along the floor **in order not to** unbalance the bus.
He lowers a man out of a window **so that** he can let the air out of the tires.

☛ Go to page 140, Master your grammar.

Practice

5 In your notebook, combine the sentences using *to, in order (not) to,* or *so that*.

1 Kevin wanted to pass the test. He studied hard. (in order to)
Kevin studied hard in order to pass the test.
2 I didn't want to forget her phone number. I wrote it on my hand. (in order to)
3 Please turn off your cell phones. Don't annoy other people on the train. (so that)
4 My brother moved to Chicago. He wanted to find a better job. (to)
5 He wanted to lose weight. He started jogging. (to)
6 You should take a guided bus tour. Then you won't miss the important sights. (so that)

6 Match the pairs of sentences. In your notebook, make changes and combine each pair using *so that (not)*.
1-e) I need some money so that I can buy a CD.

1 ~~I need some money.~~
2 He keeps his passport in a special place.
3 She is careful about what she eats.
4 We should talk more quietly.
5 I put the cola in the fridge.

a) We don't want people to hear us.
b) I want it to get cold.
c) He doesn't want to lose it.
d) She doesn't want to put on weight.
e) ~~I want to buy a CD.~~

Vocabulary: Adjective suffixes with *-ful, -y, -ous, -ive, -al*

7a 🔊 3/09 Read the article again. Find the adjectives derived from the nouns below and write them in the chart. Then listen and check.

Noun	Adjective
profession	*professional*
beauty	
sun	
danger	
effect	

b 🔊 3/10 In your notebook, write the adjectives for the nouns below. Listen and check. Then put the adjectives in the chart above.

1 salt   2 wonder   3 imagination   4 origin
5 humor   6 thirst   7 attraction   8 use   9 music
10 suspicion   11 mystery   12 ambition

Speak

8 PAIRS Ask and answer the questions.

1 What exciting action or adventure movies have you seen recently, e.g., *Spider-Man*?
2 What difficult or frightening problems do the characters have to solve?
3 Tell the story briefly. What happens at the end?

Write

9 On a piece of paper, write about one of the movies you discussed in Exercise 8. Describe the problem in the movie and how it was solved.

> **Extra practice**
> • **Student Book, page 122, Lesson 9B**
> • **Language Builder: WB, page 68; GB, page 129**
> • **Student CD-ROM, Unit 9**

It sounds like a police siren.

Grammar	*look, seem, sound, feel, taste, smell* + adjective /*like/as if*
Vocabulary	Adjectives of texture and shape
Function	Talk about advertisements

Get started

1 *Texture* is the way something feels. What are three words that describe texture?

Vocabulary: Adjectives of texture and shape

2 (3/11) Listen and repeat. Look at the adjectives in the box. Write *T* if an adjective describes texture. Write *S* if it describes shape.

> _S_ curved __ fluffy __ hard __ oblong __ prickly __ rectangular __ rough __ round __ silky __ slippery __ smooth __ soft __ square __ star-shaped __ straight __ thick __ thin __ triangular

Read

3 (3/12) Listen and read along. Which product do you think is the best idea? Which one is the worst?

Comprehension

4 Which product . . .

1 plays music? _____*slippers*_____
2 is useful for heavy sleepers? _____
3 is for tourists? _____
4 helps you see in the dark? _____
5 might make you hungry? _____
6 moves around your room? _____

THE NOVELTY GADGETS CATALOG • *YOUR ONE-STOP SOLUTION FOR NOVELTY GIFTS*

Sensational Slippers $22.99

These soft, fluffy slippers not only feel warm and comfortable, they also look great and sound great, too. When you walk, they come alive! Tiny speakers play your favorite happy dance tunes, and small, star-shaped lights flash on and off. You'll never trip over your cat in the dark again!

SnS Postcards $4.99 each

If you go to London, send your friends an SnS postcard! They look like normal postcards, but when you follow the instructions to scratch and sniff, they smell incredible—just like the places in the photo. The postcard of Caledonian Road Flower Market smells like a real flower market, and the one of a fish and chip shop smells like real fish and chips! But don't lick them—they taste terrible!

The Rocket Alarm Clock $25.99

This rocket-shaped alarm clock looks as if it's going to blast off into space! In fact, when the alarm goes off, the top half of this rocket alarm clock takes off and lands somewhere in your bedroom. The alarm sounds like a police siren and keeps ringing until you find the top half of the rocket and turn it off. By that time, you're awake and up!!

 **Solve it!**

5 What does *SnS* in the postcard advertisement stand for?

Grammar

> **look, seem, sound, feel, taste, smell + adjective /like/as if**
>
> **look, seem, sound, etc. + adjective**
> The slippers **feel warm** and **comfortable**.
> They **sound great**.
>
> **look, seem, sound, etc. + like**
> It **smells like** a real flower market.
> It **sounds like** a police siren.
>
> **look, seem, sound, etc. + as if**
> It **looks as if** it's going to blast off into space.
> It **sounds as if** our neighbors are having a party.

☛ Go to page 140, Master your grammar.

Practice

6 Complete the sentences with the correct form of *look, seem, sound, feel, taste,* or *smell* and an adjective from the box.

> • delicious • depressed • difficult • dizzy
> • excited • horrible • numb • wonderful

1 I saw Caroline this morning. She _seemed excited_ about your trip to Mexico.
2 Your perfume _____!
  What is it? I want to get some.
3 Mike just called. He _____.
  Do you want to go and cheer him up?
4 It's so cold outside that my fingers
  _____.
5 I don't want to do that crossword. It
  _____.
6 I just tried some of that pizza. Yuck!
  It _____.
7 I _____ when I stand at the
  top of a tall building.
8 A fresh fruit smoothie _____
  when it's hot outside.

7 Complete the conversation with *look, sound, smell,* or *taste* and *like* or *as if*.

Andy: What are you watching on TV?
Betty: I'm not sure. I just turned it on.
  It [1] ___*looks like*___ a sci-fi movie.
Andy: Hey, that's Arnold Schwarzenegger.
  He [2] _____ a young man there!
Betty: Yeah—it must be an old movie. The music
  [3] _____ it's from the 1980s!
Andy: By the way, what's for dinner?
Betty: Dad's cooking, so it's probably spaghetti.
Andy: Dad's spaghetti is usually OK.
Betty: Yes, but it doesn't [4] _____
  Mom's.
Dad: Oh, NO!
Andy: Uh-oh. It [5] _____
  Dad is having some problems.
Betty: Yeah, and it [6] _____
  something is burning.
Andy: We'd better go and see if he's OK.

Listen

8  Listen to the ads. Complete the chart.

	Ad 1	**Ad 2**	**Ad 3**
Place/ product	*Blue Waves Indoor Water Center*		
Special features	1 2 3	1 2 3	1 2 3
Slogan			

Speak

9 PAIRS Discuss: Have you ever bought something or gone somewhere because of an ad? Was it as good as the ad described it? Explain.

Write

10 On a piece of paper, write an ad for a product. Use the text on page 80 as a model. Use adjectives of texture and shape, *like*, and *as if*.

> ⦿ **Extra practice**
> • **Student Book, page 123, Lesson 9C**
> • **Language Builder: WB, page 70; GB, page 130**
> • **Student CD-ROM, Unit 9**

Work experience

CONSOLIDATION

Values for living

Before you read, go to page 83.

IT'S NASTY STUFF

When Justin got home from school, he was in a good mood. His older sister, Vicky, who was a local newspaper reporter, asked him why he was so happy.

"I'm looking forward to doing my internship next week," Justin said. "I'm going to work for Richard Ross for two weeks. He owns Ross Construction. They build houses and . . ."

"I know," Vicky said. "He's a successful businessman."

"Maybe he'll offer you a job when you finish college," Justin's father said. "Make sure you work hard to impress him."

Justin promised that he would. He picked up Vicky's newspaper. The lead article was about the illegal dumping of asbestos near their town, and there was a photo of bags containing asbestos.

"It's an important story," Vicky said. "Asbestos is nasty stuff, and it can cause lung cancer if you breathe in the dust."

On Monday morning Justin arrived at Ross Construction. Richard Ross himself was waiting for him at reception.

"I'm Richard Ross. Nice to meet you, Justin. Now follow me. We have some work to do."

For the next two weeks Mr. Ross showed Justin how the company worked and spent a lot of time with him. Justin worked hard so that he would make a good impression on Mr. Ross.

On the last day Justin and Mr. Ross visited an old building. Ross Construction was demolishing it in order to build a new hotel. As they walked around the site, Justin saw workers wearing protective clothing and face masks. They were throwing bags into a big dumpster.

"What's in the bags, Mr. Ross?" Justin asked.

"Asbestos," Mr. Ross said.

"Oh, right. That's toxic, isn't it? Do you have it specially removed?" Justin asked.

"No, we get rid of it ourselves. Now come and see . . ."

Mr. Ross clearly wanted to change the subject. Justin said nothing, but he thought the bags looked similar to the ones in the newspaper photo.

"Is your newspaper still writing articles about asbestos?" Justin asked Vicky that evening.

"Yes," Vicky replied. "Why?"

Justin hesitated. What should he say?

New words and phrases

- work experience
- nasty stuff
- in a good mood
- look forward to
- impress
- dump (v)
- asbestos
- lung cancer
- breathe
- dust
- impression
- demolish
- face mask
- dumpster (n)
- toxic
- get rid of
- hesitate

Get started

1 Sometimes dangerous or poisonous materials are used in buildings. How should people throw out these dangerous materials?

Read

2 Read the story on page 82. What does Justin know that Vicky doesn't know?

Comprehension

3 Answer the questions.
1 Why is Justin happy? *He has an internship.*
2 What does Justin's father hope will happen?
3 What is the newspaper article about?
4 How did Mr. Ross treat Justin?
5 What is usually done with the bags of asbestos?

Speak your mind!

4 PAIRS Role-play: Choose one of the roles and decide what to do. Then act out the conversation.

> **Student A:** You are Vicky. Justin told you what he has seen. You want to tell your newspaper. Companies shouldn't dump asbestos illegally. The dust might kill people. Justin's information can stop the dumping.

> **Student B:** You are Justin. You have told Vicky what you have seen. Now she wants to tell the newspaper. You don't want her to do that because Mr. Ross will get into trouble and might go to jail. However, you also want to do the right thing and find a solution to the problem.

Listen

> **Learning strategy: Listen for linking phrases**
>
> A linking phrase will often tell you what kind of information is coming next. When you hear *for example, because of this*, or *as a result*, you can predict the kind of information you will hear.

5a (3/14) Listen to a telephone conversation. Does Justin tell the newspaper who is dumping the asbestos?

b (3/14) Listen again. Complete the sentences.
1 Justin calls Mr. Ross to _talk about the asbestos_.
2 Justin knows what the newspaper is going to do. They are going to _____.
3 Justin didn't want to give the name of the company that was dumping the asbestos because _____
4 Justin has found some companies that can _____
5 Mr. Ross asks Justin to _____.

Write

6 On a piece of paper, write a letter to Mr. Ross. Use the ad and the cues to help you.

Paragraph 1
– thank Mr. Ross for his help
– say why the last two weeks were a good experience for you

Paragraph 2
– give Mr. Ross the details of the asbestos removal company
– explain why it is a good idea to use the company

Paragraph 3
– thank Mr. Ross again

CLIL PROJECT, page 157

He shouldn't have left it there.

Grammar	*should have/ought to have*
Function	Apologize for past mistakes

Get started

1 Look at the photo. Carlos lost something. What do you think he lost?

Presentation

2 🎧 3/15 Listen and read along. Where is Carlos's bike?

Carlos: Great judo class! Wait a minute. Where's my bike?

Sergio: Did you lock it?

Carlos: No. I **should have locked** it, but I was late for the class and I forgot. Do you think someone's stolen it?

Sergio: What? That old wreck? . . . Well, maybe you'd better report it to the police.

Carlos: What a drag! I knew I **ought to have locked** it. OK. See you later.

Man: Hello. Are you looking for a bike?

Sergio: Yes, my friend is. Are you the custodian?

Man: That's right. I put your friend's bike behind the building. He **shouldn't have left** it against the wall.

Sergio: Oh, OK. Thanks. I'll call him.

Half an hour later:

Mom: Carlos, you're back very late. What happened?

Carlos: I couldn't find my bike, and I thought someone had stolen it. I **should have called**. I'm really sorry.

Mom: Well, at least you're back safely. Just look at your bike. I'm not surprised nobody wanted to steal it!

Phrases

🎧 3/16 Listen and repeat.

- Wait a minute.   • That old [wreck]?
- What a drag!

Comprehension

3 Answer the questions.

1 Where have Carlos and Sergio been? *at a judo class*
2 Why didn't Carlos lock his bike?
3 Who is the man?
4 Why did the man move the bike?
5 Why was Carlos's mom worried?

💡 Solve it!

4 About what time did Carlos arrive home?

Grammar

☛ Go to page 141, Master your grammar.

Practice

5 Complete the sentences with *should have* or *ought to have* and the correct form of a verb from the box.

> • ask • buy • call • give • ~~wear~~ • write

should have

1 It's freezing. I ____*should have worn*____ a hat.
2 This jacket is too small. I _____ a larger size.
3 I didn't know where you were. You _____ me.

ought to have

4 I can't remember his phone number. I _____ it down.
5 That dog looks hot. They _____ it water.
6 You used my laptop. You _____ me first.

6 Look at the picture below. In your notebook, write sentences with *should have/shouldn't have* and a verb from the box.

Max invited his friends over for pizza. When his parents saw the kitchen, they weren't happy. Why?

1 *They should have washed their dirty plates.*

> • drink • eat • empty • leave open • leave out
> • turn off • wash

Use your English: Apologize for past mistakes

7 Read the sentences below.

Complain/Ask for an explanation
• I've been waiting for you for a long time. Why are you so late?
• You're back very late. Where have you been?
• Look at this jacket! What happened?

Apologize and explain
• I'm very sorry. I couldn't find my bike.
• I'm really sorry. I missed the bus.
• I'm so sorry. I spilled some coffee on it.

Accept apology
• That's OK. We/It just started.
• Well, at least you're back safely!
• That's all right. It wasn't expensive.

Listen

8 **PAIRS** Listen. Then have similar conversations. Use the situations below.

> 1 You arrange to meet a friend, but you can't find your wallet. You eventually find it, but you show up late.

> 2 Your friend lends you a book to take on vacation. When you return it, there is sunscreen on it.

Write

9 On a piece of paper, write a paragraph about a past mistake. What should you have done instead?

I lost my backpack at a park. I should have . . . .

> **Extra practice**
> • Student Book, page 123, Lesson 10A
> • Language Builder: WB, page 74; GB, page 133
> • Student CD-ROM, Unit 10

Grammar	*must/can't/might/could* for deductions in the present
Vocabulary	Phrasal verbs with *away*
Function	Talk about hoaxes

Get started

1 Look at the photos. What do you think they show?

Read

2 Listen and read along. Who is sure that the monsters don't exist?

---

http://www.fact-or-fiction.cm

| UFOs | Ghosts | Beasts | Photos | Podcasts |

Mythical creatures: **Real or hoax?**

The Loch Ness Monster

This photo was taken in 1977 at a loch (lake) in Scotland. It claims to show the head of a huge beast called the Loch Ness Monster. Could the creature be real?

> A monster in a Scottish lake? Come on. How did it get there? The photo **must be** a fake! It **can't be** a real monster! I bet someone faked the photo and then sold it to a newspaper.
> **James Judd, 17, Houston, TX**

> Loch Ness is a huge lake. It's certainly deep enough to hide a monster. And there have been hundreds of sightings! They **can't all be** mistaken. I think a monster **really could live** in Loch Ness.
> **Olivia Zander, 16, New York**

Bigfoot

This photo is a still from a video shot in 1967 in California. It claims to show a creature called "Bigfoot."

> The creature looks enormous. It **must weigh** about 600 lbs. It **can't be** real. If it were, it wouldn't get scared and run away.
> **Eli Montoya, 17, Miami, FL**

> Roger Patterson, who shot the video, passed away five years later. As he was dying, he swore that the film was real. Why would he lie? I think Bigfoot **might** really **exist**.
> **Lynn Wu, 17, San Diego, CA**

Comprehension

3 Write *J* for *James*, *O* for *Olivia*, *E* for *Eli*, or *L* for *Lynn* after each sentence.

1 Many people say they have seen the monster. _____

2 The man who made the video said that it was real. _____

3 Someone faked the photo to make money. _____

4 A real monster of that size wouldn't be afraid. _____

5 The monster has enough space to hide in. _____

 **Solve it!**

4 What year did Roger Patterson die?

86

Vocabulary: Phrasal verbs with *away*

5 Listen and repeat. Complete the sentences with phrasal verbs from the box.

> • get away • give something (sth) away
> • go away • ~~look away~~ • pass away
> • put sth away • run away • throw sth away

1 My sister _____*looks away*_____ when there's a really scary part in a movie.

2 My mom never _____ her old clothes _____. She sells them.

3 We can use cell phones during break time but we have to _____ them _____ during classes.

4 When the dog followed me, I told it to _____.

5 Sadly, Michael Jackson _____ in 2009.

6 I couldn't sell my old CD player, so I _____ it _____.

7 Ava _____ from home, but she came back an hour later.

8 My cat tries to catch birds, but they usually _____.

Grammar

> ### *must/can't/might/could* for deductions in the present
>
> The photo **must be** a fake.
> They **can't** all **be** mistaken.
> Bigfoot **might** really **exist**.
> A monster really **could live** in Loch Ness.

☛ Go to page 141, Master your grammar.

Practice

6 In your notebook, write sentences using *must, can't, might,* or *could*.

1 His bike's not outside his house. (be at home)
   He can't be at home.
2 She didn't sleep last night. (feel awful)
3 He speaks perfect French. (be American)
4 He shops a lot. (get a big allowance)
5 She's working today. (be at the beach)
6 It looks real, but you never know. (be a fake)
7 Those pears are very hard. (be ripe)
8 Don't make so much noise. (someone/hear us)

Pronunciation: Eliding consonants

7 Go to page 131.

Speak

8 **PAIRS** Look at the photos. Do you think they are real or fake? Comment using *must, can't, might,* or *could*.

It can't be a real cat. The photo . . .

Listen

9 Listen to a podcast from a website and check your answers to Exercise 8. Then answer the questions.

1 How heavy is the heaviest cat? ___*42 pounds*___
2 How much would this cat weigh? _____
3 Who took the cat photo? _____
4 Who took the bus photo? _____
5 What ad was the bus photo used for? _____
6 What was the phrase in the ad? _____

Write

10 On a piece of paper, write a paragraph about a story you have heard that might not be true. Use *must, can't, might,* and *could*.

I've heard that there's a dog in my city who can talk. That can't be true because . . .

> **Extra practice**
> • **Student Book, page 124, Lesson 10B**
> • **Language Builder: WB, page 76; GB, page 133**
> • **Student CD-ROM, Unit 10**

He can't have drowned.

Grammar	*must have/can't have/might have/could have* for deductions in the past
Vocabulary	Crime
Function	Explain past events

Get started

1 Look at the pictures on the right. They show different parts of a story. What do you think the story is about?

Read

2 🎧 3/23 Listen and read along. When was Joe released from prison?

Third time lucky?

The first time Joe Harvey tried to disappear was when he jumped from a ferry going from mainland Italy to Sicily. He was trying to fake his own death to collect nearly $4 million in life insurance, but his plan didn't work because a passenger dove into the sea to save him. "I found him under water, breathing from an oxygen cylinder," said the passenger. "He **must have hidden** it under his coat before he jumped."

Four days later, Harvey tried again. This time he paid a tourist to help him. When the ferry reached open water, his accomplice shouted: "Man overboard!" Joe had in fact hopped off the ferry just before it left. Rescuers thought he **must have drowned**. However, when his family tried to claim the insurance money, the insurance company said, "He **can't have drowned**. We have reliable witnesses who say that they have seen him in Italy."

Four years later, police found Joe and arrested him. He was sentenced to five years in prison for insurance fraud. Then, three years after his release from prison in 1999, he went missing again. At first, his sister thought he **might have gone** on vacation. Then she became worried and called the police. After six months of searching, the police finally closed the case. This time Joe Harvey had disappeared forever.

Comprehension

3 Read the story again and number the pictures in the correct order.

 A ____

 B ____

 C _1_

 D ____

💡 Solve it!

4 In which year did Joe go missing a) for the first time? b) for the last time?

Vocabulary: Crime

5a Review. In your notebook, write lists of words next to the headings. Then check the Word bank on page 129.

Criminals: *burglar, . . .*   **Crimes:** *burglary, . . .*
Verbs + nouns: *to burgle a house, . . .*

b 🎧 3/24 Extension. Listen and repeat. Complete the article with verb phrases from the box.

> **Verb phrases connected with crime**
> - accuse somebody (sb) of   • ~~arrest sb for~~
> - charge sb with   • convict sb of
> - sentence sb to (a period of time) for (a crime)
> - suspect sb of

> **Note:** These phrases are followed by a noun or a gerund (-*ing* form).

The police ¹ *arrested* a 29-year-old man last night for breaking into a house. They ² _____ him with stealing money and jewelry. They ³ _____ him of carrying out several other burglaries in the area, but they had no proof. Police officers ⁴ _____ him of burgling other houses, but he denied it. When the case came to court, he was ⁵ _____ of burglary and ⁶ _____ to three years in prison.

Grammar

> ***must have/can't have/might have/could have* for deductions in the past**
>
> He **must have hidden** it under his coat.
> He **might have/could have gone** on vacation.
> He **can't have drowned**.

☛ Go to page 141, Master your grammar.

Practice

6 Read the police report below. Then, in your notebook, use the cues to make deductions with *must, can't, might,* or *could* + past infinitive.

> 1 When we arrived at the house at 3:30 A.M. on May 4, we found a broken window in the kitchen.
> 2 There were muddy footprints all over the house.
> 3 We found a train ticket dated May 3.
> 4 The bathroom floor was wet.
> 5 The owners can't find their TV and DVD player.
> 6 It's possible the burglar had an accomplice— the TV and DVD player are heavy.
> 7 All the jewelry is still in the house.
> 8 We found fingerprints, which weren't the owners', on the phone.

> ✓ = almost sure it's true
> ✗ = almost sure it's not true
> ? = possible but not sure

1 The burglar/break/window to get into the house. (✓)

The burglar must have broken a window to get into the house.

2 It/rain/during the night. (✓)
3 The burglar/travel/by bus. (✗)
4 He/have/a shower or/wash/his hands. (?)
5 He/steal/the TV and DVD player. (✓)
6 He/have/an accomplice to help him. (?)
7 He/see/the jewelry. (✗)
8 He/make/a phone call. (✓)

Speak

7 **PAIRS** Read the puzzle. Discuss a possible solution. Use the cues and *must have, can't have, might have,* or *could have.*

1 He can't have gone by boat.

> **Nouns:** • boat • bridge • car • clothes
> • plane • plastic bag • river • string
> **Verbs:** • drive • fly • go • jump • put
> • run • swim • tie • walk

---

http://www.puzzlespot.com

Can you solve this puzzle?

Crossing the river

A man escaped from prison in Wyoming in the U.S. A helicopter pilot soon spotted him standing on one side of a wide river. The pilot radioed the police. Not long after, the police arrived at the river and noticed that the man was now on the other side. He was still dressed in his prison clothes, which were dry. There was no bridge anywhere in sight. He was holding a plastic bag and a piece of string. There was no sign of a boat or raft. How did he get there?

Click here SOLUTION to post your answer.

(The answer is on page 129.)

Write

8 Go to the Writing bank on page 148 and complete the exercises. Then, on a piece of paper, make up a story about an unusual crime that you read or heard about.

> **> Extra practice**
> • **Student Book, page 125, Lesson 10C**
> • **Language Builder: WB, page 78; GB, page 134**
> • **Student CD-ROM, Unit 10**

Across cultures

INTEGRATED
CONSOLIDATION
SKILLS

INTERNATIONAL SOCIAL CUSTOMS

 Greeting and eating

http://www.traveltips.net

"If I meet someone my age for the first time, I just say 'Hi' and smile. If it's somebody older, like one of my parents' friends, I usually shake hands and say 'Nice to meet you.' On the other hand, if it's close family or a good friend, I just give them a hug.

If you're invited to dinner, it will probably be at about seven o'clock. It's polite to arrive on time, or up to 10 minutes late, and bring a small gift, like flowers or chocolate. It's OK to chat and laugh during the meal."

Lucy, 16, U.S.

"If I'm formally introduced to someone, I shake hands and say 'Buenos dias, señor/señora.' If it's someone I know, I shake hands and kiss them on both cheeks. It isn't a real kiss, it's an air kiss. But if it's a very good friend or relative, I'll hug and kiss them.

A dinner invitation will probably be for about nine o'clock, but it's all right to be at least 15 minutes late. The dinner will usually go on until after midnight because Spanish people like to stay up late. In spite of this, they always get up early for work! Guests usually bring a gift of flowers or a plant for the host or hostess."

Gloria, 14, Spain

"In my country greetings are formal. Consequently, people often think we're unfriendly, but we aren't. It's just tradition. Older people always bow when they meet for the first time. But when young people meet, we just nod and look at each other.

If you get an invitation to a Japanese home, arrive on time and bring something to eat or drink, or flowers or candles. But never give a gift of four items because four is an unlucky number. As soon as you enter the house, you must take your shoes off. During the meal, you should eat quietly and not talk too much."

Yosuke, 15, Japan

New words and phrases
- social • custom • shake hands • close *(adj)*
- hug *(v/n)* • kiss *(v/n)* • on time • cheek
- air kiss • go on • host(ess) • tradition
- bow *(v/n)* • nod *(v/n)* • item

Get started

1a How do you greet the following people?

- a girl or boy of your age who you meet for the first time?
- an older friend of your parents?
- a relative or a friend that you know well?

b If you're invited to a meal at someone's house, do you bring a gift? If so, what do you bring?

Read

2 Read the text. In which country is four an unlucky number?

Comprehension

3a Read the customs. Check (✓) the country or countries.

In which country or countries:	U.S.	Spain	Japan
1 ... do they kiss on both cheeks?		✓	
2 ... do family and friends hug?			
3 ... do they bow when they meet?			
4 ... is it all right to arrive a little late for social occasions?			
5 ... is it polite to take your shoes off when entering the home?			
6 ... do people eat after 9 P.M.?			
7 ... is it polite to bring flowers?			

b Answer the questions.

1 How do you greet people in Japan, Spain, and the U.S.?
2 Should you arrive on time in a) Spain? b) Japan?
3 How much conversation is it polite to make during a meal in a) the U.S.? b) Japan?

Listen

4 🔊 3/25 Listen to a woman talking about her vacation and complete the information in the chart.

Country of speaker	*U.S.*
Country she was visiting	
Occasion	
Problem	
Local custom	

Speak

Learning strategy: Practice new language

Try to use new language. Look back at what you have learned and bring it into your speech and writing.

5 PAIRS Discuss: What social customs do you think are different between your country and the U.S.? Discuss these topics:

• meeting and greeting   • meals
• other social occasions   • being on time

Write

Writing tip: *On the other hand, in spite of this, consequently, because of this*

Contrast: *If it's somebody older, I usually shake hands.* **On the other hand**, *if it's a good friend, I give them a hug.*

Concession: *Spanish people like to stay up late.* **In spite of this**, *they always get up early for work!*

Cause: *In my country greetings are formal.* **Consequently/Because of this**, *people often think we're unfriendly.*

6 In your notebook, rewrite the sentences using one of the phrases from the box above.

1 I didn't want to be late, but I didn't want to be early, either.

   I didn't want to be late. On the other hand, I didn't want to be early.

2 We had an enormous dish of pasta. I managed to eat all the dessert.

3 I offered to help clean up after the meal. I didn't get home until after midnight.

4 I wanted to bring a gift. I didn't want to bring anything too formal.

5 There was a huge traffic jam in town. I arrived at the theater late.

6 I couldn't speak very much French. I was able to chat with his parents.

7 On a piece of paper, write about your country for the website "International social customs." Use your ideas from Exercise 5 and use Lucy's text in the website on page 90 as a model.

CLIL PROJECT, page 157

Grammar (40 points)

1 Complete with causative *have*. (6 points)

0 Sarah is going to _have her portrait painted_.
(her portrait/paint)

1 I hate my curly hair. I want to _____.
(it/straighten)

2 Mom says I can _____.
(my bedroom/redecorate)

3 My watch isn't working. I'd better _____.
(it/repair)

4 Jo's at the hairdresser's. She _____.
(her hair/cut)

5 Tom _____ before he used it.
(his bike/service)

6 You need _____! (your eyes/test)

2 In your notebook, combine the sentences with *to, in order (not) to,* or *so that.* (6 points)

0 I need a box. I want to put these books in it. (to)
I need a box to put these books in.

1 They organized a treasure hunt. They wanted to raise some money. (in order to)

2 Come closer. You can see better. (so that)

3 They walked in very quietly. They didn't want to disturb anybody. (in order to)

4 He's going into the hospital. He's going to have an operation. (to)

5 I went by taxi. I didn't want to be late. (in order to)

6 Drive faster. You can pass the car in front. (so that)

3 Complete with *like, as if,* or nothing and a phrase from the box. (5 points)

> • a teacher at my school • ~~his car~~ • peppermint
> • sick • there's been an accident
> • they're having an argument

0 I think Dad's home. That sounds _like his car_.

1 Our neighbors are shouting. It sounds _____
_____.

2 I just ate 30 chocolates and I feel _____!

3 That woman looks _____.

4 This tea is interesting. It tastes _____.

5 I can see an ambulance. It looks _____
_____.

4 In your notebook, rewrite the underlined sentences with *should(n't) have* and the past participle. (5 points)

0 <u>I had coffee after dinner</u> and I couldn't sleep.
I shouldn't have had coffee after dinner.

1 <u>He ate a whole chicken</u> and now he feels sick.

2 <u>We didn't bring food</u> and now we're hungry.

3 <u>You watched the late movie.</u> Now you're tired.

4 <u>I didn't go to the dentist yesterday.</u> I forgot.

5 <u>She wore jeans,</u> but the other guests were all nicely dressed.

5 Complete with *must, can't,* or *might.* (6 points)

0 You _can't_ (be) hungry. You just ate a cake!

1 This suitcase _____ (be) mine, but I'm not sure.

2 She _____ (feel) tired after that long journey.

3 It's too hot. I _____ (wear) a coat.

4 He _____ (like) pizzas. He's ordered two!

5 You never know. The tickets _____ (be) free.

6 She _____ (be) American. Her Spanish is too good!

6 Complete with *must have, can't have,* or *might have* and the past participle. (12 points)

Holmes: Well, Watson. Who do you think stole Lady Gray's jewelry?

Watson: It [0] _can't have been_ (be) her son because he said he was in Paris last week. But that [1] _____ (be) a lie.

Holmes: I'm sure it was a lie. The gardener saw him here on Saturday, so he [2] _____ (stay) in Paris.

Watson: The gardener [3] _____ (make) a mistake. It's possible.

Holmes: No. He [4] _____ (recognize) him. Everybody knows the Gray family in this village.

Watson: So where's the son now?

Holmes: His car isn't here. He [5] _____ (take) it.

Watson: Well, he [6] _____ (go) far. Come on!

Vocabulary (40 points)

7 Complete the bike words. (7 points)

0 You put your feet on these: p _e d a l s_

1 You sit on this: s _ _ _ _

2 These are full of air: t _ _ _ _ _

3 You hold these: h _ _ _ d _ _ _ _ _ _ _ _

4 When it's dark, use your l _ g _ _ _ _

5 You use these to stop the bike: b _ _ _ _ _ _

6 There are two of these. They are round: w _ _ _ _ _ _

7 You use different ones to go up a hill: g _ _ _ _ _

8 Complete the sentences with the adjective form of the words in the box. (10 points)

- ambition • ~~humor~~ • imagination
- mystery • origin • thirst

0 It's not a serious program. It's _____ _humorous_ _____.

1 That's a really _____ idea. You should be an inventor!

2 There's some juice if you are _____.

3 His essays are really _____.

4 I want a good job, but I'm not _____.

5 No one knows who did it. It's very _____.

9 Rearrange the letters to make adjectives of texture or shape. (9 points)

0 _____ _prickly_ _____ rose (RKICLYP)

1 _____ slippers (FUFLYF)

2 _____ cushion (FOST)

3 _____ baby's skin (MOHOTS)

4 _____ icy road (PLISEPRY)

5 _____ line (VRUCDE)

6 _____ coin (UNDRO)

7 _____ picture (RACRNUGLETLA)

8 _____ road (THIRSGAT)

9 _____ box (UAQESR)

10 In your notebook, replace the underlined phrases with phrasal verbs in the correct form. (7 points)

- ~~get away~~ • give away • go away • look away
- pass away • put it away • run away • throw it away

0 I nearly caught a fish but it <u>escaped</u>. _(got away)_

1 The musician Louis Long <u>died</u> last year.

2 I <u>let someone have</u> my old phone <u>for free</u>.

3 In a horror movie, I often <u>take my eyes off the screen</u>.

4 I <u>put the empty candy wrapper in the garbage can</u>.

5 Can you make that dog <u>go somewhere else</u>?

6 I <u>placed your laptop back in its bag</u>.

7 If I saw a snake, I'd <u>go somewhere else quickly</u>.

11 Complete with the correct verbs. (7 points)

- accused • admitted • arrested • charged
- denied • robbing • sentenced • ~~suspected~~

Police [0] _suspected_ Frank Bishop of [1] _____ a bank. When they found a suitcase full of money at his house, they [2] _____ him and [3] _____ him of the robbery. Frank [4] _____ doing it. He said that he'd been at home at the time. The police collected more evidence, and finally they [5] _____ Frank with the crime. In the end Frank [6] _____ everything and he was [7] _____ to five years in prison.

Use your English (20 points)

12 Match the sentences.

0 - g) Was your phone expensive?
No, it was really cheap.

~~0 Was your phone expensive?~~

1 Do you think you could change it for me?

2 Sorry, but you'll have to rewrite this.

3 What seems to be the problem with it?

4 Is Tim fast enough to run the marathon?

5 I like your new jeans.

6 There's something wrong with my camera.

7 Come on! Let's go!

8 He had an accident.

9 We're going in my brother's car.

a) That old wreck! We'll never get there!

b) Wait a minute. Where's my bag?

c) The brakes don't work.

d) Well, they're not exactly new.

e) What exactly is wrong with it?

f) What kind of accident?

~~g) No, it was really cheap.~~

h) Yes, he's in pretty good shape.

i) I'll see what I can do.

j) What a drag! It took me two hours last time!

SELF-CHECK	
Grammar	_____ /40
Vocabulary	_____ /40
Use your English	_____ /20
Total score	_____ /100

The photos were sold.

Grammar	The passive: simple present, simple past, present perfect, past perfect
Vocabulary	The media
Function	Talk about different types of media

Get started

1 How do you find out what's happening in the world?

Vocabulary: The media

2 🎧 ³/₂₆ Listen and repeat. Match the words in the box to their meanings.

___ blog	___ newspaper	_1_ channel
___ editor	___ headline	___ magazine
___ podcast	___ report	___ tabloid

1 a TV station and its shows
2 a radio show you can download from the Internet
3 a publication that features sensational news stories
4 a person who decides what goes into a newspaper
5 a personal diary on the Internet
6 a daily publication that features serious news stories
7 a spoken or written news story
8 the title of a news story
9 a publication that features photos and articles, sold weekly or monthly

Speak

3 PAIRS Ask and answer the questions.

1 Have you ever downloaded a podcast or read a blog? What was it about?
2 What's your favorite TV channel? Why?
3 What are the most popular newspapers in your country? Which ones are tabloids?
4 What are the headlines today?

The paparazzi

The paparazzi are back in the news again. Several celebrities have complained that their children **have been followed** on their way to school. The paparazzi usually sell their photos to gossip magazines and tabloid newspapers for large sums of money. But the paparazzi **are** often **accused** of "hunting" celebrities to get a good photo.

Some celebrities say that their private lives **have been destroyed** by the paparazzi. For example, Miley Cyrus says that paparazzi have ruined her life. She **is photographed** every time she goes out, so she has to stay at home a lot of the time. "I have nightmares about paparazzi. I always have these flashing things in my dreams. They're so scary," Miley says.

In a famous case, the paparazzi **were accused** of putting lives in danger. When Princess Diana **was killed** in a car accident in Paris, France, she **had been followed** by the paparazzi, who were chasing her car on motorcycles.

Read

4 🎧 ³/₂₇ Listen and read along. Vote in the "Your opinion" poll at the end of the article. How did you vote and why?

Comprehension

5 Answer *T* for *true*, *F* for *false*, or *NI* for *no information*.

_T_ 1 The paparazzi are often in the news.
___ 2 They take photos of celebrity children every day.
___ 3 Selling photos is a way of making money.
___ 4 The paparazzi let celebrities have private lives.
___ 5 Miley Cyrus has been hurt by paparazzi.
___ 6 The paparazzi were chasing Princess Diana on the night of her accident.

Who needs them?

Your opinion
What do you think? Do we need the paparazzi? Vote now.

✓ Yes, we do. They give us the photos we want to see.

✗ No, we don't. They don't allow celebrities to have a private life.

Grammar

The passive: simple present, simple past, present perfect, past perfect

Miley Cyrus **is photographed** a lot.
Princess Diana **was killed** in a car accident.
Their private lives **have been destroyed**.
She **had been followed** by the paparazzi.

☞ Go to page 142, Master your grammar.

Practice

6 In your notebook, write passive sentences.

1 Oh, no! I think my wallet/steal!
   Oh, no! I think my wallet has been stolen!
2 You can't leave your car here. Parking/not/allow.
3 When/the first computer/invent?
4 The watch didn't work because it/drop.
5 I don't know the price. It/not/decide/yet.
6 Millions of cell phones/sell since 1990.
7 The story that/write/about Jay-Z wasn't true.
8 The cat was very hungry because it/not/feed.

7 Complete with the correct form of the passive.

💻 Online news

Every day, millions of newspapers ¹ _____ are sold _____ (sell). Until recently, most of them ² _____ (read) by commuters on the train to work, but these days, a lot of newspapers ³ _____ (read) online. Media blogs have also become very popular. These ⁴ _____ (write) by journalists. Comments about stories on these blogs ⁵ _____ (often/send) in by readers. Most TV channels have websites, too. Over 2,000 TV shows a day ⁶ _____ (download) since 2000.

Pronunciation: Word stress in compound nouns

8 🎧 Go to page 131.

Listen

9a 🎧 [3 29] Listen. How do these people answer the question "Do celebrities need the paparazzi?" Write *Y* (Yes), *N* (No), or *S* (Sometimes).

1 Gina __Y__ 2 Juan _____ 3 Sarah _____ 4 Ali _____

b In your notebook, answer the questions.
1 Why does Gina think celebrities need the paparazzi?
   Because they want their pictures in magazines
2 What, in Juan's opinion, makes people famous?
3 Why does Sarah think that the paparazzi can be dangerous?
4 Why does Ali feel sorry for celebrities?
5 When does Ali think the paparazzi should take photos?

Write

10 On a piece of paper, write a paragraph about a celebrity and the paparazzi. Use the passive.

Angelina Jolie is photographed by the paparazzi all the time. She ...

> **Extra practice**
> • **Student Book, page 125, Lesson 11A**
> • **Language Builder: WB, page 82; GB, page 137**
> • **Student CD-ROM, Unit 11**

11B He was being chased.

Grammar The passive: present continuous, past continuous, and simple future

Function Give opinions, agree, and disagree

Get started

1 Have you ever seen a movie being filmed? What was it like?

Presentation

2 Listen and read along. What's going on in Seattle today?

Sophie: Hey, what's happening over there?

Sergio: Let's ask this guy. Excuse me. What's going on?

Man: They're filming a scene for an action movie. It**'s being shot** behind that store.

Sergio: Cool! Thanks.

Sophie: I'm not into action movies.

Lisa: Neither am I. I saw one good one where the star **was being chased** over the roof tops, but usually they're boring.

Sergio: No way! How can you say that? What about the Bourne movies?

Lisa: Well, I don't like Matt Damon that much. He never smiles in his movies, and I don't think he's particularly good-looking.

Sergio: What?! He's cool and he's tough. What more do you want?

Carlos: Stop arguing, guys. Here's someone from the film crew.

Sergio: Maybe we**'ll be asked** to be extras!

Sophie: Dream on!

Comprehension

3 Write the correct name.

1 Who likes action movies? *Sergio*
2 Who doesn't like action movies?
3 Who likes Matt Damon? Why?
4 Who doesn't like Matt Damon? Why not?
5 Who doesn't think the friends can be extras?

Phrases

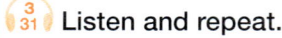 Listen and repeat.

- What's going on?
- I'm (not) into • that much
- What more do you want?
- Dream on!

Grammar

The passive: present continuous, past continuous, and simple future

Present continuous passive

It**'s being shot** behind that store.
They **are being followed** by an assassin.

Past continuous passive

The star **was being chased**.
Some scenes **were being shot** in Seattle.

Simple future passive

Maybe we**'ll be asked** to be extras.

☛ Go to page 142, Master your grammar.

Practice

4 Read about the day a movie was being shot. In your notebook, change the sentences into the passive form.

What was happening a few hours ago?

1 A man was interviewing Leonardo DiCaprio.
  Leonardo DiCaprio was being interviewed.
2 They were writing a new scene for Leonardo DiCaprio.
3 They were closing some of the roads.

What is happening now?

4 They are telling people to be quiet.
5 They are turning on special lights.
6 They are shooting a scene at a bus stop.

What will happen next?

7 They will edit the scenes.
8 They won't release the movie until next March.
9 A woman from *People* magazine will photograph Leonardo DiCaprio.

Use your English: Give opinions, agree, and disagree

5 Read the phrases below.

Give an opinion
- I think it's right/good/great that . . .
- I think it's a good/great/bad/terrible idea.
- I think it's wrong/bad/terrible/unfair that . . .

Agree
- I agree./I think so, too. • I think you're right.
- Me, too./Right!

Disagree
- Sorry, I don't agree./I think you're wrong.
- No way!/What?! • How can you say that?

Concede
- I see what you mean. • Maybe you're right.
- OK. You win!

Speak

6 GROUPS Imagine you are extras in the movie that is being filmed in Exercise 2. Discuss the rules for extras below. Give your opinions.

A: *I think it's right that extras will not be allowed to talk on the set . . .*

Rules for Extras

1 Extras will not be allowed to talk while they are on the set.
2 Extras will be asked to wait until the film crew has eaten before they have lunch.
3 Extras will not be allowed to talk to or take pictures of movie stars on the set.
4 Extras who arrive late for a shoot will be sent home immediately.

Write

7 On a piece of paper, write about the rules for extras in Exercise 6, or rules for a performance or event that you are taking part in. Use the passive.

In my school play, actors are being asked to make their own costumes. I think that's a good idea . . .

 Extra practice
- **Student Book, page 126, Lesson 11B**
- **Language Builder: WB, page 84; GB, page 137**
- **Student CD-ROM, Unit 11**

97

11c It ought to be stopped.

Grammar	The passive: modals, gerund (-*ing* form), and infinitive
Vocabulary	Adjective and noun formation
Function	Give your opinion on an issue

Get started

1 If you were ruler of the world for a year, what would you change?

Read

2 Read the quiz. Write a topic from the box below next to each statement.

> a) the environment b) fair wages c) ~~education~~
> d) the media e) scientific research f) the Internet

---

http://www.changetheworld.nt

HOME NEWS **WATCH** CONTACT

GET INVOLVED NOW!

THE WEBSITE FOR TEENAGERS WHO WANT TO CHANGE THE WORLD

Do you have what it takes to change the world? Take our quiz and find out.

Choose A, B, C, or D for each question. **A** = I strongly agree. **B** = I agree. **C** = I disagree. **D** = I don't know.

 1 Teenagers **shouldn't be asked** to take so many tests. It's too stressful.
A B C D TOPIC: _education_

 **2** Using animals in experiments **ought to be stopped**. It's cruel and unnecessary.
A B C D TOPIC: _____

 **3** Something **must be done** to help victims of online bullying.
A B C D TOPIC: _____

 **4** Sixteen-year-olds **should be paid** the same as everyone else if they do the same job.
A B C D TOPIC: _____

 **5** Magazines show too many images of youth and beauty. They destroy people's confidence.
A B C D TOPIC: _____

 **6** Most of the things you throw away **can be recycled**. Don't wait **to be told**, just recycle!
A B C D TOPIC: _____

CHECK YOUR ANSWERS

KEY: **A** = 3 points **B** = 2 points **C** = 1 point **D** = 0 points

0–6 points: Changing the world is not your priority.
7–12 points: You have some strong views.
13–18 points: You really want to change the world.

READ ABOUT OUR LATEST CAMPAIGNER
Omar Wilson, 16, from Chicago
AND WATCH HIS VIDEO.

Be nicer to strangers!

I feel we are too greedy and selfish in our society. But we can change that. We can show that helping other people is as satisfying as **being helped**. For example, we can carry a bag for a stranger or share a snack. So join my campaign and start to make a difference!

JOIN OMAR'S CAMPAIGN

3 PAIRS Take the quiz. Compare your answers with a partner. Check your profile in the quiz key.

Speak

4 Which statement (1–6) from the quiz do you agree or disagree with strongly? Why?

Grammar

> ### The passive: modals, gerund (-*ing* form), and infinitive
>
> **Modals**
>
> It **ought to be stopped**.
> Something **must be done** to help the victims.
> Sixteen-year-olds **should be paid** the same.
> Things **can be recycled**.
>
> **Gerund (-*ing* form)**
>
> Helping is as satisfying as **being helped**.
> No one likes **being ignored**.
>
> **Infinitive**
>
> Don't wait **to be told**.

☛ Go to page 142, Master your grammar.

Practice

5 Complete the statements. Use the cues.

1 Teachers ___*must be paid*___ a fair wage. (must/pay)
2 More parks _____ in our cities. (should/create)
3 Refugees _____ to our country. (ought to/welcome)
4 The rainforest _____. (shouldn't/cut down)
5 Seventeen-year-olds _____ the vote. (should/give)
6 Animals _____ to make fur coats. (mustn't/kill)
7 Musicians _____ by illegal downloading. (can/hurt)
8 Teenagers _____ children. (hate/call)
9 Cyclists _____ by drivers! (don't like/shout at)

Vocabulary: Adjective and noun formation

6a Complete the chart with adjectives or nouns from the website on page 98.

Adjective	Noun
cruel	cruelty
	stress
young	
beautiful	
confident	
	greed
different	

b 🎧 3/32 Copy the chart into your notebook. Add the adjectives and nouns in the box to it. Write the missing forms. Use a dictionary if necessary. Then listen and check.

Adjectives	Nouns
high	*height*

> **Adjectives:** 1 high 2 poor 3 proud
> 4 hopeful 5 brave 6 wise
> **Nouns:** 7 strength 8 truth 9 success
> 10 courage 11 luck 12 anger

Write

7 Choose an issue from the website on page 98 or think of another issue. On a piece of paper, write a paragraph giving your opinion about the issue. Use Omar Wilson's paragraph on the website to help you with ideas.

I believe that using animals in experiments ought to be stopped. I feel that . . . For example . . .

>  **Extra practice**
> • **Student Book, page 126, Lesson 11C**
> • **Language Builder: WB, page 86; GB, page 138**
> • **Student CD-ROM, Unit 11**

INTEGRATED CONSOLIDATION SKILLS

Before you read, go to page 101.

Curriculum link: Science

SCIENCE TODAY

The Nano Revolution

FACTFILE: Nanotechnology

- *Nano* means "one-billionth," so a nanometer is one-billionth of a meter.
- Nanotechnology works in sizes of less than 200 nanometers (a human hair is 80,000 nanometers wide).
- The term *nanotechnology* was first used in the 1970s.

Nanorobots working in the brain

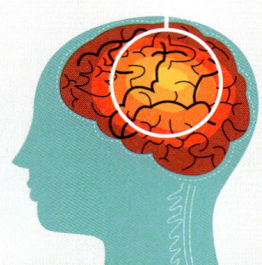

What is nanotechnology?

Nanotechnology is the science of using atoms and molecules to build new machines and materials.

What is it being used for now?

Nanotechnology can be used to create materials like sunscreen, paint, and clothes. Nanotech sunscreen stays on the skin longer and is transparent. American submarines are coated with a special nanotech paint that protects them from rust, and there are nanotech clothing materials that can't be stained or creased. Already there are around 1,000 nanotech products.

What are the future applications?

Transportation

In the future, nanotechnology might produce super-strong, super-light materials that can be used to build new aircraft and cars. These will be far more environmentally friendly because they will be light and will use less fuel.

Energy

A nanotech coating on the glass in our houses may be able to collect and store energy from the sun. We will then have a free supply of energy that isn't damaging to the environment.

Medicine

Doctors hope that, one day soon, microscopic nanorobots will be able to diagnose illness. These tiny robots will be injected into our bodies to conduct tests, deliver drugs, or do surgery when needed.

It looks as if the future is going to be interesting, exciting and very small!

New words and phrases
- nanotechnology • billionth • nanometer • atom • molecule • sunscreen
- transparent • coat *(v)* • rust • stain *(v)* • crease *(v)* • fuel • coating
- store *(v)* • supply *(n)* • microscopic • diagnose • tiny • inject

Get started

1 Look at the picture on page 100. What are the blue and black objects? What are they doing?

Read

2 Read the article on page 100. How many uses of nanotechnology are mentioned?

Comprehension

3 Complete the sentences.

1 Nanotech sizes are less than _____ nanometers.
2 Nanotech sunscreen is more effective because _____.
3 Nanotech paint is especially useful for protecting _____.
4 Cars that use nanotech products will be _____.
5 A nanotech coating on the windows of a house will be able to _____.
6 Doctors hope that microscopic nanorobots will _____.

> **Learning strategy: Dictionary skills (4)**
>
> When you look up a word in a dictionary, make a note of other related words or information.

4 Look up *product, coat, crease, inject,* and *stain* in a dictionary. Answer the questions in your notebook.

1 What part of speech is it?
2 What other related words are given?
3 What other useful information is given?

Now write an example sentence for each word.

Sunscreen is a product that protects people from the sun.

Listen

5 (3 33) Listen to a teacher talking to his class. In your notebook, answer the questions.

1 How far above Earth will the space elevator travel?
62,137 miles
2 Where might it be attached to Earth?
3 How will the cable stay tight?
4 What will travel up and down the cable?
5 Why will the elevator be better than a rocket?
6 How will nanotechnology be useful for this?

Speak

6 PAIRS Look at the list of nanotechnology benefits below. Put the benefits in order from 1 (very important) to 6 (not important at all). Then discuss your order with another pair.

THE BENEFITS OF NANOTECHNOLOGY

In the future we could see

- an elevator that can transport people into space _____
- clothes that will never stain or crease _____
- a glass surface that can store the sun's energy _____
- a submarine that can't rust _____
- planes that use less fuel _____
- a robot that can diagnose and cure disease _____

Write

7 On a piece of paper, write a short article for a school magazine about the benefits of nanotechnology. Use your first three choices from Exercise 6 and give reasons why you chose them.

Nanotechnology
I think nanotechnology is the most exciting thing that I've read about for years! It will bring us many benefits. In my opinion, . . . is the most important benefit because . . . Another exciting idea is . . ., because . . . Finally, I think that . . .

CLIL PROJECT, page 157

If she hadn't been so generous, . . .

Grammar	Conditional: *if* clause + past perfect
Vocabulary	Verbs connected with money
Function	Talk about how to deal with money

Get started

1 Do you think lotteries are a good idea? Why or why not?

Read

2 (3/34) Listen and read along. Was winning the lottery good for the people in the article? Explain.

Lottery winners lose everything

Many people dream of winning the lottery. But for some lottery winners, the reality is more like a nightmare.

Evelyn Adams used to think she was very lucky. She won the New Jersey lottery not once, but twice. She got $5.4 million. But today, all the money is gone, and Evelyn lives in a trailer. "Everybody wanted my money. Everybody had their hand out. I never learned one simple word in the English language — 'No,'" Evelyn says. If she hadn't been so generous, she wouldn't have spent all her money.

Janite Lee from St. Louis, Missouri, also gave away a lot of money after she won $18 million in a lottery. First, she splurged on a million-dollar house and cars for herself. Then she donated huge amounts of money to a university, President Clinton, and even the family of a

South Korean church pastor. But it was her gambling habit that used up the last of her money. If she hadn't gambled so much, she wouldn't have gone bankrupt in 2001.

Ken Proxmire won $1 million in the Michigan lottery. He used the money to move to California to open a chain of sporting goods stores. But Ken didn't know much about running a business. Several years later, his business failed, and Proxmire was $100,000 in debt. Then his wife left him. If Ken had found out more about running a business before he started the chain of sporting goods stores, it probably would have been more successful.

Sadly, Evelyn, Janite, and Ken probably would have had happier lives today if they had never won the lottery!

Comprehension

3 Answer the questions.

1 Why did Evelyn use to think she was lucky?
   Because she won the lottery twice
2 What did Evelyn and Janite both do with their money?
3 Why did Janite go bankrupt in 2001?
4 Why did Ken's business fail?

💡 Solve it!

4 Who lost the most money in the article?

Speak

5 PAIRS Discuss the questions.

1 What do you think Evelyn, Janite, and Ken should have done with their money?
2 Do you think the people they gave money to should now give back the money? Why or why not?

Grammar

Conditional: *if* clause + past perfect

If she **hadn't been** so generous, she **wouldn't have run** out of money.

They **would have had** happier lives **if** they **hadn't won** the lottery.

☛ Go to page 143, Master your grammar.

Practice

6 In your notebook, rewrite the sentences using *if* clauses + past perfect.

1 He borrowed his friend's bike. He arrived on time.

If he hadn't borrowed his friend's bike, he wouldn't have arrived on time.

2 I passed my final. My parents bought me a TV.
3 I didn't have a map. I got lost.
4 He dropped the ball. We didn't win the game.
5 Lucy complained about the meal. She got a free dessert.
6 The movie wasn't interesting. I fell asleep.

7 Read Maria's story. In your notebook, write sentences with *if* clauses + past perfect.

1 a) + b) If it hadn't started to rain, she wouldn't have gone into a second-hand store.

Maria was on her way to buy a new armchair.
a) It started to rain.
b) She went into a second-hand store.
c) She bought an old painting.
d) Her art expert friend saw it.
e) Maria discovered that it was valuable.
f) She sold it for a lot of money.
g) She bought a new house and a new armchair!

Vocabulary: Verbs connected with money

8a 🔊 3/35 Listen and repeat. Look at the article in Exercise 2 again. Underline the verbs that are in the article.

- afford • be in debt • borrow (from) • ~~donate (to)~~
- earn • gamble • give (away) • go bankrupt
- inherit (from) • invest (in) • lend (to) • lose
- make • owe (to) • pay • pay (someone back)
- repay • save • spend (on) • splurge (on) • win

b Complete with verbs from the box above.

Teacher gives winnings to charity

A TEACHER has [1] *donated* her $3 million lottery win to charity. Lorna Davies, 49, [2] _____ the money last month, but instead of [3] _____ on the usual luxuries, she gave the money away. Lorna, who [4] _____ about $40,000 a year, said, "I don't really need the money. I don't have any debts to [5] _____ and I don't [6] _____ the bank any money. I have simple tastes and I can [7] _____ to buy what I need." Lorna's children, who won't now [8] _____ the money when she dies, had no comment, but her husband, Bill, said, "If she had [9] _____ some of the money in the stock market or [10] _____ some on a new house, I would have been happier."

Write

9 Go to the Writing bank on page 149 and complete the exercises. Then, on a piece of paper, write an essay arguing for or against this statement: "Winning a lot of money is usually a bad thing for people."

> **Extra practice**
> - **Student Book, page 126, Lesson 12A**
> - **Language Builder: WB, page 90; GB, page 140**
> - **Student CD-ROM, Unit 12**

Grammar *wish/if only* + past perfect
Vocabulary Phrasal verbs with *out*
Function Talk about regrets

Sweet Success

Adrian Pritchard interviews 17-year-old Evie Cole about her very profitable luxury chocolate business.

How did you get started?

When I was 10 and my brother was 13, we made some chocolates and took them to our local market. People loved our chocolates because they were homemade, and we sold out in an hour. Sometimes I **wish** we **hadn't been** such a success, because that gave us the idea of going into business, and it hasn't always been easy. We set up a company and a website, but the website took far too long to design. We didn't really have a clue how to do it. It turned out all right in the end, but looking back, I **wish** we**'d hired** somebody to do it for us.

How did you manage school and your business?

It was kind of difficult. At first, we got a lot of orders, and I had to work two hours every day after school and three hours on the weekend. We went through a really bad stage for about a year. The fridge was always full of chocolates, and it was driving Mom crazy. Then my school work began to suffer, and I failed some classes. In the end, we figured out that we could afford to employ other people to make the chocolates. **If only** we**'d had** the money for that earlier!

Do you have any regrets?

Not really. Even the mistakes we made helped us to learn. Maybe I have one regret—I **wish** I **hadn't given up** language classes at school. I sell chocolates to lots of countries, and I'd like to be able to talk to some of my customers in their own language.

Get started

1 Do you know any teenagers who have started their own businesses? What kind of businesses? Would you like to have your own business? Explain.

Read

2 🎧 3/36 Listen and read along. Why did Evie's school work suffer? _____

Comprehension

3 Complete the sentences.

1 Evie was ___*10*___ when she started selling chocolates.
2 Evie sold her first chocolates at _____.
3 It took _____ to sell the chocolates.
4 It was difficult to set up the website because _____.
5 At first they put the chocolates in _____.
6 Soon they could afford to _____.
7 Evie says the mistakes helped them _____.

 **Solve it!**

4 How many hours a week did Evie work at first?

Vocabulary: Phrasal verbs with *out*

5 🎧 3/37 Listen and repeat. Complete the sentences with the correct form of phrasal verbs from the box.

> • eat out • figure out • find out • leave out
> • point out • ~~sell out~~ • throw out • turn out

1 I tried to buy the new *Twilight* book, but the store _____*had sold out*_____ of them.
2 Can you _____ the answer to the math problem?
3 Evie had some problems with her business, but it all _____ well in the end.
4 You wrote a really good essay, but unfortunately you _____ the introduction.
5 I thought I looked so cool until my friend _____ I had toothpaste on my nose!
6 Don't _____ my old books! I need them!
7 I don't feel like cooking. Let's _____ tonight.
8 Did you _____ what time the bus leaves?

Grammar

> ### wish/if only + past perfect
>
> I **wish** we**'d hired** somebody to do it for us.
> **If only** we**'d had** the money for that earlier!
> I **wish** I **hadn't given up** language classes.

☛ Go to page 143, Master your grammar.

Practice

6 In your notebook, write sentences with *wish* or *if only*. Use the cues.

1 Today I kept falling asleep. (go/bed/earlier)
  I wish I'd gone to bed earlier!
2 I bought some sneakers and now I'm broke! (not/spend/all my money)
3 I broke my watch. (be/more careful)
4 It's freezing. (bring/sweater)
5 I didn't know it was Jack's birthday. (buy/birthday present)
6 I did what Carla told me, but it wasn't good advice. (not/listen to/Carla)

7 Complete the story with *wish* or *if only* and phrases from the box.

> • give her a nicer surprise
> • look where I was going • not answer the phone
> • ~~not try~~ • read the recipe more carefully

Cooking catastrophe

I decided to make a cake for my mom's birthday. [1]I ___*wish I hadn't tried*___ to be so ambitious! Everything went wrong. While the cake was in the oven, my phone rang, and I forgot about the cake, so some of it was burned. [2]_____. Then I tripped over the cat and nearly dropped the cake. [3]_____. When my mom tried the cake, it didn't taste good at all because I'd forgotten to put the sugar in it. [4]_____. Anyway, she was happy, but [5]_____!

Listen

8 🎧 3/38 Listen. Complete the chart with the names *Andy*, *Tony*, *June*, *Brian*, or *Cathy*. Who . . .

1 . . . stopped studying a language?	*Andy*
2 . . . didn't like living at home?	
3 . . . didn't pass some classes?	
4 . . . tried many jobs?	
5 . . . now knows that personality is more important than beauty?	
6 . . . studies after work?	

Speak

9 PAIRS Do you share any of the regrets of the people in the chart? Which ones? Why?

Write

10 On a piece of paper, write a paragraph about things you wish you had or hadn't done in the past. Use your ideas from Exercise 9.

> **Extra practice**
> • **Student Book, page 127, Lesson 12B**
> • **Language Builder: WB, page 92; GB, page 140**
> • **Student CD-ROM, Unit 12**

12c I might not have done so well if . . . .

Grammar Conditional: *if* clause + *might have*
Function Give and accept congratulations

Get started

1 Have you ever won anything or done a really good job on something? Explain.

Presentation

2 🎧 3/39 Listen and read along. Who is happy, and why?

Carlos: What are you up to for the rest of the summer, Sergio?
Sergio: I have to go to summer school. You know I failed a biology class? Well, I have to retake it.
Carlos: What a pain.
Sergio: Tell me about it! If I **'d done** a little more work last semester, I **might have passed**.
Carlos: Yeah. I think I **might have gotten** a better grade in history if I **'d read** a few more books.
Sophie: Guess what! I'm in the final of the "Young Business Person of the Year" contest! They really liked my T-shirts.
Lisa: Wow! Congratulations! You must be thrilled.
Carlos: Yeah. Great job! That's fantastic!
Sophie: Thanks. But I **might not have done** so well if you **hadn't helped** me with my application form.
Sergio: That's not true! You worked really hard. You deserve it.
Sophie: Thank you. Anyway, let's celebrate. They make a wicked brownie in that café. How about it? It's on me.
Lisa: My favorite! Lead the way!

Comprehension

3 Match the names with the phrases. More than one answer may be correct.

_a)_ 1 failed a class   a) Sergio
___ 2 didn't study enough   b) Sophie
___ 3 is happy for Sophie   c) Lisa
___ 4 wants to treat friends   d) Carlos
___ 5 loves brownies

Grammar

Conditional: *if* clause + *might have*

If I**'d done** more work last semester, I **might have passed**.

I **might not have done** so well if you **hadn't helped** me.

☛ Go to page 143, Master your grammar.

Practice

4 Complete the sentences with *if* clauses + *might have*.

1 If they _____*had tried harder*_____ (try) harder,
they _____*might have won*_____ (win).

2 He _____ (not crash) if he
_____ (drive) too fast.

3 If the weather _____ (be) better, we
_____ (go) for a bike ride.

4 I _____ (not finish) my homework if you
_____ (not give) me some help.

5 If Dan _____ (not be) so tired,
he _____ (enjoy) the party more.

5 Write sentences with *if* clauses + *might have*.
Use the cues.

1 Sophie/listen to her parents → take music instead
of art classes.
If Sophie had listened to her parents, she might
have taken music instead of art classes.

2 she/not work so hard in her free time → not become
so successful.
_____
_____

3 her aunt/not take such an interest in her work →
she/not be able to sell her clothes in the market.
_____
_____

4 her friends/not help her → miss the application date.
_____
_____

5 the judges/not like her T-shirts → she/not get into
the final.
_____
_____

Pronunciation: Weak form: /əv/ *might have*

6 🎧 Go to page 131.

Use your English: Give and accept congratulations

7 Read the sentences below.

Announce your news
- Guess what! I'm in the finals!
- You'll never guess—I got an A!
- Believe it or not, I just won $50!

Congratulate the person
- Congratulations! You must be thrilled!
- Great job! That's fantastic!

Accept congratulations
- Thanks. I couldn't have done it without you.
- Thanks. I never believed it would happen.
- Thank you. It must have been my lucky day!

Respond
- Don't be silly. I knew you could do it.
- That's not true. You worked really hard.
- Not at all. You deserve it.
- Let's go and celebrate! Lunch is on me.

Listen

8 🎧 ³/₄₃ **PAIRS** Listen to the conversation. Then
have similar conversations using the cues below.

1 You just passed your driving test.
2 You got into the final of a contest.
3 You got an A in English for your last essay.

Write

9 On a piece of paper, write a paragraph about
something that might or might not have happened
if you had done something.

If I had come home earlier, my parents might not
have gotten angry at me last night . . .

> ### Extra practice
> - **Student Book, page 127, Lesson 12C**
> - **Language Builder: WB, page 94; GB, page 141**
> - **Student CD-ROM, Unit 12**

INTEGRATED CONSOLIDATION SKILLS

Values for living

Get started

1 If you inherited $1,000, what would you do with the money?

Read

2 Read the article below. What are Leyla's four options?

"You're only young once!"

Unlike her older brother, Amin, Leyla was very close to her grandmother. Leyla played the guitar in a band and always visited her grandmother after rehearsals. Her grandmother often gave Leyla good advice. For example, Leyla would have taken a Saturday job at the local supermarket if her grandmother hadn't advised her against it.

"You're too young to have a job and worry about earning money," her grandmother said. "Why don't you just enjoy playing the guitar? You're only young once! Besides, you're very good at it, so maybe you can teach others. You'd be surprised how rewarding it is!"

"That's easy for you to say," Leyla replied, laughing. "I want to go to college when I finish school, and that costs a lot of money. I have to save up for it."

Even though she really needed to earn some money, Leyla followed her grandmother's advice. She started working with a local music charity, and she loved the work. The charity taught children from poor families to play musical instruments, particularly the piano. They had over 30 students who came every week. The only problem was that they needed a new piano. Without one, they might have to close down. The cheapest piano they could find was $750, but the charity didn't have any money.

Leyla's brother, Amin, was also having a few problems. He was in his last year at college and had a big paper to write. His laptop was old and slow and crashed a lot of the time. He needed a new one. He'd seen the most recent model advertised for $800. "I'm worried that I won't get my coursework finished unless I get a new laptop," said Amin to his sister.

One evening, as Leyla was walking home, she stopped outside a guitar store. There, in the window, was a beautiful electric guitar. The price was $1,000. If she'd been able to afford a new guitar, Leyla would have chosen this one.

Then her grandmother died. Leyla missed her a lot and often thought about her. A few weeks after her grandmother passed away, Leyla found out that she had inherited $1,000. It was all the money her grandmother had owned. Now Leyla had to decide what to do with it. It seemed that there were four different options.

New words and phrases
- inheritance • rehearsal • advise against
- close down • model • coursework

Comprehension

3 Answer the questions.

1 Why didn't Leyla's grandmother want her to take the supermarket job?

She thought Leyla was too young to have a job.

2 Why did Leyla need to earn some money?
3 What did the charity need, and why?
4 What did Amin need, and why?
5 What did Leyla want to buy for herself?
6 What happened when Leyla's grandmother died?

Speak your mind

4 **GROUPS** Role-play: Choose one of the roles below and prepare your arguments. Then discuss what Leyla should do with the money.

Student A: You are Leyla's brother. You want Leyla to lend you money for a new laptop.

Student B: You are Leyla's father. You think that she should save the money for college.

Student C: You are from the charity. You would like Leyla to spend $750 on a new piano.

Student D: You are Leyla. You want to give the money to everyone, but you also want to spend some on yourself. You must decide what to do.

Listen

5a 🎵 3 44 Listen to Leyla talking to her friend Michael from her band. What does Leyla decide to do with the money?

b 🎵 3 44 Listen again and complete the sentences.

1 It's Tuesday evening and Leyla and Michael just finished *band practice* .
2 They decide to go and have a _____.
3 Leyla didn't buy the guitar because if she'd bought it, she would _____.
4 Leyla bought her brother a computer that cost _____.
5 Amin had to promise to pay her back when _____.
6 Leyla gave the rest of the money to _____.
7 Leyla's father thinks she should have _____.
8 Leyla's grandmother was named _____.

Speak

6 **PAIRS** Discuss the questions.

1 Do you think Leyla made the right decision? If not, what would you have done?
2 Should people give some of their money to charity every year? Why or why not?

Write

7 On a piece of paper, write a formal thank-you letter from the charity to Leyla. Mention the points below.

– Thank Leyla for the $600.
– The rest of the money for the piano ($150) was donated by a local businessman.
– The children are happy.
– The piano will be delivered next week.
– Thank Leyla again.

CLIL PROJECT, page 157

Grammar (40 points)

1 Complete the news report with the correct form of the passive. (8 points)

"A $10,000 diamond necklace ⁰ _has been stolen_ (steal) from the singer Angelica's hotel room in Las Vegas, U.S. The necklace ¹ _____ (take) this afternoon while she was out. Angelica ² _____ (give) the necklace by her husband. The rapper BeeJay, who is staying at the same hotel, ³ _____ also _____ (rob) the same night. Some computer equipment ⁴ _____ (take) from his room. The police in Las Vegas ⁵ _____ (already/call in), but nobody ⁶ _____ (yet/charge). The hotel, which ⁷ _____ (often/use) by celebrities, ⁸ _____ (vote) 'Hotel of the Year' last year."

2 Change the active sentences into passive sentences. (8 points)

0 They won't make a decision until next week.
A decision won't be made until next week.

1 They will sell the new *Twilight* book online.
_____

2 They were making a video of our show!
_____

3 I hope they won't ask us to show our passports.
_____

4 They're awarding the prizes on Monday.
_____

3 Complete the sentences with the correct form of the passive. (4 points)

0 Nurses ought _to be paid_ (pay) more.
1 I don't enjoy _____ what to do. (tell)
2 She shouldn't _____ alone at home. (leave)
3 I asked _____ early. (wake up)
4 Dictionaries must not _____ out of the library. (take)

4 Write *if* clauses + past perfect sentences. Use the cues. (8 points)

0 I didn't wear a coat. I was cold.
If I had worn a coat, I wouldn't have been cold.

1 I didn't run. I didn't catch the bus.
_____

2 The train was late. I missed the start of the movie.
_____

3 He didn't set the alarm. He overslept.
_____

4 Julia got lost. She didn't have a map.
_____

5 Rewrite the sentences using *if* clauses + *might have*. (8 points)

0 They didn't study. They didn't pass the test.
If they had studied, they might have passed the test.

1 He ate three burgers. He was sick.
_____

2 She didn't wear boots. She slipped.
_____

3 He had a guitar lesson. He didn't come.
_____

4 I missed the bus. I was late.
_____

6 Rewrite what people said about a party with *wish/if only* + the past perfect. (4 points)

0 I wore my high heels.
I wish I hadn't worn high heels.

1 Anna didn't hire a DJ.
_____

2 Anna didn't invite Mark.
_____

3 We had the party outdoors.
_____

4 Maria didn't show up.
_____

Vocabulary (40 points)

7 Complete the media words. (6 points)

0 A n_ewspaper_ is a serious publication.
1 A t_____ is a sensational newspaper.
2 A h_____ is the title of a newspaper article.
3 Download a p_____ from the radio website.
4 A b_____ is an online diary.
5 A c_____ is a TV station.
6 A journalist writes r_____s.

8 Complete the sentences with the noun form of adjectives from the box. (18 points)

> • beautiful • courageous • cruel • different • high
> • poor • proud • successful • stressful • strong

0 I'm a vegetarian, so I hate _cruelty_ to animals.
1 There's no _____ between these two brands of cola.
2 Too many people are living in _____.
3 You should always take _____ in your work.
4 His business was a great _____, and he got rich.
5 I think _____ isn't as important as personality.
6 What's the _____ of Mount Everest?
7 To make a speech, you need _____.
8 You need _____ to lift that suitcase.
9 Applying for college can cause _____.

9 Complete the paragraph with the correct form of verbs from the box. (10 points)

> • afford • borrow • earn • inherit • lend
> • make • owe • pay • save • spend • splurge

I ⁰ _earn_ about $50 a week. I ¹ _____ about $5 a day on travel. Last week, I ² _____ my friend $10. He ³ _____ me nearly $30 now, but I know he'll ⁴ _____ me back. I never ⁵ _____ on expensive things because I prefer to ⁶ _____ my money. I can't ⁷ _____ to go out much, but I don't like to ⁸ _____ money from my parents. Last year, I ⁹ _____ $500 from my uncle. After college, I'd like to ¹⁰ _____ money by designing websites.

10 Circle the correct phrasal verbs. (6 points)

0 We're (eating)/finding out in a restaurant tonight.
1 Al can't **figure/turn** out why his TV won't work.
2 **Throw/Point** out that he needs to turn it on.
3 Did you **find/sell** out about the train times?
4 I'm sorry, but the tickets are **sold/figured** out.
5 My sister is **turning/throwing** out her old guitar.
6 The class was hard, but it all **turned/figured** out well in the end.

Use your English (20 points)

11 Complete the conversations with the correct responses from the box. (14 points)

> • Dream on! • Great job! You must be thrilled.
> • It's on me • Lead the way! • Tell me about it!
> • What a pain. • What are you up to?
> • What more do you want?

0 **A:** Hi, John. ⁰ _What are you up to?_
   B: Hi, Kate. Not much. I'm watching TV.
1 **A:** Let's get a coffee. ¹ _____
   B: OK. Thanks! ² _____
2 **A:** Guess what? I passed the test!
   B: ³ _____
3 **A:** Wow! You have a lot of work to do!
   B: ⁴ _____ I'm going to start tonight.
4 **A:** I hate Robert Pattinson!
   B: He's intelligent and good-looking.⁵ _____
5 **A:** A computer virus deleted all my files.
   B: I'm sorry to hear that. ⁶ _____
6 **A:** Do you think I'll get a part in the movie?
   B: You? ⁷ _____

12 Put the conversation in order. (6 points)

☐ a) **A:** How can you say that? I think it's really unfair!
☐ b) **B:** I think that's a very sensible idea.
☐ c) **A:** Because they'll make us pay to take the test.
☐ d) **A:** OK. I see what you mean.
☐ e) **B:** Unfair? Why?
☐ f) **B:** Yes, but not very much. Anyway, cyclists will be much safer on the roads.
☑ g) **A:** Next year everyone will have to take a bike-riding test.

SELF-CHECK	
Grammar	_____ /40
Vocabulary	_____ /40
Use your English	_____ /20
Total score	_____ /100

Extra practice

Unit 1

Lesson 1A, Grammar

1 Complete the paragraph with the present continuous or simple present form of verbs from the box.

> • end • go (x2) • learn • ~~love~~
> • play • take • want • work

Sergio Perez [1] ___*loves*___ all sports, but he [2] _____ hard at school, too. This semester, he [3] _____ three honors classes at his school. He [4] _____ to go to college next year. On the weekend, he usually [5] _____ soccer or basketball, and this year he [6] _____ how to rock climb. He [7] _____ twice a week to the local climbing center. School [8] _____ in two weeks, and next summer he [9] _____ climbing in Colorado.

2 Make tag questions to ask Sergio.

1 name – Sergio (✓)
Your name is Sergio, isn't it?

2 father – American (✗)
_____

3 are in high school (✓)
_____

4 taking four honors classes (✗)
_____

5 like soccer (✓)
_____

6 like tennis (✗)
_____

Vocabulary: Clothes

In your notebook, list the clothes in the correct sections of the body (1–5).

1 bandana, baseball cap, . . .

> • ~~bandana~~ • ~~baseball cap~~
> • belt • blouse
> • boots • bracelet
> • cargo pants • coat
> • dress • fleece
> • hat • headband
> • high heels • hoodie
> • jacket • jeans
> • leggings • pants
> • sandals • shirt
> • shoes • shorts
> • skirt • sneakers
> • socks • sweater
> • sweatpants
> • sweatshirt
> • tights • T-shirt

Lesson 1B, Grammar

Read about Bill, a firefighter. Write a short paragraph about him in your notebook. Use the present perfect and simple past forms.

Job	firefighter
Started the job in	2004
Places worked?	Seattle (2004–7), Portland (2007–now)
Things he's done at work so far	rescued hundreds of people and animals in accidents, put out fires, drove the fire truck, gave talks in schools
Funniest incident	rescued cat in a tree 2008
Reason he chose the job	always wanted to help people

Bill has been a firefighter since 2004. He worked in . . .

Lesson 1C, Grammar

Complete the e-mail with *as* + adjective/adverb or the comparative form. Use an intensifier (*much*) if you see a ✓✓.

Dear Nicky,

Sorry I haven't written in a while, but I have a part-time job on the weekends selling ice cream in the park. It's certainly not [1] *as interesting* (interesting) as my last job in a music store, but it's [2] _____ (enjoyable ✓✓) than working in a supermarket.

Other news – I'm going to the gym [3] _____ (frequently ✓✓) now – sometimes four days a week, usually from 5–7 P.M., but I leave [4] _____ (early) on Wednesdays and stay [5] _____ (late) on Fridays. I don't go by bus anymore. I can get there [6] _____ (easily) by bike. I'm getting [7] _____ (thin ✓✓). I don't get out of breath [8] _____ (often) as I used to.

Bye,
Roland

💡 Solve it!

Read the sentences. Write the names of the teenagers in the order of how frequently they watch DVDs. Start with the person who watches the least.

Josie, _____

_____

- Adam watches twice a week.
- Harriet watches every Friday.
- Ben watches more frequently than Meryl.
- William doesn't watch as often as Meryl, but he watches more often than Adam.
- Josie watches once a year.
- Meryl watches two more days a week than Adam.

Unit 2

Lesson 2A, Grammar

Complete the sentences with the simple past form of the verbs in parentheses.

1 They _____ *lived* _____ (live) in California for ten years. Then they _____ (move) to New York.
2 The show _____ (be) three hours long, so we _____ (buy) some snacks during the intermission.
3 He _____ (look) at me and _____ (say) nothing for a long time.
4 My father _____ (watch) television every day last week.
5 The baby _____ (wake up) three times last night and _____ (cry).
6 He _____ (wait) for half an hour. She eventually _____ (come) at 6:30!
7 I _____ (start) to feel ill this morning.

Lesson 2B, Grammar

Match the sentences in A to the sentences in B. Then combine them in three different ways in your notebook, using *when* and *while*.

1 – d)

I was searching the Internet when my laptop crashed.
While I was searching the Internet, my laptop crashed.
My laptop crashed while I was searching the Internet.

A
1 I was searching the Internet
2 They were watching a DVD
3 She was trying on some jeans in a store
4 I was running for the bus
5 He was walking down the stairs
6 We were having breakfast
7 I was eating a salad in a restaurant

B
a) the heel of my shoe broke.
b) a police officer knocked on our door.
c) he slipped and fell.
d) my laptop crashed.
e) I saw an insect on my lettuce.
f) they heard someone in the kitchen.
g) her cell phone rang.

Vocabulary: Phrasal verbs with *up*

Replace the underlined parts of the sentences with phrasal verbs with *up*.

1 She usually <u>rises</u> when the sun rises.
  She usually gets up when the sun rises.

2 I <u>spent my childhood</u> on a farm in Wisconsin.
  _____
  _____

3 Can you wait while I <u>check</u> the times of the trains?
  _____
  _____

4 He <u>started to learn to play</u> the guitar when he was 12.
  _____
  _____

5 <u>Open your eyes!</u> It's a beautiful day!
  _____
  _____

6 Jack isn't here yet, but he may <u>come</u>.
  _____
  _____

7 We are so late, so please <u>be quick</u>.
  _____
  _____

8 Can you <u>remove</u> your clothes from the floor?
  _____
  _____

Lesson 2C, Grammar

Read the story. Then rewrite it in your notebook, in this order: E A B F H G C D. Change the simple past to the past perfect, where appropriate.
(E) Eddy's parents had a nasty scare yesterday. (A) Five-year-old Eddy had left the house at four o'clock to buy ice cream, but (B) he ...

A Five-year-old Eddy left the house at four o'clock to buy ice cream.
B He didn't return.
C Half way to the ice cream store, the boy changed his mind and walked to the station.
D He got on a train and got off at a station 60 miles away from his home.
E Eddy's parents had a nasty scare yesterday.
F The parents called the police.
G Two girls saw the boy at a train station.
H Ten minutes later, Eddie's parents received a phone call.

Unit 3

Lesson 3A, Vocabulary: Kitchen equipment

Complete with words for kitchen equipment.

1 You need a _____*kettle*_____ to boil water.
2 You can serve soup in a _____.
3 You need a _____ to open a can.
4 You use a _____ for cutting your food.
5 You usually put a _____ under a cup of tea.
6 You need a _____ if you want to weigh something.
7 You need a _____ to get small pieces of cheese.
8 You use a _____ to take the skin off potatoes.

Grammar

Circle the correct answers.

Jamie: What [1] (**are you doing** / **do you do**) this afternoon? Do you want to take a bike ride?

Glen: I don't know. I [2] **will have / 'm having** a guitar lesson at 4 P.M., so I have to be back for that.

Jamie: OK. But let's go out for an hour or two. It [3] **will being / will be** fun. Don't worry, we [4] **are / 'll be** back before your lesson.

Glen: All right! I [5] **'m telling / 'll tell** my dad.

Jamie: Oh, no! It [6] **will rain / 's going to rain**!

Glen: Well, I [7] **'m not going to enjoy / 'm not enjoying** the bike ride if it rains. Maybe my dad [8] **will take / is taking** us to a movie instead.

Lesson 3B, Grammar

Complete the sentences with *(not) have to, must (not), should,* or *shouldn't*.

1 I'd better go. I ____*have to*____ start at 8 o'clock.
2 Do you think I _____ call and say we'll be late?
3 We _____ call her now. We're going to see her this evening.
4 You _____ answer all the questions or you'll get an error message.
5 If you want my opinion, he _____ borrow your stuff without asking. It's rude.
6 It's a surprise, so you _____ open your eyes until I tell you.
7 It's your decision, but you really _____ read in the dark. It's bad for your eyes.
8 It's only an informal party. You _____ wear anything dressy.

Lesson 3C, Grammar

Complete the letter to a magazine with the correct forms of *(not) allowed to*, *make*, or *let*.

> ### Dear Problem Page, ⭐ ⭐ ⭐
>
> I [1] *'m allowed to go* (allow/go) to the youth club at night as long as I'm back by 10 o'clock. Last Friday I got home late because I lost my bus pass and I [2]_____ (not/allow/get on) the bus without it. My parents were really angry. They [3]_____ (not let/explain) and now I [4]_____ (not/allow/go) to the club anymore. Now my parents always [5]_____ (make/tell) them exactly where I am going. What's your advice?
> *Clare (15)*

Use your English

Circle the correct answers.

A: Hey, do you want [1] **go /** (**to go**) to see the new Bourne movie this evening?

B: I [2] **like to / 'd love to,** but I can't.

A: Really? Why not?

B: I [3] **have / have to** go and visit my aunt in the hospital.

A: That's [4] **good idea / too bad.** Well, would you [5] **like to go / like go** tomorrow?

B: Yes, that [6] **sounds / would sound** great!

Unit 4

Lesson 4A, Grammar

Complete the conversation with the present perfect or simple past form of the verbs.

Ann: Hi, Jack! Where [1] *have you been* (you/be)? I [2]_____ (not/see) you for a long time.

Jack: I [3]_____ (just/come) back from New York. I [4]_____ (go) there on a trip with my school.

Ann: Cool! I [5]_____ (never/be) to New York. What [6]_____ (you/do) there?

Jack: I [7]_____ (take) lots of photos, and I [8]_____ (visit) the Met.

Ann: The Met? What's that?

Jack: It's a big art museum. In fact, it's the biggest museum I [9]_____ (ever/be) to.

Use your English

Write sentences with a similar meaning.

1 I've never read such an amazing book. (read/ever)
   This is the most amazing book I've ever read.

2 Is this your first time in Miami? (be/before?)
   _____

3 He arrived a few minutes ago. (arrive)
   _____

4 I saw that movie last year. (see/already)
   _____

5 Do you know what octopus tastes like? (eat/ever?)
   _____

6 I have no idea who that girl is. (meet/never)
   _____

7 I've never played this game. (first time/ever/play)
   _____

8 I still have homework to do. (not finish/yet)
   _____

Lesson 4B, Grammar

Read each situation and write two sentences, one in the present perfect form and one in the present perfect continuous form. Use *for* and *since* where necessary.

1 Ben is writing a novel. He started three days ago and he is now on page two!
   (he/write/three days)
   He has been writing for three days.
   (he/write/two pages so far)
   He's written two pages so far.

2 Gemma is traveling around South America. She began her trip two months ago.
   (she/travel/around South America/two months)
   _____
   (she/visit/four different cities so far)
   _____

3 Thierry Henry is a soccer player. He began playing when he was nine years old. He just won "French Player of the Year" for the fifth time.
   (he/play/soccer/the age of nine)
   _____
   (he/win/"French Player of the Year" five times)
   _____

Vocabulary: Music words

Complete the paragraph with words from the box.

- album
- ~~bands~~
- beat
- charts
- lead singer
- lyrics
- single
- track
- voice

One of my favorite rock [1] ___bands___ is
Flyleaf. The [2] _____ is a woman named
Lacy Mosley. She has a great [3] _____.
Their first [4] _____ was called *Flyleaf*.
It reached number 18 in the [5] _____ in
2009. My favorite [6] _____ on it is
"All Around Me." It's great for dancing
because it's got a good [7] _____, and
the [8] _____ are simple, but very
powerful. I know all the words to it. They later
released it as a(n) [9] _____.

Lesson 4C, Grammar

In your notebook, combine the two underlined
sentences and make a new sentence with a relative
clause. Omit the relative pronoun if possible.

I recently saw a movie I will never forget.

Chuck Williams: A few of my favorite things

DVD

1 I recently saw a movie. I will never forget it. It was
called *The Last Song*.

Singer

2 Right now, my favorite singer is a woman. The
woman is named Laura Marlin.

Restaurant

3 I often go to a local Mexican restaurant. They serve
excellent food there.

Video game

4 I don't like video games. They are for young people.
The young people have quicker fingers than me.

Vocabulary: Phrasal verbs with *on*

Complete the conversations with the correct form
of phrasal verbs from the box.

- count on
- hold on
- keep on
- log on
- put on
- ~~try on~~
- turn on

Conversation 1

A: Excuse me. Can I [1] _try_ these sunglasses _on_?
B: Sure, but be careful when you [2] _____
them _____. They're very expensive.
A: Oh, no, these don't look good. No, thanks.
B: [3] _____ a minute. Try another pair.

Conversation 2

A: I'm doing my project.
B: Oh, sorry. I won't disturb you. [4] _____
doing your work. . . . Wait a minute! You're not
working. You've [5] _____ to a chat website!

Conversation 3

A: You get along with your boyfriend really well, don't
you? What's your secret?
B: We trust each other. I know I can [6] _____
him. I also [7] _____ the TV when he talks
too much!

Unit 5

Lesson 5A, Grammar

Match the cues in A and B to form sentences. In your notebook, write the sentences with *if, unless, provided that,* or *as long as.*

1 – e) He'll come with us to New York provided that his parents say yes.

A
1 He/come with us to New York
2 Someone/fall over your bag
3 I/buy those sneakers
4 I/help you with your homework
5 She/not be late for school

B
a) you help me with mine (if)
b) there/be a lot of traffic (unless)
c) you/leave it by the door (if)
d) I/manage to save enough money (as long as)
e) his parents/say yes (provided that)

Vocabulary: Landforms and the environment

Complete the facts with words for landforms and the environment.

Geography factfile

1 The deepest place in the Pacific ___Ocean___ is the Mariana Trench.

2 Angel Falls in Venezuela is the highest _____ in the world.

3 The Nile _____ in Egypt is 4,147 miles long.

4 The Atacama _____ in South America is the world's driest place.

5 Greenland is the biggest _____ in the world.

6 The huge Taiga _____ near the North Pole contains one third of all the trees in the world.

7 A _____ is always under 1,968 feet high. If it's higher, it's called a mountain.

8 _____ Baikal in Russia contains 20% of the world's fresh water.

Lesson 5B, Vocabulary: Extreme weather

Read the clues. Complete the crossword.

1 shaking and moving of the earth
2 a lot of snow coming down a mountain
3 not enough food for everyone
4 a lot of rain for a short time
5 a snowstorm
6 not enough rain for a long time
7 very strong winds and strong rain
8 small pieces of ice from the sky
9 a very big wave at sea
10 a lot of water on the ground

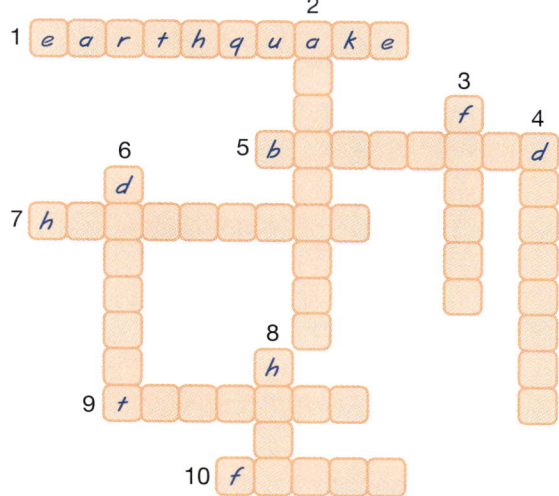

Grammar

Match the cues in A and B to form sentences. In your notebook, write the sentences with the correct forms of the verbs.

1 – c) As soon as my computer is fixed, I'll do some research online.

A
1 As soon as my computer (be) fixed
2 I think she (be) a millionaire
3 Until this blizzard (stop)
4 There (be) a prom
5 By the time Jake (arrive)
6 Simon (call) us

B
a) I (stay) at home by the fire.
b) it (be) too late to go out.
c) I (do) some research online.
d) when he (get) home.
e) before she (be) 21.
f) after the school year (end).

117

Lesson 5C, Grammar

Complete the sentences with *in case* or *if*.

1 I'm going to pack some bandages ___*in case*___ I get a blister from my new sneakers.

2 I turn the light on and read _____ I can't sleep.

3 Dan is crazy! He's taking two cell phones with him _____ he loses one!

4 Tell me _____ you're bringing Carlos to the party.

5 Set the alarm for seven o'clock _____ you oversleep.

6 The ice cream will melt _____ you leave it out on the kitchen table.

7 You should get insurance _____ you have an accident while you're skiing.

Vocabulary: Camping equipment

Read what some people say on a camping vacation and choose what they need from the box below.

> • backpack • bandages • compass • flashlight
> • matches • penknife • sleeping bag
> • sunscreen • ~~tent~~

1 "We need shelter from this rain." ___*a tent*___

2 "I have no idea which way is north."
_____

3 "Do we have something to cut this apple with?"
_____

4 "Ouch! I cut my finger." _____

5 "Watch out. You're going to get sunburned."
_____

6 "Let's light the fire." _____

7 "We need something to carry all this stuff in."
_____

8 "How are we going to see in the dark?"
_____

9 "I need something warm to sleep in."
_____

Unit 6

Lesson 6A, Vocabulary: Transitive phrasal verbs

Replace the underlined phrases in the story with the correct form of phrasal verbs from the box. Write them in your notebook.

> • ~~ask out~~ • check out • give back
> • pick up • turn off

1 ask her out

Never give up!

Liam met Catherine at a party. Catherine was his friend David's sister. Liam liked Catherine, and he decided to [1] invite her to go on a date. The next weekend, he asked Catherine if she wanted to [2] go see what the new shopping mall was like, but she couldn't go because she had to [3] bring her younger sister home from school. Liam was disappointed. On Saturday he went to David's house to [4] return a CD. Catherine was there. She was watching television. Liam suggested going bowling. Catherine [5] switched off the TV, and they went to Super Lane Bowling. Two years later, they were still together!

Grammar

1 Rearrange the words to make *if* clause and past questions in your notebook.

1 would live? were If where you rich, you
If you were rich, where would you live?

2 you which superhero, were be? would
a If you one

3 Selena Gomez, what If met you say? would
you

4 one be? would had wish, If what it you

5 you you do? what If would $1,000, found

2 PAIRS Ask and answer the questions with your partner.

Lesson 6B, Grammar

Complete the thought bubbles of teenagers at a party.

I wish I _____was_____ OR _____were_____ (be) taller.

1

I wish I _____ (not have) red hair.

2

If only we _____ (have) some live music.

3

I wish he _____ (not talk) so much.

4

If only I _____ (can) dance.

5

If only I _____ (not be) so shy.

6

Use your English

Number the sentences in the correct order.

- [ ] a) If I were you, I'd buy her some flowers.
- [ ] b) Nothing serious, but I want to apologize. What do you think I should do?
- [ ] c) Yes, that's a good idea. Thanks.
- [ ] d) I'm not sure. Flowers are too much.
- [ ] e) What was the fight about?
- [ ] f) Well, in that case I think you should e-mail her.
- [1] g) How's Samantha?
- [ ] h) She's OK. But we had a big fight.

Lesson 6C, Grammar

Complete the conversation with the correct form of the verbs in parentheses.

Jay: What do you want [1] _to do_ (do)? Do you prefer [2] _____ (watch) a DVD or a TV show?

Kim: A DVD if you promise [3] _____ (not/choose) a horror movie. I avoid [4] _____ (watch) that kind of thing before I go to bed.

Rob: I don't want [5] _____ (sit) in front of the TV. I'd like [6] _____ (keep on) [7] _____ (play) this video game.

Jay: I think you should stop [8] _____ (play) now.

Rob: No, I refuse [9] _____ (give up) now. I'm nearly at the next level.

Kim: You seem [10] _____ (spend) all day in front of your computer!

Rob: All right. If I manage [11] _____ (reach) the next level, I'll stop.

Kim: And then you can enjoy [12] _____ (watch) a silly movie with us.

119

Unit 7
Lesson 7A, Grammar

Jack was interviewed for a job yesterday. Look at his notes. In your notebook, report his questions to the interviewer.

1 He asked how many weeks the course lasted.

Students required as assistants at a children's summer camp

1 How many weeks does the course last?
2 Do I have to wear a uniform?
3 How much will I earn a week?
4 Will I get free meals?
5 What time do I have to start in the morning?
6 How many other students are you interviewing for the job?

Lesson 7B, Grammar

Read the clues and write the reporting verbs in the crossword.

1 "This steak is terrible! It's raw."
2 "I'll call you when I get there."
3 "Do you want a ride?"
4 "I didn't break your favorite cup!"
5 "I didn't have my phone on me, you see."
6 "OK, it was me. I broke your cup."
7 "Would you like to come to my party?"
8 "Go to bed now."

Lesson 7C, Vocabulary: Relationship words

Complete the sentences with the correct form of the verbs from the box.

- be   - care   - drive   - ~~get~~   - treat
- trust   - worry

1 I don't like him. He _____*gets*_____ on my nerves.
2 I _____ my best friend, Joe. I can tell him anything, and I know he won't repeat it.
3 I like our new teacher. She _____ us like adults.
4 My little brother _____ me crazy! He's always borrowing my stuff!
5 I _____ a lot about my sister. I always make sure she's OK.
6 Harry _____ very close to his father. They do everything together.
7 George gets annoyed with his parents because they _____ about him too much.

Unit 8
Lesson 8A, Grammar

Combine the sentences. Use *so, such a/an, so many,* or *so much + that*.

1 He drove very fast. I was scared.
   He drove so fast that I was scared.

2 I talked very loudly. I lost my voice.
   _____

3 It was a great day. I had to write about it in my blog.
   _____

4 She got up early. She must be tired.
   _____

5 He has a lot of money. He doesn't know what to do with it.
   _____

6 Jenny had a hard day. She went straight to bed.
   _____

7 It was very hot. I wore shorts.
   _____

8 I was very happy. I sang all the way home.
   _____

Lesson 8B, Grammar

Complete the conversation with the correct forms of *used to*, *(not) be used to*, or *get used to*.

Lynn: In the studio today, we have JB, the famous rap singer, just arrived from London. How's it going, JB?

JB: Good, thanks, but I [1] *'m not used to* the time difference yet.

Lynn: Is this your first visit to New York?

JB: No, it isn't. I [2] _____ come here a lot when I first started singing. That was years ago.

Lynn: Where [3] _____ perform?

JB: I [4] _____ sing in a club in the East Village, but it's closed down now.

Lynn: Has New York changed a lot?

JB: Yes, it's much busier. There [5] _____ be so many cars on the street. I just can't [6] _____ the traffic now!

Lynn: You're giving a concert tomorrow, right?

JB: Yes. It's at Meadowlands Stadium. I [7] _____ performing in such a big place!

Use your English

Two young American students are in a restaurant in Mexico City. Complete the conversation. Capitalize if necessary.

> • a little strange • does that mean • ever tried
> • kind of • never heard • no idea • sound
> • are like • what are • what's

Ted: Are you going to have an "aperitivo"?

Max: What [1] *does that mean*?

Ted: It's the first course.

Max: Oh. Maybe. [2] _____ "queso fundido"?

Ted: It's a [3] _____ cheese.

Max: OK. I'll have that.

Ted: Have you [4] _____ tamales?

Max: No, I have [5] _____ what they are.

Ted: They [6] _____ like cornbread, but they're stuffed with sweet or salty fillings.

Max: Oh. They [7] _____ good. And there's something here called "chapulines." I've [8] _____ of them before.

Ted: I haven't either. Let's ask the waiter. Excuse me, [9] _____ chapulines?

Waiter: They are toasted grasshoppers. Would you like some?

Ted: Um . . . no, thanks. They sound [10] _____!

Lesson 8C, Grammar

Complete the ad for the Phobia Treatment Clinic with the correct form of *(not) be able to* and verbs from the box.

> • attend • cure • go • help • live • relax

PHOBIA Treatment Clinic

Here at the PTC, we treat all phobias. If you [1] *are able to attend* sessions with us, then we [2] _____. Every client receives one-to-one treatment in a safe and supportive environment.

Over the past 10 years we've helped hundreds of clients. Before they came to us, some of them [3] _____ and enjoy their yards because of a fear of spiders or birds. Others [4] _____ out of the house because of a fear of people or open spaces. Fortunately, since the clinic opened, we [5] _____ almost all our clients' phobias and enabled them to live a happy, healthy life. After just a few easy sessions you, too, [6] _____ a normal life.

Call us now at 1 800 555 2390

121

Vocabulary: Phrasal verbs with *in*

Replace the **bold** phrases with phrasal verbs from the box. Which phrasal verb is not used?

> • break in • fit in • give in • ~~hand in~~
> • move in • sink in • stay in

1 Oh, no! I forgot to **give** _____ *hand in* _____ my homework to the teacher.

2 While our neighbors were out, a man **forced his way in** _____ to their house.

3 My dad doesn't want to teach me to drive. I ask him every day, but he won't **do what I want** _____.

4 Some people don't like her because she doesn't **seem to be part of the group** _____, but I think she's great.

5 When did you **start living** _____ here?

6 It's cold outside. Let's **not go out** _____.

Unit 9

Lesson 9A, Grammar

1 Complete the conversations with causative *have*.

1 A: My brother can't see the blackboard very well.
  B: He should ____ *have his eyes tested* ____.
  (test/his eyes)

2 A: Are you going to the bike shop?
  B: Yes, I need to _____.
  (service/my bike)

3 A: Is your computer OK now?
  B: No, I'm going to _____.
  (check/it)

4 A: What's wrong with the zipper on your jacket?
  B: It's broken. I'm going to _____.
  (replace/it).

5 A: Sarah's back from the hairdresser's.
  B: Oh. Has she _____?
  (cut/her hair)

6 A: Look at that stain on the carpet.
  B: We'd better _____.
  (clean/it)

2 Circle the correct answers.

A: ¹ _____ help you?
  (a) Can I b) Do I c) Will I

B: Yes. It's my cell phone.

A: What ² _____ the problem?
  a) does seem b) seems to be c) does it seem

B: It doesn't work. ³ _____ check it?
  a) Do you b) Why not c) Do you think you could

A: I ⁴ _____ I can do.
  a) 'll see what b) see c) will try

B: And there's also a problem with the volume.

A: All right. I ⁵ _____ at it.
  a) take a look b) 'll take a look c) look

Lesson 9B, Grammar

Write sentences with *so that*, *to*, and *in order to*.

> **How can you improve your English?**
>
> 1 Read magazines or newspapers. Your grammar and vocabulary will improve. (to)
>
> 2 Talk to English-speaking people. You want to use your English. (so that)
>
> 3 Sing along to songs in English. You will improve your pronunciation. (in order to)
>
> 4 Keep a vocabulary notebook. You won't forget vocabulary. (so that)
>
> 5 Find an English-speaking pen pal. You can practice your writing. (to)

1 *Read magazines or newspapers to improve your grammar and vocabulary.*

2 _____

3 _____

4 _____

5 _____

Lesson 9C, Vocabulary: Adjectives of texture and shape

Complete the crossword with adjectives of texture (T) and shape (S).

Down

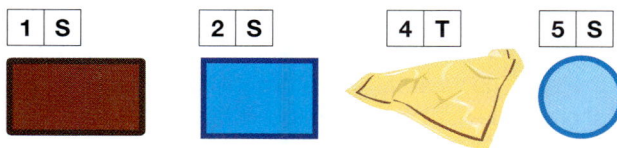

| 1 S | 2 S | 4 T | 5 S |

Across

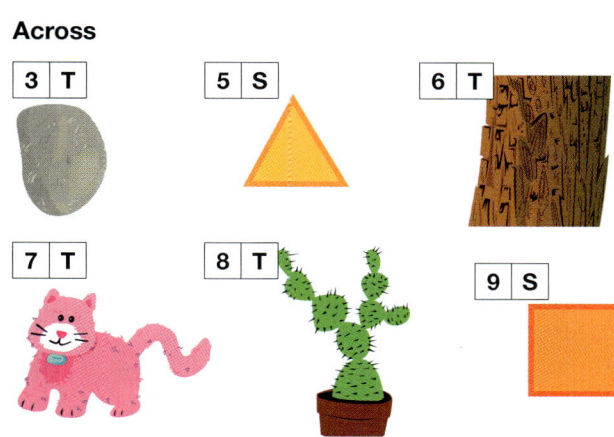

| 3 T | 5 S | 6 T |
| 7 T | 8 T | 9 S |

Grammar

Complete the conversations with *look*, *sound*, *feel*, *seem*, *taste*, or *smell*, and *like* or *as if* where necessary. Use each verb once only.

1 A: This is a photo of the beach next to our hotel.
   B: Wow! It _____*looks*_____ amazing.
2 A: I don't like the Sunrise FM breakfast show.
   B: Neither do I. The DJ _____ he's asleep.
3 A: Try this. It's chili-flavored chocolate.
   B: It _____ really strange.
4 A: What's in the oven?
   B: I can't see, but it _____ pizza.
5 A: Have you got a headache?
   B: Yes. My head _____ someone is hitting it with a stick.
6 A: Do they know each other?
   B: Well, they certainly _____ friends.

Unit 10

Lesson 10A, Grammar

Change the underlined sentences into statements with *should have* or *shouldn't have*.

1 We're going to miss our flight. <u>Why didn't we catch an earlier train?</u>
   We should have caught an earlier train.

2 It's cheaper for students. <u>We were silly not to take our ID cards.</u>

_____

3 <u>I don't understand why you were so rude to your brother.</u> It wasn't his fault.

_____

4 <u>Why didn't I buy that?</u> It was a good price!

_____

5 <u>I can't believe you didn't bring a sweater.</u> You're going to be really cold.

_____

6 He should apologize. <u>He ate all the cake.</u>

_____

7 <u>It's a shame you didn't write his phone number more clearly.</u> I can't read it.

_____

Use your English

You were on your way to return a friend's magazine when something happened. Look at the picture and complete the conversation below. Use these verbs to help you: *cross, buy, fall out of, run over.*

Friend: [1] _____ *Look at* _____ my magazine! Why are there tire marks on it?

You: I'm [2] _____!
I [3] _____ the road when the magazine [4] _____ my bag. Then a car [5] _____ it.

Friend: That's [6] _____! It wasn't [7] _____.

You: I'll [8] _____ a new one if you like.

Friend: No, that's all right. [9] _____ you're OK!

Lesson 10B, Vocabulary: Phrasal verbs with *away*

Complete the story with phrasal verbs from the box.

> • ~~get away~~ • go away • look away • pass away
> • put away • run away • throw away

Claire was alone in her grandparents' house with the cat. The weather was stormy and the cat was scared. Claire picked it up, but it [1] _____ *got away* _____ from her and [2] _____. She followed it into the big, dark library.

"That's strange," she thought. "I'm sure those books and newspapers weren't on the floor earlier." She [3] _____ the books _____ on the shelf and then [4] _____ the newspapers _____ in the wastepaper basket.

Suddenly the door closed with a bang. She heard a noise in the hall.

"Who's there?" she shouted. "Whoever you are, please [5] _____."

The door started to open. Claire was so scared that she couldn't watch; she [6] _____.

"I don't believe in ghosts," she said to herself. "When people [7] _____, they don't become ghosts." At that moment, she felt something brush against her leg. It was the cat!

Grammar

In your notebook, write sentences for each picture. Use *must be, might be, can't be,* and the cues.

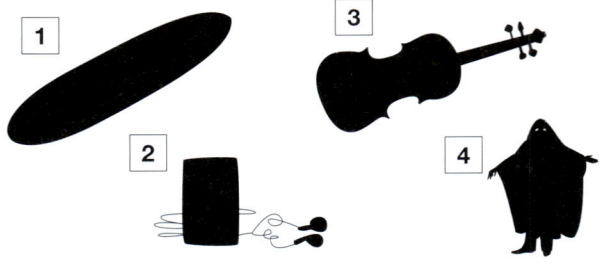

> ✓ = almost sure it is   ✗ = almost sure it isn't
> ? = possibly it is

1 a) (? surfboard/snowboard)   b) (✗ skateboard)
   It might be a surfboard or a snowboard. It can't be a skateboard.

2 a) (✗ a cell phone)   b) (✓ MP3 player)

3 a) (✗ guitar)   b) (? cello/violin)

4 a) (✗ ghost)   b) (✓ person)

Lesson 10C, Grammar

1 Write sentences with *must have, can't have,* or *might have* and the verb in parentheses.

1 Luz is over an hour late. There's no other explanation. She _must have missed_ (miss) her train.
2 You paid $200 for this phone? It _____ (cost) that much! They _____ (put) the wrong price on it.
3 No one is answering the door, and the lights are out. They _____ (go) out.
4 I'm not sure where Nadia is. She _____ (go) shopping, or she _____ (take) the dog for a walk.
5 He _____ (be) crazy to enter the marathon. He wasn't in shape at all!
6 Maria is ten minutes late. I don't know, but I think she _____ (forget) about our date.
7 Harry _____ (watch) that football game. He was at a movie all evening!
8 He lost the game very quickly. He _____ (practice) very much.

2 Read about David Blaine. In your notebook, answer the questions using *must have, can't have, might have,* and the cues.

> ✓ = almost sure it's true ? = possible but not sure
> ✗ = almost sure it's not true

In New York in 2006 David Blaine survived in a water bubble for seven days with the help of breathing apparatus. After a week, his aim was to remove the breathing tube and hold his breath to break the world record of nine minutes. He failed the very last part and was rescued after seven minutes.

1 How long did he train? (✓ train/months)
  He must have trained for months.
2 What did he eat? (✗ eat any food)
3 Why did they rescue him? (? drown)
4 How did he look when he came out of the bubble? (✗ look very healthy)
5 How did people react? (some/? be disappointed)
6 What did he do after he came out? (✓ go home/for a long rest)

Unit 11
Lesson 11A, Grammar

In your notebook, rewrite the news broadcast using the passive. Use the underlined words and phrases as the subject of each sentence.

Good evening. Here is the news. [1] *Reports of a fire in an office building have just been received.*

Good evening. Here is the news. [1] We have just received reports of a fire in an office building. The fire started last night. [2] It trapped some office workers inside the building. [3] Someone called the fire department and soon [4] the firefighters carried the people to safety. What caused the fire? [5] Someone had left an electric heater on near a pile of papers. [6] People cause accidents when they don't think, according to the fire department. [7] Luckily, this time, the fire hurt no one.

Vocabulary: The media

Find nine media words in the wordsearch.

C	H	T	S	E	O	B	E	H	W
H	M	A	G	A	Z	I	N	E	T
A	E	B	D	L	I	N	C	A	P
N	N	L	A	B	N	D	H	D	O
N	A	O	A	L	I	X	A	L	D
E	D	I	T	O	R	E	N	I	C
L	M	D	L	G	T	Z	I	N	A
N	I	B	H	U	B	R	E	E	S
N	E	W	S	P	A	P	E	R	T
T	R	E	P	O	R	T	N	O	N

Lesson 11B, Grammar

In your notebook, rewrite the paragraph using the passive.

A few weeks ago I read in the paper that ¹ teenage boys and girls were being auditioned for . . .

A few weeks ago I read in the paper that ¹ *they were auditioning teenage boys and girls* for the next *High School Musical* movie. When I got to the audition, which ² *they were holding* in Memphis, there were over 500 people there. The director said: "Today ³ *we will give all of you* a chance to sing and dance. Then ⁴ *we will choose six boys and six girls* to come for a final audition in Los Angeles." I was one of those lucky six boys. I thought: "I'm sure ⁵ *they won't choose me* for the main part," but I got the part. And guess what—next week ⁶ *they're interviewing me* for our local newspaper.

Use your English

Number the sentences in the correct order.

☐ a) **Sue:** Two hours! That's awful!

☐ b) **Tim:** Because it means we won't get so much homework on the weekend.

☐ c) **Jake:** I know. It's really unfair.

☑ d) **Jake:** Guess what! Next semester, we're going to get two hours of homework every day.

☐ e) **Tim:** Unfair? No way! I think it's good.

☐ f) **Jake:** OK. You have a point.

☐ g) **Sue:** Good? Why?

Lesson 11C, Grammar

Complete each question with the appropriate active and passive form of the verbs.

1 Do you prefer *telling people what to do* or *being told what to do* ? (tell people what to do)

2 Is it better *to love your friends* or *to be loved by your friends* ? (love your friends)

3 Do you prefer _____ or _____? (give presents)

4 Which do you prefer, _____ or _____? (film with a video camera)

5 Is it worse _____ or _____? (shout at a friend)

6 Which one is more unusual for you, _____ or _____? (smile at a stranger)

Vocabulary: Adjective and noun formation

Complete the website comments with the noun form of the adjectives in parentheses.

http://www.careeradvice.gov

File   Edit   View   History   Bookmarks   Tools   Help

What qualities do you need to be successful in different jobs?

Successful business people need ¹ _courage_ (courageous) and ² _____ (lucky).

If you have a lot of ³ _____ (angry) or ⁴ _____ (proud), you won't be a good politician.

Good athletes need speed and ⁵ _____ (strong).

It's important for actors and actresses to have ⁶ _____ (confident) in their ability.

In every job you need the ⁷ _____ (wise) to distinguish the ⁸ _____ from lies.

Good police officers and firefighters have to show ⁹ _____ (brave).

Models need to be beautiful, but remember, ¹⁰ _____ (beautiful) is only skin deep.

Unit 12

Lesson 12A, Grammar

Match cues in A and B to form *if* clause and past perfect sentences. Write the sentences in your notebook.

1 - c) If I had known the movie was so bad, I wouldn't have bought the DVD.

A
1 If I/know/the movie was so bad
2 If I/invite/her to the party without her boyfriend
3 If you/tell/him how much it cost
4 If he/not learn/Spanish
5 If I/go out/last night
6 If/her camera/not be broken

B
a) he/have/a difficult time in Mexico.
b) he/not believe/you.
c) I/not buy/the DVD.
d) she/take/a photo of them.
e) she/not come.
f) I/miss/*Dancing with the Stars* on TV.

Vocabulary: Verbs connected with money

Circle the correct verbs to complete the newspaper article.

Kind-hearted neighbor

A family has [1](inherited)/invested/won $40,000 from their 80-year-old neighbor, Mrs. Trellis, who passed away last week. The family had thought that Mrs. Trellis was poor as she had no relatives and sometimes had to [2] save/earn/borrow money from them. It seems, however, that Mrs. Trellis had [3] spent/afforded/owed all the money she had [4] invested/lent/saved during her life on building up a valuable stamp collection. The family inherited it and sold it for $40,000. They have decided to [5] pay back/donate/splurge some of the money to charity and to use the rest to [6] repay/owe/afford the money that they had [7] made/borrowed/lent from the bank last year to build a new garage for their house.

Lesson 12B, Grammar

In your notebook, write sentences with *wish* or *if only* and the past perfect using the cues in parentheses.

1 I didn't have my umbrella and it rained. (take)
   I wish/If only I'd taken my umbrella.

2 I went to the party, but I didn't enjoy it. (not/go)

3 When I was on vacation, I put on 10 pounds! (not/eat/so many chips)

4 My best friend moved to Costa Rica and I miss her. (my friend/stay in the U.S.)

5 It's a pity that only 50 people came to our concert. (more people/come)

6 My brother borrowed my cell phone and dropped it. (he/be/more careful with)

Vocabulary: Phrasal verbs with *out*

Replace the phrases in parentheses with the correct form of the phrasal verbs from the box.

- figure out • find out • point out • ~~sell out~~
- throw out • turn out

Sticky tickets!

I went into town to buy tickets for a rock concert, but when I got there, the tickets had [1] _____sold out_____ (all been sold). I called my friend Nina, and she [2] _____ (gave me the information) that people sometimes had extra tickets that they sold on the Internet. Luckily, it [3] _____ (happened) that there were a few tickets for sale. They were kind of expensive, but I [4] _____ (calculated) that I had just enough money. The tickets arrived a few days later. That day I went to school happy. But when I got home, I [5] _____ (discovered) that Mom had [6] _____ (put in the garbage can) the tickets! The tickets were a little dirty and sticky when I got them out of the can, but it was worth it—the concert was great!

Lesson 12C, Grammar

Match cues in A and B to form *if* clause and *might have* sentences. Write the sentences in your notebook.

1 – b) I might have passed if I'd answered all the questions.

A
1 I (pass)
2 She (sing) in the concert
3 I (do) some work
4 She (not come)
5 You (not burn) the cake

B
a) you (not give) her a ride.
b) I (answer) all the questions.
c) you (check) the oven.
d) she (not catch) a cold.
e) I (take) my laptop with me.

Word bank

Unit 1

1A Clothes, styles, accessories, and patterns

Clothes
- boots • coat • dress • fleece • flip flops
- hat • high heels • hoodie • jacket • jeans
- pants • shirt • shoes • shorts • skirt
- sneakers • socks • suit • sweater • T-shirt
- tie • tights

Styles
- baggy • casual • dressy • sleeveless • tight

Accessories, etc.
- belt • gloves • pocket • scarf • zipper

Patterns
- checkered • flowery • patterned • plain
- polka-dotted • striped

1B Jobs
- actor • administrative assistant • artist
- beautician • builder • carpenter • cashier
- chef • dentist • detective • director • doctor
- electrician • engineer • farmer • firefighter
- hairdresser • homemaker • journalist • manager
- mechanic • model • musician • nurse
- pilot • plumber • police officer • politician
- receptionist • reporter • store assistant
- ski instructor • taxi driver • teacher
- TV presenter • vet • waiter/waitress

Unit 2

2C Transportation
- bike • boat • bus • car • ferry • helicopter
- moped • motorcycle • plane • ship • subway
- taxi • trailer • train • tram • truck • van

Unit 3

3A Food and drink

Fruit
- apple • banana • grape • lemon • melon
- orange • peach • pear • strawberry

Vegetables
- bean • carrot • cucumber • lettuce • mushroom
- onion • pea • pepper • potato • tomato

Meat
- beef • chicken • lamb • steak

Fish
- salmon • shrimp

Dairy
- butter • cheese • cream • egg • milk • yogurt

Drinks
- apple juice • coffee • cola • decaffeinated coffee
- fruit juice • hot chocolate • lemonade
- mineral water • orange juice • tea

Snacks/Fast food
- baked potato • burger • cake • chips • cookies
- French fries • hamburger • hot dog • pizza
- sandwich • soup

Restaurant food
- apple pie • cheesecake • dessert • fruit salad
- garlic bread • green salad • ice cream
- lasagna • mashed potatoes • ravioli • salad
- spaghetti Bolognese

Other
- bread • honey • nut • olive • olive oil • pasta
- rice • salt • sugar • vinegar

Unit 4

4B Musical instruments
- cello • clarinet • drums • flute
- guitar (acoustic, electric, bass) • keyboard
- piano • saxophone • trumpet • violin

Unit 5

5A Landforms and the environment
- bush • cliff • coast • coastline • desert
- forest • harbor • hill • island • lake • mountain
- ocean • path • river • rock • sea • stream
- tree • valley • waterfall • wood(s)

Unit 7

7C Relationship phrases

- ask someone out
- break up with someone
- fall in love with someone
- get along well with someone
- get divorced from someone
- get engaged/married to someone
- go out with someone
- have an argument with someone
- make up with someone

Unit 10

10C Crime

Verbs + nouns	Crimes	Criminals
break into [a building]	breaking in	
burgle [a house]	burglary	burglar
catch/arrest a criminal		
commit a crime		
go to prison		prisoner
mug [a person]	mugging	mugger
pay a fine		
pick someone's pocket		pickpocket
rob [a bank/person]	robbery	robber
shoplift	shoplifting	shoplifter
steal [some money]	theft	thief
vandalize property	vandalism	vandal
write/draw graffiti		

Lesson 10C Exercise 7 Answer to puzzle:
He took off his clothes, put them in the plastic bag, and tied it
very tightly with the string. Then he tied the bag to his head.
He swam across the river. On the other side, he opened the
bag and got dressed again.

Pronunciation

Unit 1A Exercise 9

a [1 05] Listen and repeat.

A: You're American, aren't you?   B: Yes, I am.
(The falling intonation means that you are sure of the answer.)

A: You aren't American, are you?   B: No, I'm not.
(The rising intonation means that you are not sure of the answer.)

b [1 06] Listen and say if the speaker is sure or not sure of the answer.

1 You're over 16, aren't you?
2 Your mother isn't Italian, is she?
3 He goes to the same school as you, doesn't he?
4 She has a nice jacket, doesn't she?
5 They don't like skateboarding, do they?

c Now listen and repeat the sentences.

Unit 2A Exercise 7

a [1 15] Listen and repeat.

1 Where were you born?   4 How long did you stay?
2 When did you start?   5 Why did you stop?
3 What happened?

b [1 16] Use the cues to ask questions in the past tense. Then listen and check.

1 Where/you/go to school?
2 What time/it/start?
3 When/you/do your homework?
4 Who/he/have lunch with?
5 Why/they/leave so early?

Unit 3A Exercise 3

a [1 24] Listen and repeat. Copy the intonation.

1 We have apples, oranges, and pears.
2 There's a kettle, a saucepan, and a frying pan.
3 Sorry, no fast food, electricity, or running water.
4 I'm going to buy a CD, a book, and a DVD.

b [1 25] Answer the questions with the correct intonation.

1 What did you eat for breakfast today?
2 What are your three favorite sports?
3 Who are your three favorite movie stars?

Unit 4A Exercise 7

a [1 35] Listen and repeat.

1 Wow! That's amazing!   4 That's horrible!
2 Oh, no! That's too bad.   5 Good job!
3 How great!

b [1 36] Use the cues and react to the news. Then listen and check.

1 I have a new TV in my bedroom. (awesome)
2 My brother found a great new job. (Wow!/fantastic)
3 The weather was really bad. (Oh, no./terrible)
4 I'm sorry, I can't come to the party. (too bad)

Unit 5C Exercise 8

a [2 09] Listen and repeat.

1 a dollar, please . . . Lend me a dollar, please . . . Could you lend me a dollar, please?
2 call me . . . Ask him to call me . . . Can you ask him to call me?
3 your bike . . . could I borrow your bike . . . Do you think I could borrow your bike?
4 your jacket . . . moving your jacket . . . Would you mind moving your jacket?

b [2 10] Read aloud. Then listen and check if your intonation is the same as the speaker's.

1 Do you think I could use your phone?
2 Do you think you could help me with this job?
3 Could I borrow your dictionary, please?
4 Would you mind turning the music down a little?

Unit 6C Exercise 8

a [2 20] Listen and repeat. Underline the stressed syllable in each word.

1 solution   5 disappointment
2 decision   6 arrangement
3 explanation   7 difficulty
4 development

b [2 21] Read aloud with the correct word stress in the underlined words. Then listen and check.

1 Please write your corrections on your homework.
2 The discovery of America was an important event.
3 This puzzle tests your mathematical ability.
4 Video games are great entertainment.
5 Playing tennis involves very good coordination.

Unit 7A Exercise 7

a 🎧 2/26 Listen and repeat. Underline the stressed syllables.

1 He asked me what I was doing.
2 She told him where she'd been.
3 I said that we'd leave soon.

b 🎧 2/27 Read these sentences and underline the stressed syllables. Then listen and check.

1 She said that she'd seen it before.
2 I told him that we were going to play football.
3 David said that he couldn't help me.

Unit 8B Exercise 5

a 🎧 2/37 Listen and underline words with extra stress.

1 I'm used to looking right, not left.
2 I used to live in Ecuador, not Peru.
3 Kate is coming on Tuesday.
4 Kate is coming on Tuesday.

b 🎧 2/38 Listen to the questions and say the answers below with the extra stress on the correct word. Then listen and check.

1 No, look under the table.
2 No, look under the table.
3 No, I gave the book to him.
4 No, I gave the book to him.
5 No, I usually visit her on Sunday.
6 No, I usually visit my grandmother.

Unit 9A Exercise 8

a 🎧 3/05 Listen and underline the words that are stressed. Then listen and repeat.

1 I'll have it tested tomorrow.
2 I'm having it fixed on Friday.
3 He had it serviced last week.

b 🎧 3/06 Practice saying the sentences. Replace the words in bold with the words in parentheses. Then listen and check.

1 I'll have it **tested** tomorrow. (checked/serviced)
2 I'm having it fixed on **Friday**. (Monday/Wednesday)
3 He had it **serviced** last week. (removed/changed)

Unit 10B Exercise 7

a 🎧 3/20 Listen and repeat.

1 That can't be a monster.
2 She wants a hot dog and a cold drink.
3 It's a great photo.
4 I don't know why.
5 She told Pete.

b 🎧 3/21 Underline the sounds that will disappear in these sentences. Then listen, check, and repeat.

1 I can't believe it.
2 Emma bought a big pizza!
3 She could be the girl we saw last week.

Unit 11A Exercise 8

🎧 3/28 Listen to the compound nouns and repeat. Stress the underlined syllables.

1 cell phone
2 news story
3 gossip magazines
4 car accident
5 television show
6 train station
7 parking lot
8 shopping center

Unit 12C Exercise 6

a 🎧 3/41 Listen and repeat.
might have
would have
should have
may have
must have
can't have

b 🎧 3/42 Underline the weak forms in these sentences. Then listen and repeat.

1 I wouldn't have recognized him.
2 He might have been sick.
3 She must have liked the movie.
4 You might have hurt yourself.

Lifestyles

Complete the example sentences and the grammar rules that follow.

Lesson 1A, page 4

Simple present	Present continuous
I **like** these clothes.	I**'m working** at the market today.
He **studies** every night.	He _____ **studying** for a test right now.
We **play soccer** every weekend.	We **are playing** soccer on Saturday.

- Use the _____ for permanent situations, daily routines, scheduled events in the future, and stative verbs (such as *be*, *like*, *need*, etc).
- Use the _____ for things that are happening now and for future plans.

Tag questions

Questions	Expected answers
I **look** nice today, **don't** I?	Yes, you **do**.
You _____ from Peru, **aren't** you?	Yes, I **am**.
He **doesn't know** Sophie, **does** he?	No, he **doesn't**.
She **has** a blue bag, **doesn't** she?	Yes, she _____.
That**'s** a cool shirt, _____ it?	Yes, it **is**.
We **haven't met** before, **have** we?	No, we **haven't**.
They **went** shopping, **didn't** they?	Yes, they **did**.

- A tag question is a question that is added at the end of a sentence when the speaker expects a certain answer.
- Use auxiliary verbs in tag questions:
  *He **doesn't** know Sophie, **does** he?*
- If the main verb is positive, the question tag is _____.
- If the main verb is negative, the question tag is _____.

Lesson 1B, page 7

Present perfect with *for* or *since*; simple past

Present perfect	Simple past
Lisa **has worked** as a pilot **for** 10 years. **Since** 2009, she**'s flown** 300 times.	Lisa **learned** to fly at the age of 25. She **flew** for the first time in 1996.

- Use the _____ to talk about past activities that happened at an unspecified time or more than once, or activities that aren't finished yet.
- Use the _____ for past activities that are finished or happened at a specific time in the past, such as *last Saturday*.
- Use *for* to talk about a period of time. Use _____ to talk about a point in time.

Lesson 1C, page 9

Intensifiers *much*, *a lot*, *a little* with comparative adjectives and adverbs; *(not) as . . . as*

Comparative adjectives

It's **much/a lot cheaper** to eat at home **than** to eat in a restaurant.
This pear tastes **a little better** _____ that pear.

Comparative adverbs

You can get a job in a store **a little more easily than** in an office.
His job is **much/_____ harder than** her job.

(Not) as . . . as

This job is **(not) as easy as** people think.
A college degree doesn't cost **as much** _____ you think.

- Use comparative adjectives and adverbs to compare things to each other.
- To make a comparison stronger, add intensifiers like _____, _____, and *a little* before a comparative adjective or adverb.
- Use _____ when comparing two things that may be the same:
  *Coffee costs **as much as** tea.*

2 Life stories

Complete the example sentences and the grammar rules that follow.

Lesson 2A, page 13

Simple past

Regular verbs	Irregular verbs
I **walked** home.	I **hurt** my head.
I **didn't walk** to school.	I **didn't hurt** my hand.
Did you _____ home?	**Did** you **hurt** your head?
Yes, I **did**. / No, I _____.	Yes, I _____. / No, I **didn't**.
When _____ you **walk** home?	When **did** you _____ your head?
Yesterday.	(I **hurt** it) yesterday.

- To form the simple past of most regular verbs, add _____ to the base form of the verb: *walked*
- Some verbs have irregular past forms. Go to www.pearsonlongman.com/insync/grammarreference for a list of irregular verbs and their past forms.

Lesson 2B, page 15

Past continuous and simple past with *while* and *when*

Past continuous + simple past with *while* and *when*

While he **was filming** the movie, he **hurt** his back.

He **hurt** his back **while** he **was filming** the movie.

He _____ **filming** the movie **when** he **hurt** his back.

Simple past + simple past with *when*

What **did** you do **when** you **got** home?

I **called** my sister _____ I **got** home.

- Use the past continuous with the simple past to talk about an action that happened at the same time as another action. Use the past continuous for the longer action that was "in progress" at a time in the past. Use _____ for the shorter, finished action.
- *While* means *during that time*. We usually use *while* with the _____ tense.
- *When* means *at that time*. We usually use *when* with the _____ tense.

Lesson 2C, page 17

Simple past and past perfect

The police officers **went** to the house. They **caught** a robber. He **had broken** into the house, and he _____ **stolen** a TV and a CD player. They **took** him to jail.

- Use the simple past and the past perfect to talk about two or more events that happened at different times in the past. Use the _____ for the event that happened first.

after/before + gerund (*-ing* form)

After calling the fire department, she waited for the firefighters outside the house.

Before calling the fire department, she tried to put out the fire.

- Use _____ + gerund for an event that happened before another event:
  After calling the fire department, she waited for the firefighters outside the house. (= She called the fire department. Then she waited for the firefighters.)
- Use _____ + gerund for an event that happened after another event:
  Before calling the fire department, she tried to put out the fire. (= She tried to put out the fire. Then she called the fire department.)

Complete the example sentences and the grammar rules that follow.

Lesson 3A, page 23

Future tenses: *will*, *be going to*, present continuous

will

It **will be** an exciting show.
There **won't be** any electricity.
We**'ll pick** you **up** next week.

be going to

I**'m going to e-mail** them tomorrow.
It**'s going to be** a lot of fun.

Present continuous

We**'re watching** the show tonight.

- Use _____ for predictions, future facts, and promises.
- Use _____ for plans and predictions.
- Use the present continuous for scheduled arrangements in the _____.
- Complete the examples with the correct form of *play*:
  People _____ soccer in the future.
  I _____ soccer at 3 P.M. this afternoon.
  We _____ soccer in college next year.

to be about to + infinitive

The show **is about to start**. Come sit down.

- Use the verb *to be* + _____
  _____ + infinitive for something that will happen very soon.

Lesson 3B, page 25

must, need to, should, ought to, had better, (not) have to

You **must** listen to your boss.
You **must not** lie in a job interview.
We **need to** get up early tomorrow.
You **have to** be polite to the customers.
You**'d better** be careful.
He **should**/**ought to** take English classes.
He **shouldn't** stay up late.
You **don't have to**/**don't need to** have any cooking skills for this job.

- Use *must (not)*, *need to*, and _____ for rules or obligations (things that it is very important for someone to do).
- Use *should/ought to*, *shouldn't*, and *had better* to give advice or to talk about what is right or wrong to do. *Had better* is stronger than *should/ought to*.
- Use _____/_____ to talk about things that are not necessary to do.
- Complete this example:
  You _____ go to school on Mondays, but you _____ go to school on Sundays.

Lesson 3C, page 26

make, let, allowed to

He **made her do** her homework.
Please **let me go** to the movies.
I**'m not** _____ _____ **use** my dad's computer.

- Use *make* to talk about obligation. Use *let* and *allowed to* to talk about permission.
- *Make* and _____ are followed by an object pronoun and the base form of a verb (without *to*).
  *He made **her do** her homework.*
- *Allowed to* does not have to be followed by an _____ _____:
  I'm allowed to stay out late.

Complete the example sentences and the grammar rules that follow.

Lesson 4A, page 31

Present perfect with *already*, *before*, *never*, *ever*, *yet*

I**'ve already played** that game.
I **haven't played** that game **yet**.
Have you **ever played** that game?
I**'ve never played** that game.
I**'ve played** that game **before**.

- You can use time adverbs like *already, before, never, ever,* and *yet* with the _____ tense.
- *Already, never,* and _____ come before the past participle in a present perfect sentence.
- *Before* and *yet* come at the _____ of a sentence.
- Use *ever* for questions. Use *never* and *yet* for _____ sentences.

Superlatives with the present perfect

This is **the best** vacation I**'ve ever had**!

- A superlative comes _____ the main verb in a present perfect sentence.

Lesson 4B, page 33

Present perfect and present perfect continuous with *for* and *since*

Present perfect

I **haven't played** soccer **for** five years.
He**'s been** a musician **since** 2005.

Present perfect continuous

I**'ve been playing** soccer **for** five years.
He**'_____ been singing** in a band **since** 2005.

- Use either the _____ or the _____ for past activities that aren't finished yet.
- You can use either the present perfect or the present perfect continuous with *work* and *live*:

He**'s worked** as a teacher **since** he graduated from college. OR He**'s been working** as a teacher **since** he graduated from college.

- Use the _____ with stative verbs like *be, have, see,* and *like*.

Present perfect with numbers and amounts

She **has been** to New York five times.
We _____ **recorded** six albums.

- Use the _____ to talk about how much or how many things you have done.

Lesson 4C, page 35

Relative clauses

Restrictive relative clauses

People **who/that** want to be famous go on reality shows.
Any musician **whose** songs are good can perform on the show.
People like TV shows **that** are exciting.
This is the place **where** they film that reality show.
People vote for the singer (**who**/_____) they like the best.
A TV show (**that**) everyone is talking about is *Star!*

Nonrestrictive relative clauses

Alice May, **who** is 16, performs on the show.
Alonzo Perez, _____ voice is good, is 25.
Reality shows, **which** are cheap to make, are very popular.

- Use _____ relative clauses to give necessary information about a subject. Use _____ relative clauses to give information that is not necessary.
- _____ relative clauses can use *that*. _____ relative clauses can use *which*.
- Only _____ relative clauses have commas around them.
- You can leave out the relative pronoun (*who, that* etc.) in restrictive relative clauses when it is the object of the clause:
a show that everyone likes OR *a show everyone likes*

Natural world

Complete the example sentences and the grammar rules that follow.

Lesson 5A, page 41

Conditionals with *if*, *unless*, *provided that*, *as long as*

If they **build** the mall, our town **will get** too crowded.
Unless they **build** the mall, our town **won't get** too crowded.
Provided that they **build** the mall somewhere else, there **won't be** a problem.
As long as they _____ the mall somewhere else, the town **won't suffer**.

- _____ has a similar meaning to *if + not*.
- *Provided that* and _____ have a similar meaning to *if*.
- In conditional sentences, the main verb in the *if* clause is in the _____ tense.
- Complete the examples with *if*, *unless*, *provided that*, or *as long as*:
  _____ the mall has good stores, I will shop there.
  _____ the mall has good stores, I won't shop there.

Lesson 5B, page 42

Future time clauses with *when*, *until*, *as soon as*, *by the time*, *before*

When the storm **starts**, we'll leave the area.
He won't be able to leave **until** he **has** some money.
She's going to leave the area **as soon as** she **can**.
By the time the tornado **hits**, it will be too late.
We'll buy some food **before** we **leave**.

- In future time clauses, the verb in the time clause is in the _____ tense. The verb in the main clause is in the _____ tense.

- Complete the example with the correct form of *stop*:
  When the rain _____ , *we'll go home.*
- *When* means *at a certain time*. *Until* means *up to a certain time*.
- *As soon as* expresses that idea that something will happen immediately after something else happens.
- *By the time* expresses the idea that an action is completed before another action.
- For example:
  Grandma: *I'm worried about you walking home in the storm. Call me* **as soon as** *you get home! I won't go to bed* **until** *you call me.*
  Maria: *But Grandma,* **by the time** *I get home, it will be midnight! I can't call you then!*

Lesson 5C, page 45

in case + simple present

We're taking shorts **in case** it **gets** hot.
She wants an umbrella **in case** it **rains**.

- Use *in case* + _____ to talk about the need to be ready for something.
- *In case* does not have the same meaning as *if*:
  We're taking shorts **in case** *it* **gets** *hot = we are taking shorts.*
  We're taking shorts **if** *it* **gets** *hot = we may not take shorts (if it is cold).*

6 Imagination

Complete the example sentences and the grammar rules that follow.

Lesson 6A, page 49

Conditional: *if* clause + past

If she **had** a camera, she **could take** pictures.
If they **saw** Taylor Swift, they **might ask** for her autograph.
What **would** you **do** _____ you **were** famous?
I'd fly around the world **if** I **was**/_____ rich.

- Use *if* + simple past conditional sentences to talk about things that are contrary to fact or the opposite of the true situation:
  *If she **had** a camera, she could take pictures (= She doesn't have a camera, so she can't take pictures).*
- For *if* + past conditional sentences, use the _____ tense in the *if* clause. You can use *would, might,* or _____ in the main clause.
- Use a comma when the *if* clause comes at the _____ of the sentence.
- *If I were* is more formal than *if I _____.*

Lesson 6B, page 51

wish/if only + simple past

I **wish** I **had** a better cell phone!
If only we **didn't have** a test tomorrow.

- Use *wish/if only* + _____ to talk about regrets.
- *If only* is a little stronger than _____.
- Complete the example with the correct form of *be*:
  If only I _____ famous.

Lesson 6C, page 53

Verb + infinitive or gerund

Verb + infinitive

We **decided to buy** a new computer.
They **promised not to play** too many video games.

Verb + gerund

My son **enjoys playing** video games.
She **can't stand not watch**_____ TV every day.

Verb + infinitive or gerund

I **hate** _____ **play** video games. OR
I **hate playing** video games.

- Use verb + _____ with the following verbs: *agree, decide, expect, forget, help, hope, manage, offer, promise, refuse, seem, try, want,* and *would like.*
- Use verb + _____ with the following verbs: *admit, avoid, can't stand, deny, enjoy, finish, give up, keep, miss, not mind, practice,* and *stop.*
- Use verb + _____ or _____ with the following verbs: *hate, like, love, prefer,* and *start.*
- For negative sentences, put *not* between the verb and the infinitive or gerund:
  *I promise **not to forget** your book.*
  *I like **not living** in the city.*
- Complete the examples with forms of *play*:
  I avoid _____ soccer because I don't like it.
  I prefer _____ volleyball.
  I would like _____ volleyball tomorrow.

7 Communicate

Complete the example sentences and the grammar rules that follow.

Lesson 7A, page 59

Reported statements and questions

Reported statements

"I **live** near here." ➔
He said that he **lived** near here.
"I'**m buying** clothes **today**." ➔
I told him that I _____ **buying** clothes **that day**.
"She **bought** clothes **yesterday**." ➔
He said that she **had bought** clothes **the previous** _____.

Reported questions

"**Do** you **make** T-shirts?" ➔
He asked me **if/whether** I _____ T-shirts.
"How much **is this** T-shirt?" ➔
I asked him how much **that** T-shirt **was**.

- Use _____ statements and questions to report a speaker's exact words.
- Verb forms, pronouns, and time-related expressions in the speaker's words are usually changed in reported statements and questions: for example, the simple present tense changes to the _____ tense.

Lesson 7B, page 61

Reporting verbs

I **asked** her **to come**.
She **told** him **not to leave**.
He **invited** her **to go** to a movie.

You **promised to get up** early.
He **offered** _____ **give** them a ride.
He **refused to take** the bus.

They **admitted losing** the money.
They **denied spending** the money.
He **suggested hav**_____ a party.
He **apologized for being** late.

I **explained that** I **couldn't** help them.
He **complained** _____ the food **tasted** bad.
He **admitted/denied that** he **had lost** the money.

- *Ask, tell, invite, persuade,* and *order* are followed by an _____ and an infinitive:
  ask **him** to come
- *Promise, offer, refuse,* and *agree* are followed by an _____:
  promise **to buy**
- *Admit, deny, suggest,* and *apologize for* are followed by a verb in the _____ form:
  deny tak**ing**
- *Complain* and *explain* are followed by _____ and a clause:
  explained **that** I lost
- *Admit* and *deny* are sometimes followed by _____ and a clause:
  admitted **that** he had broken

Lesson 7C, page 63

Subordinating conjunctions that show contrast: *although, in spite of/despite, however, on the other hand*

Although I argue with my parents a lot, we love each other.
In spite of being angry at me, they didn't punish me.
Despite our problems, we are a happy family.
However, I get angry when they treat me like a child.
On the other hand, I sometimes act like a child.

- _____, *however,* and *on the other hand* are usually followed by a subject and a verb:
  Although **I argue**
- *In spite of* and _____ must be followed by a noun or a gerund:
  Despite our **problems**
  In spite of **being**

138

Complete the example sentences and the grammar rules that follow.

Lesson 8A, page 67

> **so + adjective/adverb (*that*); such a/an + adjective + noun (*that*); so many/much + noun (*that*); verb + so much (*that*)**
>
> **so + adjective/adverb (*that*)**
>
> It was **so cold (that)** we wore ski jackets.
> I ran **so quickly (that)** I won the race.
>
> **such a/an + adjective + noun (*that*)**
>
> This is **such a funny story (that)** you'll laugh when you hear it.
> The birds were _____ **pretty colors (that)** we took pictures of them.
>
> **so many/much + noun (*that*)**
>
> There are **so many fish (_____)** it's fun to snorkel around here.
> She drank **so much seawater (that)** she felt sick.
>
> **Verb + so much (*that*)**
>
> It **hurt** _____ **much (that)** I cried.

- *So* and _____ mean *very* when used before an adjective or adverb.
- The adjective or adverb comes _____ *so* or *such*.
- Use *such a/an* and *so many/much* with _____:
  such a funny **story** that
  so many **fish** that
- Use *so much (that)* after a _____:
  It **rained** so much that
- Complete the example with *so* or *such*:
  I was _____ *hungry that I ate a whole pizza.*

Lesson 8B, page 69

> **used to/be used to/get used to**
>
> **used to**
>
> I **used to take** the bus to work.
> He **didn't use** _____ **eat** meat.
> **Did** they _____ **to live** in London?
>
> **be used to**
>
> I**'m not used to wearing** a school uniform.
> They**'**_____ **used to eating** American food.
>
> **get used to**
>
> She**'s getting used to taking** the subway.
> **Are** you _____ _____ **to driving** on the right side of the road?

- Use _____ to talk about past habits that you don't do anymore.
- Use _____ to talk about present habits.
- Use _____ to talk about changes in your life or new experiences that you are learning about.
- Use the gerund after *be used to* and _____.

Lesson 8C, page 71

> **be able to**
>
> **Will** you **be able to** come over tonight?
> She**'ll be** _____ _____ ride a bike soon.
> We **weren't able to** find the house.
> You**'ve always** _____ **able to** talk in front of lots of people.

- Use *be able to* to talk about ability.
- For sentences with *be able to*, use a form of _____ + *able* _____ + an infinitive:
  Will you be able to
  Were you able to
  Have you **been** able to
  Are you able to

Complete the example sentences and the grammar rules that follow.

Lesson 9A, page 77

Causative *have*

I **have** my car **serviced** every year.
Has she **had** her TV **repaired**?
We should **have** our car **cleaned**.

- Use _____ to talk about something that someone else does for you.
- For sentences with causative *have*, use a form of _____ + the past participle of a verb.
- Put a noun or pronoun between *have* + the past participle:
  *have **it** repaired*

Lesson 9B, page 79

Clauses of purpose: *to, in order (not) to, so that*

To make more money, she found a new job.
She found a new job **in order to** make more money.
We studied hard **in order not to** fail the test.
We studied hard **so that** we wouldn't fail the test.

- *In order to,* _____, and *to* are followed by the infinitive:
  *in order **to make***
- _____ is followed by a clause with a subject and a verb:
  *so that **we wouldn't fail***

Lesson 9C, page 81

look, seem, sound, feel, taste, smell + adjective /*like*/*as if*

look, seem, sound, etc. + adjective
These shoes **look great**.
They **feel soft** and **comfortable**.

look, seem, sound, etc. + *like*
This toy **sounds like** a real cow.
This yogurt **smells** ____ strawberries, and it **tastes like** candy.

look, seem, sound, etc. + *as if*
It **seems as if** it might break easily.

- Use *sound/taste/feel,* etc. + _____ before a noun:
  *sounds **like** a cow*
- Use *sound/taste/feel,* etc. + _____ before a clause:
  *seems **as if** it might break*
- Complete the examples:
  She looks _____ a doll.
  She looks _____ she is going to fall asleep soon.
- Note: you can use *like* before a clause, but you can't use *as if* before a noun:
  CORRECT: *Paul looks **like he is tired**.*
  NOT CORRECT: *Paul looks **as if a cowboy**.*

10 Right or not?

Complete the example sentences and the grammar rules that follow.

Lesson 10A, page 85

should have/ought to have

You **should have brought** an umbrella.
I **ought to have worn** a jacket.
He **shouldn't have forgotten** his wallet.

- To make a recommendation in the past, use _____ or *ought to have*.
- To form sentences with *should have/ought to have*, use *should have/ought to have* + the _____ of a verb.
- In American English, we do not say _____ *not to have*.

Lesson 10B, page 87

must/can't/might/could for deductions in the present

I don't believe that story. It **must be** a hoax.
The monster **can't be** real. It's too big!
Sea monsters **might** really **exist**. They **could live** deep in the ocean. We don't know what's down there!

- Use *must, can't, might*, and *could* to make deductions or judgments in the _____.
- Use _____ to talk about things you are almost sure are true.
- Use _____ to talk about things you are almost sure are not true.
- Use _____ or _____ to talk about things you think are possible.
- Complete the example:
  They're moving to Alaska. They _____ like cold weather.

Lesson 10C, page 89

must have/can't have/might have/could have for deductions in the past

She **must have stolen** the money.
They **can't have died**.
He **might have/could have broken** into the house.

- For past deductions, use *must/can't/might/could* + _____ + the past participle of a verb.
- *Might have* and _____ have a similar meaning.
- Complete the examples with *must have, can't have, might have*, or *could have*:
  A: *I can't find my wallet. I _____ left it at the supermarket, but I'm not sure.*
  B: *You _____ left it at the supermarket. I saw you put it in your backpack after you paid for the food.*

Complete the example sentences and the grammar rules that follow.

Lesson 11A, page 95

The passive: simple present, simple past, present perfect, past perfect

Simple present passive

You **are not allowed** to take pictures here.
Photographers _____ **accused** of ruining the lives of celebrities.

Simple past passive

She **was photographed** in a restaurant.
They _____ **asked** to leave.

Present perfect passive

The story **has been told** many times.

Past perfect passive

The star was angry because his house **had** _____ **broken** into **by** paparazzi.

- Use the _____ when the subject of a sentence did not perform the action.
- To form passive sentences, use a form of _____ + the past participle of the main verb:
  are allowed
- Use _____ to mention the person or thing that performed the action:
  was photographed **by** paparazzi

●

Lesson 11B, page 97

The passive: present continuous, past continuous, and simple future

Present continuous passive

The star **is being interviewed** right now.
Reporters _____ **being asked** to wait outside the film set.

Past continuous passive

A year ago, the star of the movie **was being chosen**.
The sets for the film **were** _____ **prepared**.

Simple future passive

I hope we'**ll be invited** to the movie premiere!

- Use the verb form _____ in present continuous and past continuous passive sentences.
- Use the verb form _be_ in simple future passive sentences.

Lesson 11C, page 99

The passive: modals, gerund (-ing form), and infinitive

Passive + modals

The victims **ought to be helped**.
They **must be given** food and water.
They **should be treated** by doctors.
Doctors **can** _____ **sent** to the area.

Passive + gerund

Being paid a decent salary is important.
People appreciate _____ **helped**.

Passive + infinitive

These boxes are going **to be recycled**.

- Use the verb form _be_ in most passive + _____ sentences.
- Use the verb form _being_ in passive + _____ sentences.
- Use the verb form _to be_ in passive + _____ sentences.

12 Money

Complete the example sentences and the grammar rules that follow.

Lesson 12A, page 103

Conditional: *if* clause + past perfect

If I **had saved** more money, I **would have been** rich.

_____ he **had been** more careful, he **wouldn't have spent** all his money.

They **wouldn't** _____ **won** the lottery **if** they **hadn't bought** lottery tickets.

- Use *if + would have* conditional sentences to talk about past situations that are contrary to fact. The past situation never happened. For example:
  If I had saved more money, I would have been rich (= I didn't save more money, so I am not rich now.).
- For *if + would have* conditional sentences, use the _____ tense in the *if* clause. Use *would* _____ + the past participle in the main clause.

Lesson 12B, page 105

wish/if only + past perfect

I **wish I'd gone** to bed earlier.

If only we'_____ **studied** Spanish in school.

I _____ I **hadn't bought** these shoes.

- Use *wish/if only* + _____ to talk about regrets in the past.
- _____ is stronger than *wish*.

Lesson 12C, page 107

Conditional: *if* clause + *might have*

If I **had tried** harder, I **might have won**.

_____ her aunt **hadn't helped** her, she **might not have been** so successful.

We _____ **have had** fun at the park **if** it **hadn't rained**.

- Use *if + might have* conditional sentences to talk about past situations that are contrary to fact. Use *might have* if you are not sure about what would happen if the *if* clause were true.
- For *if + might have* conditional sentences, use the _____ tense in the *if* clause. Use *might have* + a _____ in the main clause.
- Complete the example:
  If it _____ snowed, we _____ _____ gone skiing last weekend.

Writing bank

Lesson 2B

Biographies

> **Writing tips**
> 1 Divide your biography into paragraphs.
> 2 To show the order of events, use time words and phrases.

Example biography

1 Complete the example biography with the correct time words and phrases from the box.

> **Time words and phrases**
> * at the age of * currently * during
> * in (x 3) * later * not long after
> * since * soon * when (x 2) * while

2 Number the sentences below about Nicole Kidman (1–10) in the order in which they happened.

a) ☐ While she was making *Moulin Rouge*, she and Tom Cruise broke up.

b) ☐1 Nicole Kidman was born in 1967 in Hawaii.

c) ☐ Kidman currently lives on a farm in Tennessee in the U.S.

d) ☐ One year later, at the age of 20, she starred in her first big Hollywood movie, *Days of Thunder*.

e) ☐ She moved to Australia when she was three years old.

f) ☐ She was only 19 when she made her first film, *Dead Calm*.

g) ☐ Not long after, she married Tom Cruise, her co-star in *Days of Thunder*.

h) ☐ In 2001, she starred in *Moulin Rouge*, one of her biggest movies.

i) ☐ At the age of 10, she started to take drama lessons.

j) ☐ During her teenage years, she studied acting.

3 Match the sentences in Exercise 2 to a paragraph title.
Paragraph 1: Early life ___*Sentence b), e), ...*___
Paragraph 2: Career success _____
Paragraph 3: Current situation _____

4 Find some information about your favorite movie star and write a short biography. Divide your biography into paragraphs.

Johnny Depp

Johnny Depp was born [1] ____*in*____ 1963 in Kentucky, in the U.S., but he grew up in Florida. [2]_____ he was studying at school, he became interested in rock music. [3]_____ he left school [4]_____ 16, he sang in a band called The Kids. However, he [5]_____ gave up the dream of becoming a musician, and instead became a salesman of ballpoint pens.

Then one day, [6]_____ a visit to Los Angeles, Depp met actor Nicolas Cage. Cage persuaded Depp that his career was in acting. [7]_____ this, Depp won his first role in *Nightmare on Elm Street*. It wasn't a major role, but it was a start and three years [8]_____ he became famous in the American TV series *21 Jump Street*.

[9]_____ 1990, [10]_____ he was 27, Depp starred in the movie *Edward Scissorhands*, and more leading roles quickly followed. [11]_____ 2003, Depp became an international celebrity with the movie *Pirates of the Caribbean*. [12]_____ then, he has made several movies, but none of them quite as successful as *Pirates of the Caribbean*.

Depp [13]_____ lives in France with his partner, Vanessa Paradis, and their two children, Lily and Jack.

Lesson 4D

Book reviews

Writing tips

1 Divide your review into three paragraphs.
2 Where possible, combine your sentences using relative pronouns.
3 Use other conjunctions, too. See the list below.

Conjunctions of contrast and time

Contrast	• although • however
Time	• at first
	• a few days/weeks/months/years later
	• one day/morning/afternoon/evening

Example review

1 Read the example book review. In your notebook, rewrite it using relative pronouns to combine the parts in italics.

The Turn of the Screw is a ghost story by [1] Henry James, who was a famous American author.

2 Write a review of a book you have read recently. Use relative pronouns, conjunctions, and the questions below to help you.

Paragraph 1: Introduce the book
• What type of book is it?
• Who wrote it? When?
• Where is it set?
• What is the book about?

Paragraph 2: Describe the main characters and events
• Who are the main characters?
• What happens to them?

Paragraph 3: Give your opinion
• What did you think of the book?

THE
TURN
OF THE
SCREW

The Turn of the Screw is a ghost story by [1] *Henry James. Henry James was a famous American author.* He wrote [2] *the book in 1898. The book is set in England.* It is about [3] *a young governess*. The governess arrives at a big house* to teach two orphaned children and starts to see ghosts in the house.

The main character is [4] *the governess. Her* job is to look after the children, Miles and Flora. At first she feels comfortable with the children and [5] *the house. The house* is very old and beautiful. However, one night she hears the sound of [6] *a footstep outside her door. This scares* her. A short while later, she thinks she sees an intruder**. When she comes around [7] *the corner – the intruder was standing at this corner* – he has vanished. One evening the ghosts of the old valet*** and [8] *the old governess – this governess once had her job* – come to haunt her. She almost goes crazy as she tries to protect the children from [9] *the evil spirits. These spirits are everywhere in the house.*

I enjoyed the book very much, but it's pretty scary. It's [10] *that kind of book. It keeps you awake at night.* I thought about it for days afterwards.

* governess: a female teacher in the past, who lived with a rich family and taught their children at home
** intruder: someone who illegally enters a building
*** valet: a male servant who looks after men's clothes

Lesson 6B
Informal letters

> **Writing tips** (look at the number labels in the letter below)
> 1 Write your address [but not your name] in the top right hand corner.
> 2 Write the date beneath it.
> 3 Start your letter: *Dear (Emma),* using the first name of the person you are writing to.
> 4 Divide your letter into three paragraphs.
> 5 Finish your letter with *Take care* or *Love, . . .*

Example letter

1a **Choose words from the box to complete the expressions in the letter.**

• a long time • all • arrived • hear • love
• ~~much~~ • write • see • soon • stop

1 21 Barrington Road
   Seattle, WA

2 April 4, [year]

3 Dear Emma,

4 Thank you very a) _____much_____ for your letter.
   It b) _____ yesterday, and I feel very guilty.
   It seems c) _____ since I last wrote!

   I've been very busy these last few months. I just joined a photography club at school, and we meet twice a week. It's a lot of fun, and I spend hours on my computer uploading photos. Did you know that my brother Sam is now going out with a girl from the band Mad Morning? That reminds me – how are you doing with Joseph? Are you still going out with him?

   I'm sorry I don't have time to write any more now. I promised to help Mom make a pizza for dinner. Write d) _____.

5 e) _____,

   Kate

b Now use the rest of the words from the box to complete the expressions below.

1 It was great to _____ from you.
2 Well, that's _____ for now.
3 Sorry I didn't _____ sooner.
4 I hope to _____ you soon.
5 I have to _____ writing now. I have to do some homework.

c In your notebook, write the expressions from parts a) and b) under the correct headings.

Starting a letter   **Ending a letter**

Thank you very much for your letter.

2 In your notebook, write an informal letter to an English-speaking friend who you haven't seen in a while. Your friend is coming to visit you. Use the letter guide below.

Opening paragraph
• Thank your friend for his or her letter.
• Say when it arrived.

Middle paragraph
• Advise your friend on the best way to get to your house.
• Tell him or her to bring some outdoor clothes and something dressy. Explain why.
• Mention your family and any friends you both know.

Closing paragraph
• Say you have to end the letter. Explain why.
• Ask him or her to give your love to his or her parents.
• Say when you hope to see him or her.

Lesson 8D
Formal application letters

Writing tips (look at the number labels in the letter below)
1 Write your address [but not your name] in the top right hand corner and the date beneath it.
2 Write the name or position (e.g., *Club Secretary*) and address of the person you are writing to above the greeting: *Dear . . .*
3 If you know the name of the person you are writing to, start with: *Dear Mr./Mrs./Miss/Ms. (Hudson)*, and end with *Sincerely yours.* If you don't know the name, start with: *To whom it may concern.*
4 Start a new paragraph for each topic.
5 Sign the letter with your full name.

Example letter

1a Complete the letter with words from the box.

- advertised • application • apply for • forward • good at • grateful
- interested • interview • know • meeting • work experience • working

1 6 Barnes Road
Seattle, OR 98104

June 10, [*year*]

2 Ms. J. Hudson
Redmond Community Center
Seattle, WA 98053

3 Dear Ms. Hudson,
I would like to a) ___*apply for*___ the job of swimming class instructor that I saw b) _____ in a student newspaper.

4 I am 16 years old, and I live in Seattle. I just finished my junior year, and I will go back to school next September. Unfortunately, I haven't done this kind of work before, but I come from a large family, I am c) _____ swimming, and I like being with children. I want to help other people, and it would give me valuable d) _____ during the summer vacation.

I hope you will consider my e) _____. I would be able to come for an f) _____ on any weekday after 3 P.M. or on a Saturday.

I look g) _____ to hearing from you.

Sincerely yours,

5 *Jonathan Flyte*
Jonathan Flyte

b Now use the rest of the words from the box to complete the expressions below.
1 I look forward to ___*meeting*___ you.
2 I am very _____ in this kind of work.
3 Please let me _____ if you would like some more information.
4 I am used to _____ with young people.
5 I would be very _____ if you could contact me at this number.

2 In your notebook, write an application letter for a job. Use the advertisement and the guide below.

Sundale
Community Center

Sundale Community Center is looking for a sports assistant aged 16+ to help run our busy Community Center during the summer vacation.

Write to David Ortega at PO Box 251, Sacramento, CA 95814

Opening paragraph
- Say why you are writing.
- Say where you heard about the job.

Middle paragraph
- Give your age and say where you come from.
- Say how good your English is.
- Mention any hobbies or skills.
- Mention any previous experience.
- Say why you would like the job.

Closing paragraph
- Say when you could come for interview.

Lesson 10C

Stories (Narratives)

Writing tips

1 Divide your story into paragraphs.
2 Use the simple past and past continuous tenses.
3 Use time expressions to show the sequence of events.
4 For dramatic effect, use interesting adverbs and phrases of manner and mood. See the lists below.

Time expressions, adverbs, and adverb phrases

Time	• at first • then • later (on) • afterward • after that • not long after • soon • the next day • in the end • finally • a few years/months/weeks/days/minutes/seconds later
Manner	• suddenly • immediately • quickly • quietly • as quickly/quietly as possible • shaking with fear • slowly • carefully • with (masks on their faces) • without (stopping to think)
Mood	• to her horror • to her amazement
Comment	• luckily • unluckily • not surprisingly • strangely

2 In your notebook, make up a story about an unusual crime that you witnessed. Give the story a title. Use adverbs and phrases like the ones in Exercise 1. Use the questions below to help you.

Paragraph 1: Set the scene
• When did the incident happen?
• Where were you?
• What were you doing at the time?
• How were you feeling? Why?

Paragraph 2: Describe the event
• What happened? • How did you react? • What did you do?

Paragraph 3: Give the ending
• What was the result? • How did you feel?

Example story

1 Complete the example story with words or phrases from the box above.

The quick getaway

It was Saturday afternoon, and 18-year-old Monica was in a good mood. She had just passed her driving test that morning, and some friends were coming over to watch some DVDs. Her parents were out shopping, and her only job was to do the laundry before they came back.

She was putting some clothes in the washing machine in the basement when [1] _____suddenly_____ she heard voices in the living room upstairs. [2] _____ she thought her parents must have left the TV on. Then, a few seconds [3] _____, she heard some footsteps. Shaking [4] _____, Monica tiptoed back upstairs and [5] _____ opened the living room door. [6] _____ horror, two men with masks on their faces were trying to unscrew the TV from the wall. [7] _____ for her, they didn't see her, and she left the house [8] _____ possible. On her way out she saw the burglars' get away car outside the house. [9] _____

amazement, the car door was open and the engine was running. [10] _____ stopping to think, she jumped in the car and drove off to a friend's house around the corner.

Not [11] _____, when the burglars saw that their car had disappeared, they panicked and ran off. [12] _____ for them, the TV was too heavy to carry, so [13] _____ end they left it on the doorstep. Monica was very relieved when her parents [14] _____ arrived home! The police caught the burglars a few weeks [15] _____ when they were trying to steal another car!

Lesson 12A
Discursive essays

> **Writing tips**
> 1 Divide your essay into paragraphs.
> 2 Use linking phrases to make your points. See the lists below.

Linking phrases

Lists	• first • second
Addition	• in addition • what's more • furthermore • not only . . . (but also)
Contrast	• although • however • on the other hand
Example	• for example • such as
Opinion	• in my opinion • as far as I'm concerned • I think/feel
Conclusion	• on the whole • to sum up • in conclusion

Example essay

1 Read the example essay. Circle the correct linking words or phrases.

"Should older teenagers be paid to go to school?"

In the U.S. and the U.K., people are discussing the idea that older teenagers should be paid to go to school. [1] *Although/However* this shocks many people, others think that it is a good idea.

There are several reasons why people are in favor of paying teenagers to go to school. [2] *In conclusion/First/What's more*, it encourages teenagers to stay in education and get better qualifications. [3] *Furthermore/On the whole/However*, the extra money that teenagers earn can be very useful to pay for necessities [4] *in addition/in my opinion/such as* travel, books, and food.

[5] *On the other hand/Such as/To sum up*, many people feel that paying older teenagers to learn is a bad idea. They say it is expensive, and the government can't afford the money. [6] *I think/On the whole/In addition*, they argue that it may encourage some students to stay in school for the wrong reasons; [7] *however/for example/what's more*, because they want to earn the money and not because they want to study.

[8] *To sum up/Furthermore/First*, there are strong arguments for and against paying older teenagers to study. [9] *On the other hand/Such as/In my opinion*, it is a bad idea because it encourages the wrong kind of attitude toward learning.

2 You are going to write an essay arguing for and against the topic "Winning a lot of money is usually a bad thing for people." Match the paragraphs (1–4) to the opening sentences (A–D).

> 1 Introduction
> 2 "For" paragraph
> 3 "Against" paragraph
> 4 Conclusion

A On the other hand, there are several reasons why winning a lot of money can be a good thing. _____

B On the whole, I feel that winning a lot of money can have positive/ negative effects on people's lives, because _____

C Some people are lucky enough to win a lot of money in a lottery. _____

D Some people think that winning a lot of money only causes trouble. _____

3 Look at the notes below and list your main points for each paragraph. Then write your essay. Try to include linking phrases in your essay.

Paragraph 1: Introduction
• Start with a statement about the essay title. • Say that there are two sides to the argument.

Paragraph 2: "For" paragraph
• Write a topic sentence to introduce the points for the statement.
• Give two or three main points.
• Include examples or explanations.

Paragraph 3: "Against" paragraph
• Write a topic sentence to introduce the points against the statement.
• Give two or three main points.
• Include examples or explanations.

Paragraph 4: Conclusion
• Write a short summary.
• Give your opinion and a reason.

Word list

Unit 1
Lesson 1A

Clothes, styles, accessories, and patterns

bandana
baseball cap
bracelet
cargo pants
headband
leggings
polo shirt
sandals
sweater
sweatshirt
sweatpants

design
enterprising
extend
market
original
range
stall
try on
wedding
weird

What are you looking for?
something [plain]
Anyway
How's it going?
every other [Saturday]

Lesson 1B
bone
break down
brightly colored
bull rider
clown
currently
distract
escape
excitement
fall off

high-rise
ideal
incident
injured
interview (v)
previous
rodeo
route
so far
storm chaser
studio
tornado

Lesson 1C

Adjectives to describe work

badly paid
boring
creative
dangerous
dull
educational
exciting
glamorous
interesting
rewarding
safe
stressful
tiring
well paid
worthwhile

backpacking
better-qualified
choice
conduct
degree
freedom
frequently
full-time
graduate
recording studio
sound technician
temporary job
trouble
volunteer work

Lesson 1D
bargain
beyond someone's budget
child labor
designer
developing
emphasis
ensure
ethical
factor
fair trade
fashion item
fashionable
garage sale
image
influence
live and breathe
look (n)
manufacture
media
mix and match
plant (v)
product
realistic
recycled
reflect
renewable
salary
source
stuff
suitability
tend to
unusual

Unit 2
Lesson 2A
avoid
balance (n)
bleeding
concern
enter
hard times
helmet
kneepad
swerved

No problem
I bet you're glad . . .
get the hang of it
I'd better get going.

Lesson 2B

Phrasal verbs with *up*

get up
grow up
hurry up
look up
pick up
show up
stand up
take up
wake up

assassin
audition
childhood
crack
dieting
direction
drop out
drug-addicted
gain
go out (lights)
golf course
lead role
medication
part
path
rib
script
soldier
struggling
take notice
ten-pin bowling
upwards

Lesson 2C
alarm (v)
amazement
automatic pilot

check-in desk
cockpit
cruise ship
emergency parachute
emergency services
four-seater
knock down
mid-flight
overboard
parachutist
railway official
trauma
wave

Lesson 2D
achievement
advertisement
affect
air show
ambitious
apply
break (a record)
candidate
challenge (n)
circle (v)
crew
forever
hero/es
hot-air balloon
long-distance
media
member
milestone
set up
solo
space agency
space program
space shuttle
spot (v)
steering
tragically
vocation

Unit 3

Lesson 3A

Food and kitchen equipment
bowl
can opener
cheese grater
cup
cutting board
dishes
fork
frying pan
kettle
knife
peeler
plate
saucepan
saucer
scale
sieve
silverware
spoon
utensils

accepted
basic
book (v)
camera crew
canned
consist
experience
flour
hit show
open fire
reality show
screening
take part
tough
uninhabited

Lesson 3B

Part-time jobs
babysitting
delivering
  newspapers
dog walking

helping in a
  retirement home
mowing lawns
painting and
  decorating
teaching computer
  skills
washing cars
weeding yards
working in a store

campfire
charge per hour
energetic
essential
get (sb) into
  trouble
in good shape
make your bed
mealtime
open to new ideas
opportunity
own (adj)
part-time
patient
provide
push yourself
responsibility
safe
skills
suggestion
valuables

Lesson 3C

allowed to
car (train)
come over
departure lounge
fasten
let
make (somebody
  do something)
seatbelt

Lesson 3D

apply
armed

border
capital
civil war
eldest
eventually
fear
pay back
peaceful
pride
refugee
refugee camp
respect (v)
situation
trust (v)
visa

Unit 4

Lesson 4A

amazing
awesome
cards
cheer up
darts
fair
fantastic
Good job!
horrible
install
knock down
lyrics

that great
try
up for it
really easy
Bad luck.
It's my turn.
Way to go!

Lesson 4B

Music words
album
backup singer
band
beat
charts

lead singer
lyrics
producer
rapper
single
songwriter

bring up
driver's license
electric guitar
formula
foundation
funk
on average
on the move
pass the time
race
racing driver
release
time to kill
tune

Lesson 4C

**Phrasal verbs
  with on**
count on
hold on
keep on
log on
put on
try on
turn on
work on

a thing of the past
boredom
broadcast
built into
clubber
encourage
entertainment
headphone
hi-tech
innovation
instant
online

password
recording booth
rely on
round-up
silent
specs
station (TV)
submit
switch on
take place
talented
trainee
tutorial
user name
wireless

Lesson 4D

author
book review
child-like
creature
disease
evil
excerpt
fight (v)
forecast (v)
genetically
  modified
gentle
insect
living conditions
low intelligence
machine
main character
mysteriously
notice
nuclear war
physically
predict
social
underground
violent
weak
weed

151

Unit 5

Lesson 5A

appalled
argument
as long as
benefit
community
disturb
expected
fuss over nothing
in favor of
legal action
local council
prevent
principal
provided that
reassure
resident
suffer

Lesson 5B

Extreme weather and natural disasters

avalanche
blizzard
downpour
drought
earthquake
famine
flood
gale
hail(storm)
heatwave
hurricane
landslide
lightning
snow(storm)
storm
thunder and lightning
thunder(storm)
tornado
tsunami
volcanic eruption

ability
by the time
cause
chemical-filled
cloud-seeding
control
create

crops
principle
rocket
sheep farm
starving
surgery
swing

Lesson 5C

Camping equipment

backpack
bandages
camping stove
can opener
compass
flashlight
hiking boots
insect repellent
matches
painkillers
penknife
sleeping bag
sunscreen
tent
waterproof jacket

refuse
sales assistant
swimsuit
towel
waterproof

[I'll] open it up
What are you looking for?
I only have [a dollar] on me.
How sad is that!

Lesson 5D

chunk
compact (adj)
connection
constant
continuous
cover (v)
cubic
downhill
float (v)
form (v)
fresh water
frozen
glacier
global warming

hole
iceberg
land
major
melt
ocean liner
polar bear
radio operator
region
release (v)
rise
sea level
seal
sinking
snowfall
soil
steel
worldwide
worm

Unit 6

Lesson 6A

Transitive phrasal verbs

ask out
check out
find out
give back
pick up
put down
put on
take off
turn on
turn off
turn up
turn down

document
for free
government
intelligence agency
invisible
secret
split up
stay up

Lesson 6B

accept
afford
cute
grab
out of date
over the top
refund

reject
voicemail

See you in . . .
Hands off!
Come on.

Lesson 6C

Noun suffixes -ion, -ment, -ity, and -y

able/ability
accurate/accuracy
brave/bravery
coordinate/ coordination
correct/correction
decide/decision
difficult/difficulty
disappoint/ disappointment
discover/discovery
entertain/ entertainment
excite/excitement
explain/explanation
imagine/imagination
improve/ improvement
move/movement
organize/ organization
possible/possibility
real/reality
similar/similarity

Verb with infinitive

agree
decide
expect
forget
help
hope
manage
offer
promise
refuse
seem
try
want
would like

Verb with gerund

admit
avoid
can't stand

deny
enjoy
finish
give up
keep
miss
not mind
practice
stop

Verbs with infinitive or gerund

hate
like
love
preter
start

article
chord
comment
controversial
expert (n)
eyesight
generally
isolated
post
precise
professor
risk (v)
strengthen
text

Lesson 6D

afford
atmosphere
available
blame
budget
charge
decorate
decorated (adj)
disappointed
elect
election
hire
prom
school hall
strike (v)
student president
venue
vote for
wicked (= great)

Unit 7

Lesson 7A
design (v)
get back
incoming
outgoing
reach
right now
stock
take a call

Thanks for calling back.
Well, . . .
Actually, . . .
let me guess . . .

Lesson 7B
aggressive
assertive
change channels
come over
communicate
complain
diplomatic
glass pot
hope for the best
offend
stand up for
takeout

Lesson 7C
Relationship words and phrases
ask someone out
be close to someone
break up with someone
care about someone
fall in love with someone
get along well with someone

get divorced from someone
get engaged/ married to someone
get on someone's nerves
go out with someone
have a good relationship with someone
have an argument with someone
make up with someone
treat someone like [a grown-up]
trust someone [to make the right decision]
worry about someone

a quiet life
although
cry on [someone's] shoulder
definitely
despite
however
independent
in spite of
moody
on the other hand
reputation
upset

Lesson 7D
all in favor of
blog
contact (n)
digital
exchange visit

IM (Instant Messaging)
keep an eye on
keep in touch with
landline
lifeline
peaceful
phone bill
photographic record (n)
regularly
screen
screen-free
social networking
survey
via
waste (v)
webcam

Unit 8

Lesson 8A
Adjectives of emotion
afraid
amused/amusing
angry
annoyed/annoying
anxious
ashamed
bored/boring
calm
cheerful
confused/ confusing
depressed/ depressing
embarrassed/ embarrassing
excited/exciting
frightened/ frightening
frustrated/ frustrating

happy
lonely
nervous
proud
sad
scared
shocked/shocking
terrified/terrifying
thrilled/thrilling
worried/worrying

backward
clumsy
contestant
cringe
fall over
fins
hug
judge
mask
paragliding
react
shake
snorkel
snorkeling
turtle
waves

Lesson 8B
baked beans
black pudding
casually
Cornish pasty
fares
full English
grits
rugby
sausage
school uniform
scones

Watch out for [that taxi!]
That was close!
You know, . . .

Lesson 8C
Phrasal verbs with in
break in
fit in
give in
hand in
move in
sink in
stay in

achievement
clinic
extreme
height
hopefully
incredible
lie
open space
overcome
phobia
public speaking
session

Lesson 8D
branch
charity
conservation
donation
emergency
endangered
impressed
in need
involve
leading
medical
operate
persuade
poverty
protect
raise
staff
vaccination
volunteer

Word list

Unit 9

Lesson 9A

Parts of a bike
back light
brakes
chain
frame
front light
gears
handlebars
pedal
seat
tire
wheel

crash
flat tire
memory
pierced
second-hand
service (v)
shorten
wobble

it's not exactly
  [new]
in pretty good
  shape
It's a complete
  wreck!

Lesson 9B

**Adjective suffixes
  with -ful, -y,
  -ous, -ive, -al**
ambition/
  ambitious
attraction/
  attractive
beauty/beautiful
danger/dangerous
effect/effective
humor/humorous
imagination/
  imaginative
music/musical
mystery/
  mysterious

origin/original
profession/
  professional
salt/salty
sun/sunny
suspicion/
  suspicious
thirst/thirsty
use/useful
wonder/wonderful

announce
counterbalance
edge
gas tank
in order (not) to
lads
lower
lose weight
reduce
rock
sight
tip over
ton
unbalance

Lesson 9C

**Adjectives of
  texture and
  shape**
curved
fluffy
hard
oblong
prickly
rectangular
rough
round
silky
slippery
smooth
soft
square
star-shaped
straight
thick
thin
triangular

ad
blast off
catalog
come alive
dizzy
flash
gadget
go off
heavy sleeper
lick
novelty
numb
police siren
sci-fi
scratch
sensational
slippers
sniff
speaker
trip over

Lesson 9D

asbestos
breathe
concrete
contain
demolish
dump (v)
dust
face mask
get rid of
hesitate
illegal
impress
impression
in a good mood
internship
jail
look forward to
lung cancer
nasty stuff
protective clothing
removal company
skip (n)
toxic
work experience

Unit 10

Lesson 10A

custodian
judo class
safely
spill
torn

Wait a minute.
That old [wreck]?
What a drag!

Lesson 10B

**Phrasal verbs
  with away**
get away
give something
  away
go away
look away
pass away
put something
  away
run away
throw something
  away

beast
fake
ghost
hoax
mythical
ripe
sighting
swore

Lesson 10C

Crime
accuse somebody
  of
arrest somebody
  for
charge somebody
  with
convict somebody
  of

sentence
  somebody to (a
  period of time)
  for (a crime)
suspect
  somebody of

accomplice
case
claim
death
fingerprint
footprint
fraud
go missing
hop off
life insurance
mainland
muddy
oxygen cylinder
proof
raft
release
reliable
rescuer
string
witness

Lesson 10D

air kiss
bow (v/n)
cheek
close (adj)
consequently
custom
formally
go on
greet
host(ess)
hug (v/n)
item
kiss (v/n)
nod (v/n)
on time
shake hands
social
tradition
unlike

Unit 11

Lesson 11A

The media
blog
channel
editor
headline
magazine
newspaper
podcast
report
tabloid
  (newspaper)

commuter
paparazzi
poll
publication
sensational
sum

Lesson 11B
edit
extra
film crew
particularly
replace
roof tops
scene
set
shoot

What's going on?
into
that much
What more do you
  want?
Dream on!

Lesson 11C

**Adjective and
  noun formation**
angry/anger
beautiful/beauty
brave/bravery
confident/
  confidence

courageous/
  courage
cruel/cruelty
different/difference
greedy/greed
high/height
hopeful/hope
lucky/luck
poor/poverty
proud/pride
stressful/stress
strong/strength
successful/
  success
true/truth
wise/wisdom
young/youth

campaign
cruel
destroy
experiment
fur coat
involved (get)
online bullying
priority
selfish
victim

Lesson 11D
aircraft
atom
attached
billionth
cable
coat (v)
coating
collect
conduct
crease (v)
cure
damaging
deliver
diagnose
fuel
inject
material

microscopic
molecule
nanometer
nanotechnology
product
qualified
revolution
rust
space elevator
stain (v)
store (v)
submarine
sunscreen
supply (n)
surface
term
transparent

Unit 12

Lesson 12A

**Verbs connected
  with money**
afford
be in debt
borrow (from)
donate (to)
earn
gamble
give (away)
go bankrupt
inherit (from)
invest (in)
lend (to)
lose
make
owe (to)
pay
pay (someone)
  back
repay
save
spend (on)
splurge on
win

chain
lottery

luxury
no comment
responsible (for)
run a business
stock market
taste
trailer

Lesson 12B

**Phrasal verbs
  with out**
eat out
figure out
find out
leave out
point out
sell out
throw out
turn out

catastrophe
drive (someone)
  crazy
employ
essay
go through
  (experience)
have a clue
homemade
introduction
order
profitable
recipe
regret (n)
stage
toothpaste

Lesson 12C
application form
brownie
deserve
fail
retake

What are you up
  to?
What a pain.
Tell me about it!

How about it?
It's on me.
Lead the way!

Lesson 12D
advise against
close down
concerned about
coursework
inheritance
model
option
rehearsal

Irregular verbs

Infinitive	Past	Past participle	Infinitive	Past	Past participle
be	was/were	been/gone	light	lit	lit
beat	beat	beaten	lose	lost	lost
become	became	become	make	made	made
begin	began	begun	mean	meant	meant
bend	bent	bent	meet	met	met
break	broke	broken	must	had to	(had to)
bring	brought	brought	oversleep	overslept	overslept
build	built	built	pay	paid	paid
burn	burned	burned	put	put	put
buy	bought	bought	read	read /rɛd/	read /rɛd/
can	could	(been able)	ride	rode	ridden
catch	caught	caught	ring	rang	rung
choose	chose	chosen	run	ran	run
come	came	come	say	said	said
cost	cost	cost	see	saw	seen
cut	cut	cut	sell	sold	sold
do	did	done	send	sent	sent
draw	drew	drawn	set off	set off	set off
dream	dreamed	dreamed	shake	shook	shaken
drink	drank	drunk	shine	shone	shone
drive	drove	driven	show	showed	shown
eat	ate	eaten	shut	shut	shut
fall	fell	fallen	sing	sang	sung
feel	felt	felt	sink	sank	sunk
fight	fought	fought	sit	sat	sat
find	found	found	sleep	slept	slept
fly	flew	flown	smell	smelled	smelled
forget	forgot	forgotten	speak	spoke	spoken
get	got	gotten	spend	spent	spent
give	gave	given	spread	spread	spread
go	went	gone/been	stand	stood	stood
grow	grew	grown	steal	stole	stolen
hang	hung/hanged	hung/hanged	sting	stung	stung
have	had	had	swim	swam	swum
hear	heard	heard	take	took	taken
hide	hid	hidden	teach	taught	taught
hit	hit	hit	tear	tore	torn
hold	held	held	tell	told	told
hurt	hurt	hurt	think	thought	thought
keep	kept	kept	throw	threw	thrown
know	knew	known	understand	understood	understood
learn	learned	learned	wake	woke	woken
leave	left	left	wear	wore	worn
lend	lent	lent	win	won	won
			write	wrote	written

CLIL PROJECTS

Go to www.pearsonlongman.com/insync/projects

CLIL Project 1D, page 11
Social Studies

GROUPS Discuss: What kinds of clothes do teenagers wear in your country now? In the past? Then make a collage of teen fashions. Go to the website above, find CLIL Project 1D, and print out the instructions.

CLIL Project 2D, page 19
History

PAIRS Brainstorm: Choose a type of transportation, such as cars, trains, or airplanes. What do you know about its history? Who invented it and how did it develop over the years? Then make a historical timeline for the type of transportation. Go to the website above, find CLIL Project 2D, and print out the instructions.

CLIL Project 3D, page 29
Ethics

GROUPS Discuss: What is a *refugee*? What is it like to be a refugee? Then make a wordweb about refugees. Go to the website above, find CLIL Project 3D, and print out the instructions.

CLIL Project 4D, page 37
Literature

GROUPS Discuss: What kinds of books do you like to read? Then do a survey about your classmates' reading habits. Go to the website above, find CLIL Project 4D, and print out the instructions.

CLIL Project 5D, page 47
Geography

PAIRS Discuss: What are some major disasters that happened in recent years? Which disaster was the most serious, and how can people prevent it from happening again? Then prepare a presentation on the disaster. Go to the website above, find CLIL Project 5D, and print out the instructions.

CLIL Project 6D, page 55
Ethics

GROUPS Brainstorm: What kinds of things do people do at fun parties? Then plan an end-of-year party for your class. Go to the website above, find CLIL Project 6D, and print out the instructions.

CLIL Project 7D, page 65
Social Studies

GROUPS Discuss: What English abbreviations and expressions do people use when they write text messages or chat online? Then choose a paragraph from a book and rewrite it as if it was a text message. Go to the website above, find CLIL Project 7D, and print out the instructions.

CLIL Project 8D, page 73
Social Studies / Ethics

GROUPS Discuss: What are some charities that work to solve problems in your neighborhood, town, or city? Then prepare a presentation on a charity. Go to the website above, find CLIL Project 8D, and print out the instructions.

CLIL Project 9D, page 83
Ethics

GROUPS Discuss: What are some right or wrong things that people do in the workplace? Then choose a workplace situation or dilemma and decide what to do. Go to the website above, find CLIL Project 9D, and print out the instructions.

CLIL Project 10D, page 91
Cultural / Social Studies

PAIRS Discuss: What are some unusual social customs from around the world? Then make a poster about an unusual social custom. Go to the website above, find CLIL Project 10D, and print out the instructions.

CLIL Project 11D, page 101
Science

PAIRS Discuss: Some people like nanotechnology and other people don't. Why? Then prepare a presentation on nanotechnology. Go to the website above, find CLIL Project 11D, and print out the instructions.

CLIL Project 12D, page 109
Ethics

GROUPS Discuss: Who are the wealthiest people in the world? What are they doing with the money they have? Then prepare a presentation on a wealthy person. Go to the website above, find CLIL Project 12D, and print out the instructions.